Work and Family Commitments of Low-Income and Impoverished Women

Work and Family Commitments of Low-Income and Impoverished Women

Guilt Is for Mothers with Good Jobs

Judith Hennessy

LEXINGTON BOOKS
Lanham • Boulder • New York • London

Published by Lexington Books
An imprint of The Rowman & Littlefield Publishing Group, Inc.
4501 Forbes Boulevard, Suite 200, Lanham, Maryland 20706
www.rowman.com

Unit A, Whitacre Mews, 26-34 Stannary Street, London SE11 4AB

British Library Cataloguing in Publication Information Available

Library of Congress Cataloging-in-Publication Data

Hennessy, Judith.
Work and family commitments of low-income and impoverished women : guilt is for mothers with good jobs / Judith Hennessy.
pages cm
Includes bibliographical references and index.
ISBN 978-0-7391-8679-4 (cloth : alk. paper) -- ISBN 978-0-7391-8680-0 (electronic)
1. Work and family--United States. 2. Working mothers--United States--Social conditions. 3. Working poor--United States--Social conditions. 4. Poor women--United States--Social conditions. I. Title.
HD4904.25.H364 2015
306.3'6--dc23
2015000318
ISBN 978-1-4985-5054-3 (pbk : alk. paper)

∞ ™ The paper used in this publication meets the minimum requirements of American National Standard for Information Sciences Permanence of Paper for Printed Library Materials, ANSI/NISO Z39.48-1992.

Printed in the United States of America

Contents

Chapter One

The Paradox

The year 1997 marked two milestones in work and family life in the United States: The workforce participation rate of married mothers reached its all-time high (it has since decreased) the same year welfare reform was implemented in all fifty states, requiring that poor mothers go to work. The 1996 overhaul of the Aid to Families with Dependent Children (AFDC) program (what most Americans refer to as "welfare") abolished sixty years of poor mothers' entitlement to welfare assistance to care for dependent children and replaced it with a block grant program called Temporary Assistance to Needy Families (TANF), tying eligibility for cash support to paid employment. When policy makers overhauled welfare, they argued that supporting poor women to remain at home to care for children was no longer feasible now that most mothers work outside the home (Weaver 2000, 70). The question asked by policy makers as well as by the American public (whether fairly or not) was why poor women on welfare should be able to stay home and take care of their children when other mothers have to go to work. This question still resonates today. As a nation we have yet to overcome our ambivalence about the impact of mothers' workforce participation on children and family life. [1] At the same time, we hold contradictory expectations for the work and family responsibilities of poor and low-income mothers.

As the number of welfare caseloads plummeted and more single mothers entered the workforce once welfare reform became the law of the land, policy makers declared welfare reform a major social policy achievement (Haskins 2006). Paradoxically, despite the public policy "success" of increased work participation for poor mothers, the American public continues to express concern over the degree to which working mothers across the United States struggle to balance the needs of families with the demands of the workplace (Warner 2005, Peskowitz 2005, Parker 2012). Why does this

1

remarkable contradiction rarely surface in contemporary work and family debates? Rather than acknowledge the difficulties faced by poor mothers, we instead engage in recurrent skirmishes of the "mommy wars" generated by elite working mothers going public with their decisions to leave the workplace to care for children (Douglas and Michaels 2004). It appears that the modern-day poster child for work-family conflict is the professional woman "opting out" of a lucrative career to stay home and raise children. The flip side of these images endures as the poster child for poor women: the responsible (read good) single mother who does the right thing for her family by going to work (Cohen and Bianchi 1999, Hays 2003).

In the pages that follow, I argue that concerns over women's work and family responsibilities are as much moral as economic. In this book, I explore the underlying, often contradictory, cultural and moral forces that drive why stories about middle-class and professional women "opting out" of the workplace to stay home with children strike such a chord with members of the American public who at the same time demand that poor women "opt in" rather than rely on welfare to care for their children.

A widely cited example of the interest in professional women's work and family lives is the media frenzy set off in 2003 by Lisa Belkin's influential *New York Times Magazine* article, "The Opt-Out Revolution," about professional women leaving their jobs to stay home with children. *Time* magazine followed with a cover story "The Case for Staying Home: Why More Young Moms Are Opting Out of the Rat Race," in which Claudia Wallis (2004) wrote about professional working mothers ultimately doing the right thing for their families by limiting employment to devote themselves to children. A deluge of articles, commentary, and opinion pieces appeared in response, reigniting the mommy wars with salvos from progressives that the articles were harmful to women's gains in the workplace, countered by responses from conservatives who lauded the articles for pointing out the "false promise of feminism" (Schlafly 2004). Others, such as family historian Stephanie Coontz (2006) and legal scholar Joan Williams (2010), challenged the characterization of women as "choosing" to opt out, rather than being shut out by hostile workplaces and draconian family policies. The issue surfaced again in 2012 with Anne-Marie Slaughter's article, "Why Women Still Can't Have It All," in the *Atlantic* describing how even powerful women at the top of their profession (with accommodating spouses) leave work due to family demands. In the renewed attention to elite women's struggles, why do we not hear more concern for the work-family challenges faced by poor women who are required to work for low wages at jobs that are far less accommodating to family demands?

This pervasive double standard may be the result of a general understanding that poor women have little if any choice in whether to work outside the home. Yet this leaves us with the simplistic assumption that poor and working-class mothers work because they have to and others because they choose to. An alternative view is that all women work because they need to; thus, choices about work and family boil down to rational economic considerations. In this scenario no one really has a choice, and poor women's choices are obliterated altogether. In addition, people's identities as workers and mothers become irrelevant in shaping how and where they devote their time and energy. Multiple studies on work and family tell us otherwise. Examples can be found in classic works such as Arlie Hochschild's *The Second Shift* (1989), in which Hochschild argued that at the heart of the conflict between work and family lies a struggle over the meanings of paid work and caregiving. In spite of the immense change in women's work and family attachments, "the cultural landscape of family life today is one that continues to be strongly shaped by gendered beliefs" (Bianchi, Robinson, and Milkie 2006, 125). At its heart, work-family conflict is not simply the outcome of juggling too many demands but results from contradictions between taken-for-granted expectations about what it means to be workers and mothers (Hays 1996, Garey 1999, Blair-Loy 2003).

WOMEN'S WORK AND FAMILY CHOICES

In 2012, 70 percent of all mothers with children under age eighteen worked outside the home. This figure includes 65 percent of moms with children under age six and 57 percent of mothers with infants less than one year of age (U.S. Department of Labor 2013). However, despite the fact that most mothers today combine paid work with motherhood, we have yet to overcome the legacy of work and family as separate and oppositional domains; women must be either devoted to work *or* devoted to children. This influential yet outdated cultural model continues to shape women's decisions about wage earning and child care (the broader implications of the cultural influences on women's choices are explored throughout this book). Because this model constructs paid work and family life in opposition and because women (more so than men) are expected to have greater responsibility (both morally and practically) for home and children, hours devoted to employment are hours children are deprived of their mothers' care. Anita Garey noted that this model of work and family portrays working-class employed mothers "as needing to work to support their families and it is assumed that they would choose to be at-home mothers if their husbands earned a family wage" (1999, 44). In other words, if mothers could afford to stay at home and raise their children, they would and *should.* On the other hand, professional women in careers or employed mothers married to men with substantial earnings are viewed as choosing to work and placing self-fulfillment, status, and occupational success over the well-being of children (Garey 1999, Blair-Loy 2003,

Warner 2005). The criticism leveled against professional women for wanting
to "have it all" but dare to talk about the constraints that family demands
place on their careers serves as a contemporary example of this model.

OPTING OUT

In *Opting Out*, Pamela Stone focused on professional women who quit their
jobs to stay home with children. She describes these women as a group who
at least "theoretically have a choice" compared to poor women leaving welfare who "must" work (2007, 15). Her book explored factors that drive
professional women who have more resources and options—college degrees,
rewarding careers, dual-earner spouses, access to quality day care, and other
advantages—out of the workforce and back to their homes and the consequences of their decisions. She argued that the rhetoric of choice masks the
structural constraints faced by women who expected to have it all but whose
choices were limited by the demands of family and careers. In contrast to
individuals choosing to opt out, Stone uncovered workplace and family arrangements that push or shut out high-achieving women when they become
mothers.

Studies such as Stone's showing that professional women are often
pushed out of the workforce rather than voluntarily return to home and hearth
are a welcome challenge to individualistic ideas about women's preferences.
They are important in pointing out how work and family arrangements are
structured in such a way as to limit mothers' abilities to act on their preferences (Risman 1998). Yet, even as these studies debunk the characterization
of professional women's choices as opting out, they miss the opportunity to
address the moral and cultural influences that shape women's preferences.
They do not answer the question as to why these choices are so emotionally
wrenching. Although it is clear that moral concerns fuel debate over whether
women (both professional and those with more limited "choices") *should* go
to work *or* stay home with children, the point is rarely made explicit in our
studies on work and families.

The language of choice that dominates public discussion of work and
family demands tends to focus on people's individual preferences and fails,
at least explicitly, to acknowledge the broader moral and cultural underpinnings of debates over what women *should* do. Furthermore, moral evaluation
of poor single mothers' work and family choices is quite different from
evaluation of mothers at the center of the opt-out debate. Moral apprehension
over work and family choices directed toward women's individual preferences is almost always expressed as concern over the well-being of children
when their mothers go to work. For example, when professional married
mothers leave promising careers, they may struggle with a loss of identity in

addition to foregone economic opportunities (Blair-Loy 2003, Stone 2007), however, they gain moral currency from the American public as they are praised for doing the "right thing" for their children. The opposite is true for poor single mothers who may also feel the need to leave low-wage jobs due to family demands but will not find their choices extolled for being in the best interest of their children.

In contrast to poor women on welfare, it is rare to hear of professional women in careers, or even married working-class mothers, proclaimed as morally worthy for their devotion to their careers or jobs.[2] Missing from both public debate and studies on work and family are the moral and cultural influences that differentiate the ways more educated professional women approach work and family choices—including the evaluation and consequences of those decisions—from the perspectives of working-class and poor women.

In this book, I focus on poor and low-income women to shed light on the work and family obligations of a group of women whose lives are rarely front and center in the work and family debate. It is true that just as greater financial resources provide professional women with opportunities, financial hardship constrains the choices of low-income women compared to more advantaged mothers. But this is too simplistic an explanation as to why choices are so limited even for women who seemingly have a wide array of options, and so agonizing for women whether professional or working class. What is clear when we listen to poor and working-class women is that work and family decisions also involve moral and emotional commitments that are not fully explained as simply responses to economic forces. Thus, the central focus of this book is the broadly shared and influential moral and emotional forces that shape how poor and low-income women, both on and off welfare, see themselves as workers and mothers and view their commitments to caring for and providing for children.

Mary Blair-Loy in her book *Competing Devotions* (2003), provided a particularly insightful analysis of the cultural and moral forces that shape elite professional women's career and family decisions. She argues that understanding the work and family choices of even successful women requires us to look beyond individual explanations or economic factors to the taken-for-granted ideals that shape how individuals see themselves and others, what they value, and what gives their lives meaning. She asserts that choices about work and family are not made apart from the social and cultural environment in which people live and interact with others. "To confront work-family conflict is to grapple with profound issues of moral commitments and social and individual identity, as shaped by the cultures and communities in which we are immersed" (2003, 4). Blair-Loy found that in spite of tremendous financial resources, elite educations, and well-paying jobs at the top of their professions, the women she interviewed could not live up to the contradictory demands of the cultural models she refers to as "devotion schemas." Yet her analysis of the work and family lives of elite women offers little insight into the lives of poor and working-class women.

I agree with Blair-Loy that, at its heart, conflict between work and family commitments is tied to individual identity and to how we evaluate others and ourselves as competent moral adults. My question: what are the cultural and moral models—devotion schemas—that inform how poor and low-income women go to work and care for their children?

To answer this and other questions we need to go back to the issue of why leaving paid work to care for children earns professional, married mothers kudos for doing the right thing (Stone 2007), and, why, at the same time, policy makers and the American public applaud work requirements for poor and low-income mothers who might otherwise rely on welfare to stay home with *their* children. What do we make of this contradiction from the vantage point of impoverished and low-income women as they respond to changes in welfare policy that mandate participation in paid work? How do these demands help shape the moral commitments of low-income women in meeting their responsibilities as workers and mothers? I explore these contradictory cultural models of work and motherhood as they are filtered through the experiences of low-income and impoverished women.

WELFARE ASSISTANCE AND WORK-FAMILY DECISIONS

Few will be surprised to learn that poor single mothers experience considerable hardship both on and off welfare assistance in trying to make ends meet (Edin and Lein 1997) and that poor, middle, and upper middle-class professional working families experience work-family conflict (Jacobs and Gerson 2004). We are well acquainted with stories about dual-earner parents who work in demanding jobs and feel constantly pulled or torn between work and family—where balancing jobs, kids, day care arrangements, and housework shapes decisions about work and family roles (Hochschild 1997, Williams 2010). Harried middle-class mothers (and fathers) trying to balance the demands of paid work with the needs of children, spouses, and housework depend on a variety of available resources both material and symbolic that help shape their choices.

Yet, in contrast to how we think about middle and upper middle-class families, we are less likely to consider how public assistance shapes the work and family choices of low-income families. The material support provided by the state through cash payments, child care subsidies, food stamps, medical insurance, and other means is one way that public assistance influences work and family decisions. Additionally, welfare programs not only provide material resources, but they also supply both the public and welfare recipients an "interpretive map of normative, differentially valued gender roles and gendered needs" (Fraser 1989, 9).

Provisions in TANF specifically uphold marriage as the foundation of society as well as two-parent families and the care of children in their homes, which on the surface seems to support traditional gender roles. Yet in practice, TANF is geared toward moving single mothers into jobs outside the home. As Sharon Hays argued in her study of welfare reform, the underlying cultural logic of welfare reform views sending mothers out to work as *"rehabilitating* mothers, transforming women who would otherwise 'merely' stay at home and care for their children into women who are self-sufficient, independent productive members of society" (2003, 19). In this way the welfare system sends a normative message to women about their responsibilities as caregivers and providers that differs markedly from the gendered expectations at the heart of work and family conflict. If poor women do not engage in paid work but choose to stay home and care for their children, they are punished by the elimination or reduction of welfare benefits. The message sent to poor mothers is "good mothers go to work" (Cohen and Bianchi 1999). This is not a sentiment that holds much currency for the majority of Americans. Given our defense of motherhood as "the most important job in the world" (Crittenden 2001)—a 2012 example was public uproar over Hilary Rosen's comment that Anne Romney, the wife of presidential nominee Mitt Romney, had never worked a day in her life as a stay-at-home mother—it seems a sizeable portion of the U.S. public does not agree with this new definition of mothers' family obligations.

In fact, the transformation of welfare mothers into productive, responsible citizens calls for a revision of the opposition of work and family as competing and contradictory. This requires a revamping of deeply embedded ways of thinking about men's and women's roles, including the notion that paid work has traditionally been a way for men to fulfill their family obligations. Only poor women on welfare are encouraged to find redemption in the workplace.

DIVERGENT VALUES

Charles Murray in *Coming Apart* (2012) explored differing value systems between upper- and upper-middle-class Americans and working-class Americans. Murray argued that the lifestyles of haves (read upper- and upper-middle-class white Americans) reflect traditional moral values measured by educational attainment, industriousness, religiosity, and marriage. In contrast, the working class demonstrates a decline in such values. The groups are also spatially isolated from each other, which exacerbates the growing divide between the haves and the have-nots. Importantly, because Murray asserted that the cause of this divide or the reason we are "coming apart" is linked to values, no social policy solutions are needed.

Murray's book carries on the tradition of moral claims making that attributes poverty and disadvantage to distinct value systems that differ from those held by middle- and upper-middle-class Americans (Murray 1984, 2012, Wilson 1996). What Murray did not acknowledge was the relationship between the values he uncovered and the structural conditions he described, or the possibility of shared values. My book offers an alternative perspective through which to understand the moral and cultural underpinnings that shape people's values and how they live their lives. In contrast to Murray, I examine deeply held values as cultural and moral mandates that shape how poor and working-class women see themselves and others, their commitments to their children, and their responsibilities as mothers. I argue that social policy changes provide a lens with which to explore the moral universe of poor and working-class mothers and in doing so to expand our understanding of widely recognized and broadly shared cultural models centered on paid work and caring for children that drive work and family conflict.

Rather than rely on individualist explanations, this study considers how the particular contours of how and where individuals "choose" to devote their time and energy are shaped through broad historical and cultural forces. Poverty, welfare assistance, low-wage labor, single motherhood, and interaction with social service agencies (which promote workforce participation over raising children) are also contributing factors in how women in this study approach decisions about paid work and caring for children. As we hear from low-income women in the chapters that follow, it becomes apparent that gendered assumptions about women's responsibility for the care of children, the virtue associated with paid work, and the stigma attached to welfare assistance are compelling cultural forces that shape poor women's work and family decisions.

DEVOTION SCHEMAS

I explore the moral dimension of poor women's lives as a set of historically constructed cultural schemas. Cultural schemas are shared, publicly available cultural understandings, often taken for granted, that comprise the ideal dimension of social structure (Sewell 1992). These publicly shared, taken-for-granted cultural schemas act as emotional and cognitive scripts defining for individuals what they value in life (Blair-Loy 2003). They also help shape the institutions of work, family, and public assistance.

Mary Blair-Loy used the term *devotion schemas* to analyze the particular gendered cultural schemas that guide the work and family decisions of the elite professional women she studied. In her analysis, devotion schemas, in addition to organizing thoughts, also define what it is that provides meaning and purpose in individuals' lives. The affective content of these schemas contributes to their compelling power to constrain and enable action. Blair-Loy uses striking language to characterize their commanding emotional force: "Devotion schemas specify that which we are invited or compelled to devote ourselves to body and soul. Like pseudo religious articles of faith, they promise to provide meaning to life and a secure connection to something outside ourselves" (2001, 689). She labeled these two powerful gendered cultural models the *work devotion* and *family devotion schema.*

For elite professional women, the work devotion schema mandates long hours and tremendous sacrifice of time and energy to one's career. It shapes both the sense of duty and single-minded dedication of employees and a firm's workplace policies and practices. The family devotion schema defines marriage and motherhood as women's primary vocation. It demands intense time and emotional commitment to children, whose needs must trump all other responsibilities. Blair-Loy showed how women who by all accounts have "made it" in the world of work had difficulty reconciling the competing demands that they give unwavering devotion to careers and at the same time devote themselves to their children.

Blair-Loy's study staked out important ground in expanding our understanding of work and family conflict as more than simply juggling too many responsibilities or a matter of individual choice. The group of elite women she studied had more "choices" than most women in the United States: elite educations, rewarding careers, husbands with substantial earnings, ability to afford quality day care, housekeepers, and other support for paid work. Yet even very successful women found that they could not reconcile the competing demands of the devotion to family and work schemas. In contrast to a study of women who are frequently characterized as having it all (or criticized for such aspirations), I explore the devotional schemas that guide the choices of low-income and impoverished women. What can we learn about work-family conflict from the cultural and moral models shaping poor women's lives—lives that differ markedly from middle- and upper-middle-class women whose commitments to paid work and family life drive contemporary understandings about work and family conflict? In the pages that follow, I explore how these morally salient, gendered cultural models shape the work and family lives of poor and low-income women on and off welfare.

POOR MOTHERS' SCHEMAS

The two cultural models I use in this study of poor and low-income women's lives, the *work commitment* and the *family commitment* schemas, are broadly consistent with Blair-Loy's (2001, 2003) work devotion and family devotion schemas; however, there are marked differences. For example, the work devotion schema identified by Blair-Loy demands absolute devotion to a career, long work hours, and intense commitment to the firm. It promises status, engaging work, and significant financial rewards. In contrast, the cultural model defining poor and working-class mothers' work and family lives demands paid work as a sign of responsibility and independence. It promises self-sufficiency and relief from the stigma of welfare. To understand how poor women grapple with the expectations of where they should devote their time and energy, we have to take into account their confrontation with a system that repeatedly tells them that, in contrast to others, they are doing the right thing for their families by going to work. The reform of welfare in which poor women lost support for caring for their children unless they got a job challenges the opposition of work and family and the gendered assumptions about women's primary responsibilities.

The cultural models used in this study, the work commitment and family commitment schemas, are abstract models called *ideal types*. An ideal type is an analytical construct used as a point of comparison to ascertain similarities and differences in cases under study (Weber 1958a). It comprises essential characteristics of particular social phenomena, which allow the social analyst to compare observations of actual cases on the ground with important characteristics of cultural models. The word *ideal* used here means pure or typical rather than desirable or good. An example of an ideal typical construction would be the 1950s breadwinner/homemaker cultural model. Households (in the 1950s and today) in reality did not conform to all aspects of this model, but the model serves as a point of comparison to understand how actual households were similar to or different from the pure type construction. Similarly, we will see that individuals do not always express themselves or identify consistently in accord with all the elements of one devotional schema or the other. These models are not meant to be deterministic, but they are influential in shaping how people evaluate themselves and others. The competing and contradictory nature of the models is the source of considerable ambivalence faced by women in meeting the demands of work and family and is the heart of the cultural wars over women's roles fought among the American public.

Table 1.1 presents defining aspects of these cultural models. Subsequent chapters will show how people understand these models and use them to make sense of their lives.

Work Commitment Schema

Although paid work is increasingly expected of women across socioeconomic status, the moral dimension of work commitment as a sign of character

Table 1.1. Defining characteristics of work commitment and family commitment schemas

Work commitment	*Family commitment*
Breadwinner/good provider	Motherhood
Demonstrates responsibility	Responsibility for children
Builds character	Child care is a mother's primary duty/ calling
Work is a calling	Fulfills woman's nature
Role models for children	Children's needs come first
Independence/self-sufficiency	Financial support for stay-at-home mother

may resonate more powerfully in the lives of poor single mothers who would otherwise depend on welfare, not in the lives of married working mothers, other employed women, or stay-at-home mothers (Folbre 1994). The following example helps illustrate the different moral context in which poor women make decisions about paid work and caring for children.

Jane Peterson, twenty-four years old, never married, mother of a two-year-old daughter, works as a nurse's aide. She draws from aspects of the work commitment schema as she describes the rewards of paid work in setting an example for children and in the independence it brings. "They [women who work outside the home] show to their children that they can be responsible, and they know for their daughters you are not going to have to be a stay home, take care of your children, do what your husband—or you know, for instance, [what] the man says. I say do your part to earn money. You're bringing home the bread."

Several women who will be introduced in later chapters also hold a vision of work and family life in which providing for children through paid work is a sign of character and responsibility, in contrast to mothers who would otherwise "stay home, take care of your children." However, the image of the mother who *merely* stays at home and takes care of children in the neighborhoods of the women whose lives are presented in this book is more likely to be a woman supported by public assistance than by a wage-earning husband.

Family Commitment Schema

As an abstract model, the family commitment schema assigns responsibility for home and family to women. It orders a model of "intensive" motherhood that is time-consuming, emotionally absorbing, and centered on one's precious children (Hays 1996). It rests on an idealized notion of motherhood based on the circumstances of the white middle-class woman. Paid work outside the home is not forbidden altogether, yet must not interfere with a mother's primary duty to care for her children.

In contrast to the poor and working-class women who are the focus of this study, for professional women in careers the family, devotion schema promises financial stability in the form of a stay-at-home mother and male elite worker in addition to other intrinsic rewards such as fulfillment and intimacy in marriage and motherhood. Poor mothers also feel the powerful cultural pull of intensive mothering, but single mothers do not experience the social approval given to middle-class and professional mothers, finding their family commitment challenged by welfare work requirements (Weigt 2006, Nelson 2005).

Suzanne Cartwright, twenty-three, never-married mother of an eighteen-month-old child, moved back in with her father and began receiving welfare after she was fired from her job as a nursing assistant. Suzanne was not proud of the fact that she was on welfare and stated that she needed to work. Typical of many mothers in this study, she expressed conflicting feelings about working outside the home. As she explained,

> Single parenting is a totally different life, because you can't depend on the state to be there all the time to be able to take care of the child. So you have to have a job to be able to support them. And the ideal situation would be me not working and taking care of my kid. . . . If a child is really young, I understand that staying with them makes sense so then they have a really good bond with their children. I think that they should go out and look for a job as soon as they can. Although, it just breaks my heart to have to do it, to leave him at home myself. I had to do it.

Many working mothers of young children can relate to Suzanne's feeling of being torn over her choice. However, the fact that she is a single mother on welfare makes it far less likely that she will find much sympathy for her situation. Many Americans would agree that she should get a job—they would also share Suzanne's belief that small children should be cared for by their mothers. This poses a dilemma for mothers like Suzanne whose definition of a meaningful life pulls her in two different directions; her need to provide for her child is challenged by the family commitment schema's demand that children should be cared for by their mothers.

This next example further illustrates the influence of family commitment and also the distance of the lives of the women in this study from those who inform the work family debate in the United States. Gina Grinnell, forty-nine, is the mother of four children—three grown and one elementary-school-age daughter. Her work history includes a variety of different jobs from retail to truck driving, and she recently completed a training program in catering. Her portrayal of family commitment illustrates the oppositional model described earlier in which one must be devoted to work or to family.

She praises poor mothers for staying home with their children rather than devoting time and energy to a career even if they must rely on welfare to do so. Her characterization of "career women" illustrates how these cultural models not only shape decisions about women's actions but also help shape identities; dedication to a career comes at the expense of women's primary responsibility—their children. Thus, in contrast to negative depictions of women on welfare, devotion to children's well-being instead of to a career provides poor mothers with a widely recognized and valued identity as a good mother who puts her kids first.

> I think a lot of the women who are on welfare are probably the more maternal mothers that want to be home with their children! And I say hurrah for them! . . . Like I say there's some women that don't have much of a maternal instinct and maybe their career does come first. But I know a lot of women, you know, particularly women on welfare that their kids come first. And I don't necessarily say that women should be on welfare. But women have stayed home and taken care of their children for centuries and all of a sudden it's wrong? Come on. You know that is ridiculous.

Gina's comments illustrate the principle at the heart of family commitment: a shared belief that children's interests should trump other commitments. Although mothers in my study stated that some women did not want to stay home with their children, it was clear that they believed very strongly that most mothers do, and that they *should* stay home with children if they are financially able. Thus, devotional schemas not only inform how individual women evaluate their own decisions and identities as workers and mothers; they also shape how women evaluate others. They provide important insights into how the stigma of welfare assistance helps transform what it means to be a good mother from one of full-time homemaker to a woman who does her part and brings home the bread. Conversely, the view that work demands from the welfare office force women into making choices that cause them to abdicate their primary responsibility to care for their children reinforces the pull of family commitment toward involved motherhood. Women whose definition of a meaningful life is shaped through the family commitment's demand that children's needs outweigh all other commitments are more likely to resist the model of work and motherhood confronting them at the welfare office.

THE STUDY

Research on work-family conflict, broadly defined—and more specifically, studies on the cultural and moral structures that shape people's expectations of work and family—focuses primarily on married, middle-, and upper-class women. I wanted to explore how low-income and impoverished women differ from their middle-class counterparts in their work and family commitments and to investigate possible areas where they might share similar understandings. Given the changes in social welfare policy, I wanted to talk to working-class and poor women on and off welfare whose lives are most likely to be shaped by these changes. I combined thirty-nine in-depth interviews and responses to 257 survey questionnaires that asked poor and low-income mothers about their work and family lives to find answers to these questions. In the book I primarily focus on the interviews and women's accounts of their lives, with the addition of a chapter presenting quantitative analysis of the survey responses.

My objective in this study was to understand work and family decisions from the perspectives of poor women and the contradictory moral and cultural forces that shape these decisions. I wanted to include a diverse mix of women and was able to accomplish this through contact with women who were enrolled in or had previously attended programs consisting of workshops and pre-employment training for low-income women preparing to enter or reenter the workforce. The group included poor single mothers on public assistance, married and divorced mothers on and off public assistance, and women who had been previously married or partnered for a number of years. This particular group of women is not characteristic of women at the most extreme ends of poverty who suffer from severe social and human capital deficits. All the women in the study completed or had enrolled in classes to improve upon or gain job skills. None were homeless; although a few women lived in transitional housing, most lived in apartments and single-family homes with rental assistance. Others lived with parents or extended family members. A substantial minority of women *did* face formidable obstacles to their ability to work and care for their children: substance abuse, mental and physical disabilities, and domestic violence in addition to severe financial hardship. I bring this to the reader's attention because, as much as this book is not intended to gloss over or overlook the considerable disadvantage that poor and low-income women on and off welfare experience compared to others, neither does it intend to portray poor women as overwhelmingly victimized by circumstances beyond their control. Additionally, this group of women is predominantly white, which counters the tendency to associate poverty and welfare with urban minority communities of color.

Given assumptions about poor women and welfare assistance, readers may be skeptical that women may not provide accurate accounts of their actions—but rather socially desirable accounts. My role as a social analyst is not to evaluate whether what mothers tell me about their devotion to work and family is accurate or true. Rather, it is to understand the role of morality in shaping work and family decisions for poor women, and to understand how they see their lives affected by changes in expectations for men's and women's roles and welfare assistance. To do so, we need to be able to make sense of low-income women's perceptions of appropriate models of work and motherhood and the moral and cultural factors that help shape those perceptions.

I provide additional details on the sample, methods used, survey design, and variables used in analyses in a methodological appendix.

OVERVIEW OF THE BOOK

In chapter 2, I trace the history of welfare policy in the United States from its origins in the mothers' pension programs of the Progressive Era. This chapter presents welfare policy as a window through which to view dominant expectations of work and family life based on prevailing standards of paid work and motherhood and the erosion of support for poor mothers to stay at home with children. I show how contemporary debates over welfare policy and welfare reform reflect broader social cultural forces defining appropriate visions of who should work and who should provide. This section looks at the intersection of gender and cultural constructions of moral worth, illuminating the broad moral categories and gendered cultural models embedded in welfare assistance.

Chapters 3 through 5 examine work and family commitments based on interview data. Chapter 3 focuses on the work commitment schema, and its association of working outside the home with moral worth. In contrast to middle- or upper-middle-class mothers in careers that bring personal fulfillment and substantial financial rewards, respondents work in low-wage jobs. Yet the mothers in this study offer many of the same reasons for working as others: money, social interaction, relief from the tedium of housework, and personal fulfillment. They also earn self-respect as independent wage earners and provide positive role models for children. Some women become disenchanted with the promises of work commitment when low-wage jobs do not bring dignity or self-sufficiency and interfere with responsibility for children.

Chapter 4 unpacks the family commitment schema's powerful hold on the hearts and minds of women in this study. The family commitment schema demands that mothers put their children's interest first and foremost. Through the stories they share, it becomes clear that many mothers believe that undue commitment to paid work harms children's well-being and that children should be cared for by their mothers. Several mothers privilege their responsibility as mothers in opposition to TANF workfare polices and "career women," who defy the family commitment schema's demand to put children's needs first. Many find themselves caught in a catch-22 between their need to provide for their families financially and their belief that when mothers work outside the home children suffer.

Chapter 5 examines welfare policy in light of negative assumptions and stereotypes about women on welfare. In this chapter, respondents describe their interactions at the welfare office and provide vivid examples of resistance and change as mothers face work requirements, fill out forms for housing and food stamps, and respond to the stigma of reliance on public assistance. Respondents resist pressure by the welfare office to make hasty arrangements for daycare—at times less than twenty-four hours in advance—to attend training sessions or take low-wage jobs. They express anger at the requirement that mothers find employment or enter job training when children reach three months of age. The image of a mother forced to put her three-month-old infant in day care places the welfare system on the wrong side of a moral imperative prescribed by the family commitment's definition of children as vulnerable and in need of mothers' care.

In chapter 6, I step back from the interview data to present survey data and findings from quantitative analyses. I compare responses to questions on work and family priorities between mothers who received welfare under TANF and those who may have received welfare prior to TANF or who never received cash welfare benefits. Survey data show strong support for gendered division of labor and also a desire to engage in meaningful work outside the home. Gendered beliefs underlying the family commitment cultural model remain strong among all respondents. However, results of regression analysis show that respondents who received TANF are less likely to support requiring poor single mothers to work outside the home. Never-married mothers are more likely to see working outside the home as compatible with paid work compared to divorced mothers—a finding supported by the interview data in that divorced mothers are more likely to have envisioned being able to stay home with young children supported by a spouse's wage.

Chapter 7 discusses the implications of my findings for work and family studies and public policy. It suggests a more nuanced approach to studies of poor women, with greater attention to the complexity of poor women's lives. Not surprisingly, poor women, like their more affluent contemporaries, wish to engage in meaningful work without sacrificing their ability to care for their children. Though the conditions of poverty and welfare assistance constrain the choices of impoverished and low-income women, the mothers whose lives are represented here offer complex and varied interpretations of appropriate work and family decisions. Some view work outside the home as fulfilling their family role, filtered through the masculine work ethic in the work commitment schema. Others reject this model of family life, identifying strongly with the family commitment's rival vision that children's needs trump the demands of the workplace. Reconciling these contradictory cultural forces poses a painful dilemma for mothers, as poor women, like their middle-class counterparts, experience ambivalence over work and family choices. Individualistic values and narrow cultural arguments miss the forest for the trees in overlooking the moral salience of work and family decisions and how morality as part of social structure shapes the lives of women.

NOTES

1. See the Pew Research Center (http://www.pewresearch.org) for polls and reports on trends in American family life over a twenty-five-year span. Over time Americans have indicated greater support for working parents, but they are still concerned about the effects on children when mothers work outside the home. A 2014 report, *After Decades of Decline, A Rise in Stay-at-Home Moms*, found that 51 percent of adults surveyed said children were better off if their mothers stay home, whereas only 8 percent said that children were better off if their fathers stayed at home, and 60 percent said children are better off when a parent stays home. Seventy-four percent said that the increased number of women in the workplace made it harder for parents to raise children, but they also agreed that it helped families financially.

2. An exception is Linda Hirschman's (2006) response to the opt-out media frenzy in which she castigated mothers for staying at home to care for their children. Her criticism was directed at professional women who opt out of careers, whom she characterized as failing in their responsibility to promote gender equality in the workplace and opportunities for women.

Chapter Two

Historical Context

From Mothers' Aid to Personal Responsibility

As I began work on this book, I was often asked, "What is it about?" I would reply that I was writing about the moral context of poor and low-income mothers' work and family decisions in which if you are poor and on welfare, you are a good mom for going to work. What I heard most often in response was, "I never thought about that." This is not surprising in that most of the focus on work and family issues relates to how much time mothers in middle-class, married, dual-earner families devote to paid work and domestic responsibilities—and to evaluation of their choices. It is also because a large part of this story has to do with welfare assistance. Welfare, in contrast to work-family conflict, is foreign to most Americans' daily lives and off the public radar in debates over paid work and family obligations. Yet—as a reflected image of gender and class relations in U.S. society—welfare policy is intimately intertwined with taken-for-granted, unquestioned assumptions about women's work and family decisions.

"Nobody likes welfare" sums up how policy makers and the U.S. public, including the people who rely on government assistance, feel about welfare programs, albeit for different reasons.[1] For many Americans, the image that the word *welfare* brings to mind is one of people living off government handouts who cannot or will not work to earn enough to provide for themselves and their families. What the U.S. public and others (aside from welfare scholars) rarely consider is how welfare policy is and always has been part of a larger ideological and normative order that reflects and shapes dominant work and family relationships in our society (Katz 1996, Abramovitz 1996). Today's welfare system is no exception.

This chapter provides a brief overview of U.S. welfare policy development, beginning with the Progressive Era Mothers' Aid program, to illustrate how welfare, as a system of polices and practices, reflects and reinforces dominant social and moral conventions of the time. As poverty researchers Handler and Hasenfeld argued in *We the Poor People*, "Welfare policy both contributes to and is shaped by the larger moral debates in society" (1997, 4). In U.S. society, one of the most enduring moral debates concerns women's work and family obligations.

GENDERED CULTURAL HISTORY OF WELFARE POLICY IN THE UNITED STATES

In the United States, the cultural issue that forms the heart of the welfare debate centers on the question of who is morally excused from work and who is expected to provide (Handler 1995, Abramovitz 1996). This locates gender as central to understanding welfare policy. That is to say that any account of U.S. welfare policy would be incomplete without an emphasis on the role of gender as a societal ideal as to appropriate men's and women's roles that was highly influential in establishing the distinctive character of the U.S. welfare system. This fact is well documented by feminist scholars whose portrayals of the history of welfare policy making tell a story of continuous efforts to impose or reinforce dominant standards of paid work and care giving.[2] The often-contentious debates over welfare policy also reveal challenges to those ideals, as new models of work and family life compete with old models of dependency and categories of worthy and unworthy poor. The brief overview presented here (drawing from the excellent work of feminist scholars) describes the origins of welfare programs in the United States and the major legislative changes in welfare policy up to the contemporary time period. I focus on the particularly gendered nature of the U.S. welfare policy as it pertains to the initial development of policies that relied on the prevailing notion of (some) women's unique capacity as mothers and concerns about single parent families.

Maternalist Welfare State

In the United States, the categories that designate who is worthy of public support were molded to a great extent by Progressive Era women activists in the beginning of the twentieth century who shaped both public discourse and policies to reflect widespread beliefs about women's distinct capacities as mothers (Skocpol 1992, Gordon 1994). These early "feminist" reformers used the dominant ideal of the times—men earning wages sufficient to support women and children and women's separate sphere of domesticity and motherhood—to establish government support for poor families headed by single mothers. As a precursor to federal welfare assistance, the goal of these programs was to assist poor single mothers with children, to discourage child labor, and to enable children in mother-only families to remain in the home. Theda Skocpol's (1992) work is particularly relevant to understanding the degree to which societal beliefs about gender shaped the provision of public assistance as it developed in the United States. Although Skocpol's main emphasis was on the institutional processes that resulted in a "maternalist" welfare state, a major contribution of her work is to point out the gendered nature of widely accepted moral categories in the provision of poor relief. The shared belief in mothers and motherhood as morally valued categories legitimated mothers and children as recipients of public assistance, whereas other categories were not seen as deserving.

The recipient at that time was envisioned as a white widowed mother, and welfare assistance was designed to replace the family wage lost in the absence of a male provider (Abramovitz 1996, Gordon 1994). Although this ideal was never an accurate description of most American families (few workers earned wages that alone could support women and children, and welfare support for the poor excluded poor, immigrant, and minority families), it formed the template for welfare policy in the United States.

The maternalist U.S. welfare state began in the early 1900s as states and local governments—spurred by white, middle-class, educated women activists—established Mothers' Aid (pensions) programs to help single mothers refrain from at least full-time work so they could care for children in their homes. The belief in different social roles for men and women—the separate spheres ideology relegating men to provide and women to perform domestic duties—constrained women's involvement in public life as outside the bounds of proper womanhood. Ironically, at a time when women did not yet have the right to vote, it also provided the opportunity for this particular group of women activists to shape the course that public assistance for poor women would take in the United States (Gordon 1994). This was in keeping with the widespread valorization of motherhood and nurturing, along with ideas about women's capacity for moral leadership in the home and also in domestic areas of civic life.

Thus, the early Mothers' Aid reflected the experience of the elite white reformers who held a particular vision of family life that they used to shape public policy. Historian Linda Gordon wrote that the early maternalist reformers, "committed to women's exclusive mothering and domesticity, . . . imagined proper family life only with a male breadwinner and a full-time housewife; thus single mother families however formed were defective" (1994, 32). This was not necessarily indicative of reformers' beliefs that single mothers were to blame for their situation but rather a reflection of the cultural and class bias inherent in Mothers' Aid.

On the one hand, women as a whole were seen as naturally suited to care for children and deserving of support to fulfill their proper roles as mothers. On the other hand, poverty and single motherhood were reason enough to cast doubt on the moral fitness of mothers, even though there was sympathy and concern for children and for women who had been widowed or deserted by men. From the early days of Mothers' Aid, welfare assistance endeavored to reinforce the breadwinner/homemaker family ideal both financially and behaviorally on the part of poor mothers (Abramovitz 1996). The loss of a male wage created a dire economic situation for poor families, and welfare shored up the family wage ideal by replacing a man's contribution. Welfare also functioned as a mechanism to supervise or encourage the moral fitness of families headed by single mothers through activities to instill proper models of childrearing and domestic responsibilities (Gordon 1994). It was the task of charity workers to train poor women in the ways of proper womanhood so that they could raise children in ways deemed socially and culturally appropriate. This training, referred to as "moral uplift," provided poor, mostly immigrant women material help along with reform, discipline, and evaluative judgments of their moral fitness (Mink 1995, Gordon 1994).

The strong emphasis on separate spheres and the family wage ideal created contradictions when it came to mothers' employment. Social workers blamed issues faced by poor families such as neglect and child abuse on mothers' employment, insisting that women remain at home even though the provision of Mothers' Aid was insufficient to support full-time domesticity. This contradiction created a double bind for single mothers (familiar today) raising children with little to no support who had to work at least part time. Working out of necessity to put food on the table could jeopardize support needed to help protect children from the hardships imposed by poverty and the type of abuse and neglect charity workers attributed to single motherhood. Thus, providing aid to keep mothers out of the workforce further exacerbated the problems of single mothers as it contributed to the stigmatization of mothers who worked, and made them seem less deserving of support (Gordon 1994). In short, poor mothers in the early twentieth century were judged harshly if they worked outside the home for neglecting their children and for not living up to appropriate standards of womanhood, at the same time, Mothers' Aid was not sufficient to replace the family wage.

ADC to AFDC

Following the Great Depression, the Social Security Act of 1935 as part of Franklin Delano Roosevelt's New Deal legislation, nationalized the states' Mothers' Aid programs and established Aid to Dependent Children (ADC)—later changed to Aid to Families with Dependent Children (AFDC). Like the mothers' pensions, ADC was intended to support poor women and children who lost the support of a male wage earner by preventing mothers from having to join the paid labor force. The *Report of the Committee on Economic Security* of 1935 recommending the federal expansion of Mothers' Aid into what became ADC, described aid to "fatherless" children as "designed to release from the wage-earning role the person whose natural function is to give *her* [italics added] children the physical and affectionate guardianship necessary not alone to keep them from falling into social misfortune, but more affirmatively to make them citizens capable of contributing to society" (Abramovitz 1996, 315).

The report above illustrates how from their very early days welfare policy provisions were not simply a response to the economic upheaval or instability brought about by the Great Depression. They also served to promote the social and cultural mores of middle-class white Americans and conventional gender roles. It is also important to bear in mind the degree to which these early policies reaffirmed masculine identity and the work ethic. Keeping women out of the labor force not only promoted women's proper family roles in raising future citizens; it also reaffirmed men's rightful place in work and family life as sole providers. This result may partially explain why at the time, the ADC program was not nearly as controversial as other parts of the Social Security Act, which enjoys widespread popularity with the public today. In fact, there was more resistance to the passage of the Old Age Insurance provision (known today as Social Security) and Unemployment Insurance (UI) than there was to the ADC program due to fears that UI and SS would reward idleness and erode the work ethic (Gordon 1994). Again, in keeping with work and family arrangements of the time, poor mothers raising children "seemed the quintessentially deserving recipients" of public assistance (Gordon 2002, 15)—undoubtedly more so than unemployed workers or elderly retirees, all men, who were the intended beneficiaries of UI and Old Age Insurance.

An excerpt from the Children's Bureau magazine explaining the program to readers underscores the influence of maternalist ideals in shaping ADC policy: "Even where individual grants are small . . . the mother can feel that in doing a good job with her children she is making a genuine contribution to society" (Mink 1995, 131). However, opponents of the program expressed fears that providing aid to children would absolve fathers of responsibility and encourage single motherhood. This opposition served to limit the number of families that actually received aid as detractors of the program argued that it should only go to those "children of worthy character, suffering from temporary misfortune, and children of reasonably efficient and deserving mothers" (Handler and Hasenfeld 1997, 28). The sentiments expressed by both opponents and supporters of the program from its inception—the obligation to assist the deserving poor (mothers and children) and at the same time enforce a strong work ethic and personal responsibility (on the part of men)—emphasize the contradictory tensions that continued to shape welfare policy throughout a series of reforms and attempts at reform beginning as early as 1939 and culminating sixty years later with as Gwendolyn Mink (1998) argues, the *end of welfare* with the 1996 Personal Responsibility Work Opportunity Act (PRWORA). See table 2.1 for a timeline of welfare programs.

In 1939, a survivor's benefit was added to the Old Age Insurance program, drawing widows and children of deceased workers from the ADC program into the more generous social insurance program (Mink 1995). The result, in addition to an increasingly poor clientele on ADC, was that recipients of ADC were more likely to be deserted, divorced, or never-married

Table 2.1.   Timeline of welfare programs

Date	Program	Heading
1911–1920	Mothers' Aid established in forty states	Mothers' pensions established through state programs to support children in single-mother families
1935	Aid to Dependent Children (ADC) established as part of New Deal	Federalizes Mothers' Aid
1939	Survivors benefits added to Old Age Insurance	Widows and children of deceased workers move to Social Security program
1962	ADC changes to Aid to Families with Dependent Children (AFDC)	Emphasis on services to make families self-supporting
1967	Work Initiative Program (WIN)	Adds training and work requirements for mothers of children older than age six
1969–1971	Family Assistance Plan (FAP) fails Supplemental Security Income (SSI) established	Attempts to establish a guaranteed annual income to poor and working poor families
1988	Family Support Act (FSA) established	Reduces the child age exemption to age three; establishes Job Opportunity and Basic Skills Program (JOBS)
1996	Personal Responsibility Work Opportunity Act (PRWORA) abolishes AFDC, creates Temporary Assistance to Needy Families (TANF)	Devolves welfare programs to states in the form of block grants, eliminates entitlement, establishes work requirements, mandates five-year maximum lifetime limit

mothers, or the widows of men not covered by Social Security, which included many African American families. However, many state governments excluded African American women from eligibility for ADC benefits on the grounds that they were employable mothers (93 percent worked in domestic service or agriculture).[3] Many states, particularly in the South, also imposed restrictions, such as "man in the house," which they subsequently used to deny benefits to a woman if she was in a relationship with a man even though he was not legally responsible for her children, and "unsuitable home" rules that could be used arbitrarily to deny eligibility. For example, a nonmarital birth could indicate an unsuitable home, a determination welfare departments would use to withhold support for an entire family (Abramovitz 1996).[4] The impact of these practices was to deny benefits, force employment on minority women, and increase the hardship of impoverished families. It was also a way for welfare policy makers to exclude those who were deemed outside the bounds of proper gender relations and family formation.

The War on Poverty—1960s

In response to social, cultural, and policy changes in the 1950s and 1960s, the welfare rolls grew as the more worthy white widows on the rolls were replaced by divorced, never-married single mothers and increased numbers of racial ethnic families. A benefit for mothers was added to the ADC program in the 1950s, and eligibility was expanded as barriers to enrollment were dismantled. These changes coincided with increased hostility and stigma toward "welfare mothers" as the country headed toward the "welfare crisis" of the 1960s.

By the 1960s the increase in the size of the welfare rolls and changes in the attributes of families on the rolls prompted concerns about the character of welfare programs and the nature of poverty. The ADC program grew from 372,000 families in 1940 to 803,000 families in 1960 (Abramovitz 1996). From 1965 to 1971 the caseload more than doubled to 10.7 million persons, and state and federal costs grew from just under one billion to 6.2 billion dollars (Weaver 2000, 55). Although much of the concern over the welfare crisis was due to rising costs and the huge increase in the number of families receiving benefits, it was also due to the changing demographics of who was receiving those benefits. By 1961, widowed families made up only 7.7 percent of the welfare caseload compared to 43 percent in 1937 (Abramovitz 1996, 321). Although the notion of a crisis was couched in public concerns about family breakdown, the work ethic, and the "kinds" of families on welfare, much of the rapid caseload increase was due to Supreme Court rulings in the 1960s striking down restrictions used to deny benefits to poor families such as "man in the house" and "unsuitable home" as unconstitutional. Only 33 percent of eligible recipients received benefits in the early

1960s; by 1971, after the restrictions were legally prohibited, the participation rate was over 90 percent (Weaver 2000, 55).

In addition to increasing numbers, the racial makeup of the welfare rolls also changed. When welfare was established as Mothers' Aid at the turn of the century, the program was overwhelmingly white due to the formal exclusion of women of color (Gordon 1994, Abramovitz 1996, Mink 1995). The increase in minority participation is partially due to successful legal challenges to the restrictive welfare provisions noted above, used disproportionately as a means to deny benefits to eligible black women and children (Abramovitz 1996, Quadragno 1994). The 1960s also brought an increase in non-marital births, which was more likely among African American families. Black women were also more likely to be divorced, separated, or widowed than were white women, leading to an increase in the number of black families eligible for welfare assistance.

In response to these changes, the 1960s brought renewed national interest in antipoverty programs that contained provisions for rehabilitating families and encouraging self-support. In 1962, legislators renamed ADC to AFDC, approved federal funding for social services to the poor, and amended the Social Security Act to allow cash payments to two-parent households in which the father was unemployed, rather than limit funds to mother-only families (Weaver 2000). The new emphasis on social services in the early 1960s by the Kennedy administration stressed the need for services and rehabilitation as a major weapon in the fight against poverty and additionally suggested that mothers could obtain jobs to be self-supporting if the state provided day care for their children (Abramovitz 1996, Mink 1995). The policies in practice reinforced the male breadwinner ideal. For example, although the 1962 reforms added a provision for two-parent families, sanctions were levied for not working, and any strong work incentives were directed at unemployed fathers (Abramovitz 1996).

Work Incentive Program

In 1967, Congress passed another set of changes to AFDC with the Work Incentive Program (WIN), requiring states to register "appropriate mothers" for training and employment and to provide child care (Reese 2005, 119). (Note that policy makers refrained from using the acronym *WIP* for a program to increase work on the part of welfare recipients.) Jill Quadragno (1994) underscored how racial bias contributed to a backlash against welfare programs in her influential book, *The Color of Welfare* (see also Reese 2005). As spending increased for welfare programs in the 1960s and the rolls expanded, resentment against antipoverty programs grew among whites. Many of the programs set up in the 1960s under the Kennedy and Johnson administrations targeted blacks for enrollment in job training and employment opportunities in occupations that had been closed off to them by whites. AFDC was also becoming increasingly associated with black single mothers. Stereotypes of blacks as lazy and the notion that black mothers were "employable" at the same time that more women were entering the workforce contributed to support for the idea that *some* poor mothers on welfare should be required to work outside the home (Reese 2005). WIN also established sanctions for failure to register for training and employment. However, enforcement was lax, and the work and training provisions had little effect on workforce participation (Handler 1995). In the end, as Handler (1995) argued, WIN did little to increase the workforce participation of poor single mothers. Nonetheless, it was consequential for its symbolic impact on the acceptability and expectation that poor women should work.[5]

The Family Assistance Plan

In a major attempt at revamping the welfare system, the Family Assistance Plan (FAP), introduced in the Nixon administration, attempted to establish guaranteed income benefits for working and nonworking poor families including those with fathers present (Weaver 2000). The FAP was promoted as helping the deserving poor, reinforcing the work ethic, and encouraging responsible behavior (Winston 2002). It also attempted to enforce traditional values of the work ethic and nuclear family by incentivizing work through job training for unemployed men and by encouraging women to stay home (Quadragno 1994). Senator Patrick Moynihan's influential report in 1965 on black American families was instrumental in the development of the FAP. He argued that the disintegration of the black family was due to high rates of unemployment among men and the dominance of women, leading to high rates of single female-headed families among African Americans (Quadragno 1994). The solution was job training for unemployed black men and financial support that would allow black women to stay home, supported by a family wage (Quadragno 1994). The proposal advocated work requirements for both men and women, but like previous attempts at reform, men were clearly envisioned with greater responsibility to provide.

The goal of the FAP was to improve the conditions of the working poor, a population that policy makers at the time believed to be entirely composed of men. As a result, men received higher priority in training and employment, and married women and women with a preschool child were excused from the work requirements (Quadragno 1994, Mink 1998). Support for male breadwinner families is unmistakable in testimony from a Nixon administration official on the FAP: "Where there are two [parents] present it is more like a *normal* [italics added] family in the sense that the emphasis is on the father, the emphasis on upgrading and career development for him to get him into a better-paying job, and to pull him out of the welfare program entirely so he becomes entirely self-supporting. The mother role becomes one of supporting the family, caring for the children while he is trying to improve his income" (Mink 1998, 39). Moreover, the FAP also proposed freezing benefits and would have increased the work hours for single mothers on welfare; thus, the way for a woman on welfare to improve her financial status would be to marry a man with wages (Quadragno 1994).

The FAP was never implemented, but the debate over the program reveals the vast cultural and social changes taking place in the United States, and welfare policy was at the heart of that change. It also calls attention to the ideological forces that continue to shape welfare policy and how they are often at odds in response to these changes. The FAP targeted working poor households in an attempt to restore the traditional male-headed family at the same time that it tried to encourage poor women on welfare to work more. Liberal feminist organizations weighed in with arguments in support of women's rights in society, arguments that devalued women's traditional work in the home and that emphasized opportunities for women working outside the home for wages (Boris 1998, Solinger 2001). The result: primarily white middle-class feminist groups worked to undermine the rights of poor minority women to stay home with *their* children.

Another influential voice was the National Welfare Rights Organization (NWRO), a grassroots organization of welfare rights activists that emerged for a brief time as a political force in the 1960s and lobbied for resources for welfare recipients, including social rights for welfare mothers based on traditional female roles (Reese 2005). The NWRO opposed the FAP's work requirements as forced labor and argued for mothers' rights to a guaranteed income (Boris 1998). Welfare rights organizations and feminist groups diverged philosophically on issues of women's interests and were also separated by race and class. The NWRO comprised primarily minority, poor, and working-class women, whereas liberal feminist organizations represented white middle-class women. The division among women in welfare policy was not new. What was new, as Handler argued, was the change in the rhetorical justification for welfare due to the growing number of unmarried, minority mothers receiving welfare payments, at the same time married mothers of small children increased their workforce participation (1995). Discouraging paid work for mothers of small children had at one time been considered a benefit of welfare for single mothers. By the late 1970s, poor mothers who did not work and instead relied on welfare were considered undeserving (Handler 1995).[6] However, as Gwendolyn Mink explained, the erosion of support for paying welfare mothers to stay home with children indicated a reluctance to provide a benefit that more deserving working mothers were not allowed, not a loss of support for married mothers to engage in full-time homemaking (1998).

Retrenchment

The Reagan presidency marked the ascendance of conservative efforts to rein in government spending and cut back on welfare programs. Fueled by economic concerns and unease about the cultural and social unrest of the 1960s and 1970s, the 1980s signaled the end of policy concerns over the adequacy of benefits for poor families and increased attention to the effects of welfare dependency (Winston 2002, 35). Conservatives increasingly justified calls for reducing welfare benefits by arguing that providing benefits to families undermined family values (read married, male-breadwinner families) and the work ethic.

The Reagan administration was known for its aversion to welfare programs whose beneficiaries were poor, disproportionately black, unmarried mothers and their children. Although racialized discourse was not new as a factor in shaping the U.S. public and policy makers' depictions of welfare programs, it was under the Reagan presidency that the racist icon of all that was wrong with government assistance to poor single mothers emerged in the "welfare queen" (Reese 2005, Quadragno 1994). This was a racially coded description of a woman on welfare who was portrayed as a welfare cheat living high on the hog from all of the money she fraudulently collected from multiple welfare checks. It was used to drum up conservative support for the retrenchment of social welfare programs, which were increasingly blamed for not only poverty but also destroying the nuclear family and eroding American values of hard work and individual responsibility.

In 1984, Charles Murray published the influential *Losing Ground* where he argued that welfare assistance, not economic conditions, caused poverty. Murray blamed welfare assistance for a host of social ills, including rising crime rates. But the claim that received the most attention was that the expansion of welfare programs in the 1960s caused single motherhood and the breakdown of the family particularly among African Americans. Murray argued that welfare programs provided financial incentives for single mothers and their unmarried partners to have children on the public dole. He used the example of an imaginary couple, Harold and Phyllis, who faced with a choice between marriage and a job for Harold or staying single and going on welfare when Phyllis becomes pregnant, choose welfare. The decision-making process is laid out as a series of cost/benefit calculations: Would Phyllis be better off if she decided to give up the baby? Or would she be better off if she kept the baby and married Harold? She also could have the baby and remain single. What about Harold? Should Harold get a job and marry Phyllis or not? Or would they be better off having the baby, living together unmarried, and going on welfare? Murray portrayed the choice to keep the baby and forgo marriage as the rational one, given the couple's working-class backgrounds and the generous welfare benefits that tip any short-term cost/benefit analysis in favor of welfare dependency. This hypothetical narrative captured the American public's imagination, fueling outrage over the specter of hardworking taxpayers forced to support the immoral choices of others. It also proved to be influential in shaping policy makers' views on welfare assistance as creating dependency and eroding responsibility among primarily African American families.

The retrenchment of support for welfare coincided with a growing conservative backlash against feminism and gay rights. Conservatives promoted the ideal of the two-parent patriarchal family in response to changes in society they saw as a threat to traditional "family values." From this vantage point, the increased number of women working outside the home was seen as at least partially to blame for society's ills, thus adding fuel to the cultural wars that were raging over changes in family structure and proper roles for men and women. However, despite family values rhetoric, there was little conservative backing for poor mothers to remain at home with their children supported by public assistance. The result was further erosion of support for mothers on AFDC to remain out of the workforce. There was now growing support among policy makers on both sides of the political divide and also among the public that women who received welfare assistance should work outside the home—an idea suggesting, as Pamela Winston argued, that *some* children were better off cared for by someone other than their mothers (2002, 36).

Family Support Act

The Family Support Act (FSA) in 1988, the last attempt at welfare reform prior to PRWORA, added substantial but incremental steps to encourage paid work on the part of welfare recipients (Winston 2002, 37). The FSA established the Jobs Opportunity and Basic Skills Program (JOBS) to increase job training and education. To incentivize paid employment, the FSA increased earnings disregards (allowing recipients to keep a greater share of their wages while continuing to receive cash benefits), and states had to guarantee child care if mothers needed it to participate in JOBS training or to take a job (Weaver 2000). The FSA also increased efforts to enforce child support from noncustodial fathers by deducting child support payments from noncustodial parents' paychecks and by establishing state guidelines for mandatory paternity tests (Winston 2002).

Thus, at the same time that the FSA established that mothers on welfare were expected to work outside the home to support their children, it also instituted policies that reinforced men's responsibility for supporting women and children. Though most observers would agree that fathers should provide for their children, opponents of the FSA and advocates for poor women pointed out that these provisions reflected the experience of divorced, single mothers whose former spouses had earnings—mothers who themselves are more likely to have greater educational and job skills—not impoverished minority single mothers (Naples 1997). The same argument applies to provisions for child care, job training, and other work supports that are based on the assumption that mothers leaving welfare will enter jobs with wages that can support a family. Thus the FSA instituted a feminist vision of the family wage ideal in which a single wage earner could support a family with dependent children—an ideal as family historian Stephanie Coontz (1997) noted, with the exception of the postwar 1950s "golden age of families," was not the case for the majority of families, and it has never been the reality for racial, ethnic minority families. By the late 1980s a majority of Americans agreed that it takes two incomes to support a family (Schor 1998). Why, then, did policy makers assume that poor single mothers leaving welfare would earn wages sufficient to support their families?

Nancy Naples's analysis of the policy debates in the Senate hearings leading to the FSA helps answer this question. Naples argued that welfare policy is shaped by discursive frames—particular ways of presenting issues that resonate with popular ideology giving them status and authority and also limiting alternative perspectives from being heard. In this case policy makers began the debate based on agreement between liberals and conservatives that "poor adults who are able should be helped to work" (1997, 907). Testimony before the Senate subcommittee placed "low-income mothers in the category of the able bodied and thus undeserving of state support" redefining them as "potential yet reluctant workers" who needed to be forced to work by the state (923). Yet by defining low-income mothers as workers, albeit reluctant ones, policy makers created another problem. To set the standard for who would be required to work, they had to resolve the ideological opposition between the undeserving, able-bodied worker and a mother as the primary caregiver of children. The compromise in the final bill exempted pregnant women and mothers with children under the age of three from mandatory work (923). Naples characterized the FSA legislation as a consensus among policy makers marking a new social contract between the poor and the state based on shared beliefs about the work ethic and family responsibilities. It also, as Linda Gordon argued, represented "an alliance between those who believe that employment and reliance on wages is on the whole strengthening for women and those who would use employment as punishment for deviant women"—poor single mothers who dare to raise children outside marriage (1990, 28).

A parallel public debate about women's work and family roles was taking place that centered on college-educated women entering careers and seeking opportunities in the workplace. Progressive white feminists increasingly advocated policies that would alleviate the burdens of caregiving for working mothers, such as flextime, tax credits for day care, and family leave (Mink

1998). However, the flip side of growing support for policies that would benefit middle-class mothers as they entered employment and careers was further erosion of support for poor single mothers to remain in their homes and care for children. As Senator Moynihan, chair of the Senate hearings, stated: "A program that was designed to pay mothers to stay at home with their children cannot succeed when we now observe most mothers going out to work" (Weaver 2000, 70).

Ending Welfare as We Knew It: PRWORA

In 1996, President Clinton signed the Personal Responsibility Work Opportunity Reconciliation Act (PRWORA) into law, fulfilling his campaign promise to "end welfare as we know it." The legislation abolished the much-maligned AFDC program and ended any entitlement to cash support for poor women and their children, replacing AFDC with Temporary Assistance to Needy Families (TANF), a time-limited program making eligibility for welfare assistance contingent on looking for work, finding a job, or training for a job.[7] In a reversal of the original rationale for public assistance to poor families, the welfare reform of 1996 tied mothers' responsibility for children to their ability to provide for them rather than care for them at home. Similar to the FSA, PRWORA established that poor women should work and backed that up with support for job training, child care, and transitional Medicaid (Medicaid is the health insurance program for the poor; transitional benefits allow recipients to keep their health insurance for a time when they find a job and leave welfare). Although PRWORA's focus is on moving welfare recipients into the workforce, it also, as stated policy, promotes conventional marriage and family formation.

In the introduction, prior to setting out the specific rules to be implemented by the legislation, PRWORA first presents a set of findings whereby it articulates policy maker's views on the social and cultural priorities of U.S. society. For example, the legislation begins: "1) Marriage is the foundation of a successful society. 2) Marriage is an essential institution of a successful society which promotes the interests of children. 3) Promotion of responsible fatherhood and motherhood is integral to successful childrearing and the well-being of children." The introduction goes on to warn of the dangers of nonmarital sex and teen pregnancy and raises the alarm over out-of-wedlock births, children raised by single mothers, and absent fathers as a crisis in the country in need of legislation (U.S. Congress 1996).

The specific goals of TANF consist of providing support to poor families so that children may be cared for in their own homes or the homes of relatives; reducing the need for government benefits by promoting job readiness, work, and marriage and family guidance; preventing and reducing nonmarital pregnancies; and encouraging the formation and maintenance of two-parent families (U.S. Congress 1996). In practice, promoting job readiness and work takes precedence over the other goals and is to be accomplished with some government assistance as a *temporary* means of support.

In addition to eliminating entitlement to welfare assistance to accomplish the goals above, the main provisions of TANF include fixed-sum TANF block grants to states; a two-year limit on cash assistance without work; maximum lifetime limits of five years with states given the option to impose shorter time limits (thus the end of entitlement); giving states the option to impose a family cap (denial of benefits to families that have additional children while on TANF) or to refuse benefits to mothers under age eighteen; increased funds for child care; and requiring that recipients participate in work activities with hard sanctions to enforce work requirements. Although the foundation of TANF policy rests on the idea that the avenue out of poverty and into self-sufficiency is employment and that poor mothers can and should be required to work, it is also evident that policy makers crafting the PRWORA legislation had more in mind than jobs for single mothers.

Congress reauthorized TANF in 2005 with provisions to increase work hours and oversight of work requirements and to designate funding for Marriage Promotion and Fatherhood Initiatives (U.S. Department of HHS 2006). Policy makers today characterize the legislation as an overwhelming success, pointing to the sharp drop in welfare caseloads and increased workforce participation of single mothers (Haskins 2006). However, others argue that this "success" is mitigated by the fact that few women leaving welfare leave poverty and instead enter the ranks of the working poor (Collins and Mayer 2010, Floyd and Schott 2013, Loprest 2001). In short, the 1996 welfare reform formalized the work attachment trends of women in the United States, notably the dramatic increase in the number of women with small children who combine paid work with motherhood. Although whether children are better off when their mothers go to work remains a controversial issue in U.S. society, the message coming out of the welfare office today is that for poor mothers on welfare, *good* mothers arrange for day care for their children and go to work (Cohen and Bianchi 1999).

The Cultural Contradiction in PRWORA

In some ways the 1996 welfare reform can be seen as simply a means of altering the social contract between poor families and provisions for government assistance in light of changing conditions in society. From this vantage point, PRWORA is a reflection of the broadly shared consensus of the U.S. public: Now that most mothers work outside the home, poor mothers should also. Simply put, why should poor mothers be able to stay home with their children when others have to go to work? Isn't this a matter of providing poor single mothers a benefit that other working mothers do not have? On the other hand, it could be argued that the reform of welfare is a continuation of policy revisions that sends a broader message about society's expectations in reinforcing today's prevailing notions of paid work and motherhood.

Sharon Hays's analysis of the cultural and moral foundations of PRWO-RA in *Flat Broke with Children* took the latter view. Hays argued that the 1996 PRWORA welfare reform "is much more than a set of policies aimed at managing the poor, it also provides a reflected image of American culture and reinforces a system of beliefs about how *all* of us should behave" (2003, 9). But, as Hays points out, there is an inherent contradiction in the cultural logics that form the basis of PRWORA. The tension is between whether independence and self-sufficiency are paramount as national goals, or whether we as a nation still wish to maintain "traditional" family values.[8]

We can find the contradiction through two models of U.S. society in welfare reform, which Hays labeled the *work plan* and the *family plan*. According to the logic of the work plan, "women can and should join men in the public sphere of paid work, operating according to an individualistic ethic of personal responsibility" (2003, 16). The family plan relies on work requirements to punish single mothers for their failure to marry and stay married by forcing them to work in low-wage jobs. As Hays argued, the values reflected in welfare reform extend to broader cultural norms of dependence/independence, self-interest/obligation, paid work/caregiving. The competing cultural values in PRWORA place low-income women and welfare policy once again at the center of society's debate over men's and women's proper roles and recent changes in women's work and family attachments.

The historical record of welfare policy demonstrates the degree to which it has been shaped by and also reflects broadly shared moral and cultural expectations at the heart of work and family concerns in U.S. society. Today as in the past, the categories of deserving and undeserving set out in welfare policy parallel the American public's views on men's and women's proper family roles—however contentious this debate remains. In keeping with policies from the past, the legislation establishes categories designating who is morally excused from work and who is expected to provide. Women who will work are now deserving of support for a time; single mothers who would choose to opt out of the workforce to stay at home with their children are not.

In the early 1900s the justification for assistance to poor women was based on the family wage system, which assumed that a working spouse (white male) could earn enough to support a family, whereas women were expected to care for home and children. The rationale for today's welfare policy is the transformative quality of paid work in the lives of poor women where employment brings self-sufficiency and instills personal responsibility. Moral uplift for poor women now consists of programs geared toward learning to labor outside the home. What then does PRWORA indicate for our contemporary understanding of men's and women's roles, and what impact does this have on poor and low-income women's experiences and abilities to provide and care for their children? In this book, I argue that the changes in welfare reform help crystallize the profound changes in men's and women's work and family roles: moral and emotional as well as economic.

Middle-class men and women are torn between their desire for fulfilling work and for meaningful careers and family life—and yes, between their ability to provide materially and to maintain their families' economic well-being as well as the demands of parenting and partner roles. Yet rarely are middle-class women characterized as lazy if they choose to remain home and care for children—in fact they may be expected to feel or report feeling "guilty" for the time they spend at work instead of caring for children in the home. Juxtapose this view with the evaluation of a poor woman whose paycheck affirms her status as a "good" mother, whereas reliance on a welfare check to stay at home or to limit hours spent in the workplace labels her a "welfare mother" shirking her responsibilities as a productive member of society.

The institutionalization of the breadwinner role for women creates a dilemma for many American families, however much it has also created opportunity. It is at the center of the work and family debate that continues to capture the hearts and minds of the U.S. public, yet missing from that debate, and the subject I take up in the next chapter, is consideration of the moral basis of that debate and how it differs significantly for poor women who rely on public assistance.

NOTES

1. Social welfare assistance broadly defined refers to a variety of government assistance programs, including Social Security, unemployment benefits, Supplemental Security Income (SSI), Medicaid, food stamps—now the Supplemental Nutrition Assistance Program (SNAP), Earned Income Tax Credit (EITC), and housing assistance. However, most people refer to welfare primarily in terms of Temporary Assistance to Needy Families (TANF) and its predecessor Aid to Family with Dependent Children (AFDC). It is these cash benefit programs that carry negative connotations of welfare and assumptions about recipients, generally poor, single mothers.

2. A trove of excellent studies explains the construction and origin of the U.S. social welfare state. See Abramovitz (1996), and Mink (1998) for overviews from a feminist perspective; Reese (2005) for political and ideological processes and opposition to expansion of benefits; and Skocpol (1992) for discussion of policy provision that led to the creation of a maternalist welfare state.

3. See (Abramovitz 1996, Quadragno 1994, Weaver 2000, Mink 1995, and Gordon 1994) for discussion of the practice of limiting black women's eligibility for the ADC and states' ability to discriminate based on the view that black women were employable compared to white women. As reported in Gordon (1994), welfare administrators in southern states commonly "could see no reason why the employable Negro mother should not continue her usual sketchy seasonal labor" (276).

4. In the 1950s it was not uncommon for welfare departments to investigate whether there was a "man in the house" who could be considered a "substitute parent" responsible for

economic support, by surprise visits and searches of homes (Abramovitz 1996). See Abramovitz (1996, 318–32) for discussion of "moral fitness" provisions.

5. Handler (1995) and Handler and Hasenfeld (1997) referred to myths and ceremonies to describe the failed attempts of welfare policy makers to increase workforce participation through WIN, which as policy was a colossal failure. It was like other attempts at welfare reform, part of enduring efforts to make the poor work for welfare benefits, going back to the days of the poor house.

6. This is not to say that poor mothers and their children had not been morally suspect compared to married mothers since the beginning of poor relief. See (Gordon 1994, Mink 1995, and Abramovitz 1996). Handler also argued this point. But when nonpoor married women and mothers began to work outside the home, the idea that poor mothers and their children should be entitled to welfare benefits so that they could stay home with children was increasingly difficult to support even for liberal policy makers (1995, 28–29).

7. See (Weaver 2000, Winston 2002, and Reese 2005) for a detailed analysis of the political processes that led to welfare reform.

8. In using the word *traditional* I refer to its popular usage rather than assert the two-parent, married, breadwinner, homemaker family as reflecting historical reality.

Chapter Three

Work Commitment

Learning to Love Labor

Yeah, well it is fine if everybody has a job, but who's watching the kids? [laughs] It doesn't, it doesn't really seem too good.

—Dana

Betty Friedan (1963), in the *Feminine Mystique*, famously described the inner anxiety—"silent stirring"—felt by women whose place in society was defined by their devotion to husband, children, and home. Her bestselling book is credited for setting the gender revolution of the 1960s in motion and launching the cultural wars over work and family that continue today. Friedan gave voice to "the problem that had no name," yet the problems revealed by Friedan were those of married middle-class women while she ignored those of poor single mothers, working-class families, and women of color.[1]

At the time Friedan wrote, only 20 percent of mothers of small children worked outside the home. Friedan went on to say, rather than devotion to domesticity, if women pursued careers they would be much happier and their children and spouses would be better off. Few in society at the time were ready to accept Friedan's views, but history proved her right in many respects as society (however reluctantly) came to accept the changes taking place.

In writing about Friedan's prediction and working mothers today, family historian Stephanie Coontz (2013) notes that as late as 1977, two-thirds of Americans still believed "that it was much better for everyone involved if the man is the achiever outside the home and the woman takes care of the home and family." Compare that to contemporary views. The Pew Research Center as part of its ongoing analysis of trends in American work and family life reports that nearly three-quarters of American adults (73 percent) now agree that the trend toward more women in the workforce has been a change for the better. And 62 percent of adults believe that a marriage in which the husband and wife both have jobs and both take care of the house and children offers a more satisfying life than one in which the husband provides for the family and the wife takes care of the home (Parker 2012).[2] These findings illustrate the degree to which American attitudes have changed about women's place in society and work and family roles. However this same report found that while a majority support shared breadwinning and caregiving, they also express reservations about the social costs of mothers' increased devotion of time and energy to paid work.[3]

Only 21 percent of adults say the trend toward more mothers of young children working outside the home has been a good thing for society while 37 percent say this has been a bad thing. Others, some 38 percent, say it has not had much impact. There is also a mismatch between what working mothers prefer and their actual work and family arrangements. Most working mothers (62 percent) say that they would prefer to work part-time, compared to 37 percent who say they prefer full-time work. Only a small minority of mothers, about one in ten (12 percent) say having a mother who works full time is the ideal situation for a child (Parker 2012). Finally, to underscore the nation's ambivalence, as recently as the spring of 2014, 60 percent of Americans agreed that children are better off with a parent at home (Cohn, Livingston, and Wang 2014).

How do the findings above compare to the responses of women in this study about work and family preferences? Overall, in line with changing attitudes in the United States, the majority of women in my survey indicate support for working mothers. When asked to choose the ideal situation in decisions about paid work and caring for children, 66 percent of my survey respondents chose combining paid work and caring for children compared to 33 percent who believe that focusing primarily on child care is a better decision. Fewer than 2 percent agree that it is best for mothers to focus primarily on work. Table 3.1 provides additional results from my survey respondents.

The ambivalence in attitudes related to work and family found in national studies is also reflected in my survey results. Although there seems to be broad support for a traditional gendered division of labor, with 75 percent of my respondents agreeing that domestic duties and raising children are most important for women; 82 percent also agree that paid work is just as important for women as men. Most mothers in my survey (75 percent) believe that working mothers can maintain warm relationships with children, and 78 percent agree that when mothers do work outside the home, they provide good examples for children. How do we reconcile these responses with strong support (74 percent) for mothers to limit paid work when children are

Table 3.1. Percent agreeing with statements on mothers' paid work and child-care

Percent agreeing that . . .	
Working outside the home is just as important for women as it is for men	82.42
Taking care of the home and raising children is the most important job for a woman	75.40
Working for pay is one of the most important things a mother can do for her family	51.38
When children are born, mothers should not work outside the home	64.84
When a mother works outside the home, she sets a good example for her children	78.49
It is better for everyone if a single mother goes to work instead of stay at home and care for her children	38.89
It is better for everyone if the man in the household has a job outside the home and the woman takes care of the family	66.80
A working mother can establish just as warm and secure relationship with her children as a mother who does not work	75.30
Preschool children suffer when their mothers work outside the home	63.71
Mothers should not work full-time when their youngest child is under age five	73.71
Number of cases	253

small and the 64 percent who believe mothers' work outside the home is harmful to preschool-age children? In sum, a majority of the low-income mothers I surveyed agree that paid work is important for women. However, this coexists with even greater support for a traditional gendered division of labor and concern over the consequences for young children when their mothers work outside the home.

The ambivalence expressed above illustrates the gendered paradox in welfare assistance where support for poor women raising children is contingent on their willingness to work outside the home. It stands in stark contrast to the public debate over contemporary work-life relations, which remains centered on professional women's choices. Critics of the influence of the "opt out" thesis (elite women leaving the workplace in droves due to the pull of family demands) would argue that the focus on this particular group as the face of work-family conflict obscures the lack of options faced by most families and feeds the (real or media contrived) conflict between stay-at-home mothers versus working mothers (Coontz 2013, Peskowitz 2005, Warner 2005). Pamela Stone's (2007) study mentioned in the introductory chapter of professional women who quit or interrupted paid work, found that the premise of the debate is misleading in that the workplace pushes women out of careers when they become mothers, a fact obscured behind the rhetoric of choice.[4] Contributors to both the scholarly and mainstream literature, weary of the "mommy wars," argue that the problem facing women today is the lack of support for working families and propose an end to the debate over women's choices and whether women *should* work or not.[5] These are indeed important issues, and I agree we need policies that work for all families.

However, this unfortunately will not put an end to the conflict over women's work and family commitments. Missing from the debate over women's choices is greater attention to the social and cultural forces keeping the mommy wars alive, and how those differ between the group of women at the center of the work-life debate and women at its margins. Simply ignoring the intractable but less visible ideological and cultural factors that shape work and family decisions does not put a stop to their influence, nor does this approach help explain why even successful elite professional women with resources beyond the reach of most families, struggle to reconcile competing work and family demands (Blair-Loy 2003). The poor woman who hears that "any job is a good job" and "work is always better than welfare" from the welfare office and who characterizes working for wages as "better than sponging off the state," as one woman told me, would indeed benefit from greater material support for her family. Yet, workforce participation also frees her from the stigma of welfare mother. Thus, as she confronts her options, she finds her choices shaped by social and cultural structures where the meaning of work, in addition to full time home-making, differs markedly from married middle-class mothers, however weary we are of the debate over their choices.

Today, the "end of welfare" is praised by policy makers across the political perspective as the greatest policy achievement in recent history because of the number of poor mothers who moved off the welfare rolls into paid work outside the home (Haskins 2006). Conspicuously absent in tributes to welfare reform is acknowledgment that forcing women to work in low-wage jobs may exacerbate work and family conflict for poor and low-income single mothers (Weigt 2006, Collins and Mayer 2010). Much of the conflict, even for poor mothers, is due to their inability to reconcile contradictory expectations over where they *should* devote their time and energy; demands shaped by broadly shared understandings of the moral, the possible, and the attainable in the face of structural constraints. The contradiction between acclaim for poor women who go to work as doing the right thing for their family and fulfilling their responsibility as a mother/worker stands in stark contrast to the cultural and moral expectations for married professional and middle-class mothers. Rather than dismiss the moral assumptions underlying work and family, this book sheds light on the historical, social, and cultural structures in which choices about work and family occur and how these shape individual's interpretation of and response to their options.

THEORIZING WORK AND FAMILY CONFLICT THROUGH CULTURAL SCHEMAS

Recall from the discussion in the introductory chapter that cultural schemas are the shared cultural models we use to make sense of everyday life (Sewell 1992). They are cognitive maps that organize our thoughts and guide our actions. They also help us make sense of the actions of others. Schemas are constructed by societies over time and exist at differing levels. Deep cultural schemas operate as taken-for granted, relatively unconscious, unquestioned assumptions and practices (Sewell 1992). An example of a deep cultural schema is the gendered cultural model of separate spheres for paid work and caring for children. People rarely question why women continue to do the bulk of domestic labor and child care (outside of social science research), until some event or circumstance (e.g., welfare reform) causes hidden or taken for granted assumptions—cultural schema—to become available for examination, challenge and possible alteration.

Individuals draw upon cultural understandings as they interpret their options, but they are also widely shared by the public and shape the institutions in which individuals interact and go about working and raising their families. Particularly powerful gendered cultural understandings—the devotional schemas described in the introductory chapter—provide normative scripts or roadmaps for people's actions made up of partially internalized, broadly shared, taken-for-granted, expectations and beliefs. Within this conceptual framework, work and family conflict is "fundamentally a conflict between emotionally salient, moral definitions of what it means to be a good worker and a good parent" (Blair-Loy 2003,178).

Although influential, cultural schemas generally operate unconsciously. Low-income mothers do not "see" the structures that shape why they feel compelled to devote themselves to children. If these mothers were acting purely out of self-interest, the choice to devote more hours to paid work outside the home would make them "better off" economically, as would the choice to forgo having children altogether. Yet, even though people are for the most part unaware of their power, cultural schemas have real consequences. They influence the degree to which poor women are willing to "play by the rules" or resist work requirements. They help shape the expectations of mothers, employers, and caseworkers. They define whether a job brings independence and dignity or frustration and guilt for time spent away from children, and they affect decisions about who provides care for children and who must work. They shape women's evaluations of themselves as workers and mothers and their perceptions of how others see them within their community. They are at the heart of conflict between work and family as people face choices between irreconcilable demands where any choice is subject to moral evaluation and options are limited.

I build on Blair-Loy's study of the devotional schemas of elite women in financial careers where she challenges conventional understandings of work-family conflict as simply the result of personal or individual choices where people strategically weigh their options. Although the women she studied have greater resources than others, even women at the pinnacle of male-dominated careers "still have to confront powerful cultural notions about what constitutes an appropriate and fulfilling life in dedicating themselves to demanding careers and reconciling that with choices about motherhood (2003,8). Given the struggles of women at the top to reconcile the gendered demands of work and family, what can we learn from the struggles of women at the bottom? What cultural definitions of an appropriate and fulfilling life resonate with poor and low-income women as they make decisions about paid work and motherhood? How do they reconcile competing demands? To what extent do conditions of poverty and demands by the welfare office that mothers must leave their children and go to work shape expectations for paid work and motherhood? How do competing cultural schemas create moral dilemmas for poor women? I explore these questions through analysis of the work and family commitment schemas' definitions of paid work and motherhood and their influence in the lives of a group of impoverished and low-income women.

WORK COMMITMENT

This chapter focuses on the salience of the work commitment schema. Chapter 4 examines a powerful competing schema, family commitment. I first define work commitment as a cultural schema guiding low-income and poor women's preferences about paid work and childrearing. Next, I illustrate aspects of work commitment in terms of its rewards and consider its power as a source of transformation and identity in my subjects' lives. I also show how some women in the study experience ambivalence or outright rejection and disillusionment when low-wage jobs do not deliver on the promise of dignity and independence. The greatest threat to faith in work commitment arises from a competing cultural model—the family commitment schema's demand that mothers devote themselves to children.

Work Commitment Defined

The work commitment schema is based on a centuries-old model of capitalist society where hard work and material success are extolled as moral virtues (Weber 1958, Wuthnow 1996). As an abstract model or ideal type, the work commitment schema, traditionally masculine, is based on the self-sufficient nuclear family headed by a male breadwinner who needs no help from the government or anyone else. Working outside the home builds character and is a source of identity and fulfills one's obligation to society (Katz 1996). Thus, it has far greater meaning than the pursuit of material gains.

Public proclamations of its expectations and rewards were common in the first years of welfare reform. A 2002 speech by President George W. Bush in support of increasing work requirements for TANF recipients is typical for its promotion of the American individualist work ethic with a personal testimonial from a former welfare recipient to the saving power of work.

> Many are learning it is more rewarding to be a responsible citizen than a welfare client; it is better to be a breadwinner respected by your family. Sherrie Jordan, a mother of four children and a former welfare recipient living in Buffalo, New York, described her experience this way: "It's overwhelming. I'm very happy. There aren't many words to describe it. I'm looking forward to being financially independent. I can do it myself now." . . . Sherrie and millions of others are good people facing a tough climb. They are gaining self-confidence. They are earning the respect of their fellow citizens and their Nation. . . . Work is the pathway to independence and self-respect. . . . At the heart of all these proposals is a single commitment to return an ethic of work to an important place in all American lives. (Office of the Press Secretary 2002)

The work commitment schema defines this moral imperative for poor women in mandating paid work as fulfilling their obligation to family and community and promising independence and respect to its followers.

As a cultural model, work commitment shapes both individual understandings and actions and also the practices and distribution of benefits in welfare organizations. Women who comply with work requirements are rewarded with job training, day care subsidies, transportation vouchers, and so forth. Women who do not are punished by sanctions—reduction in cash support and other benefits. Thus, the cultural model of work commitment has both a symbolic and material dimension. Of course, one does not need to receive welfare to derive both material and non-material rewards from paid work. However, the notion that paid work is good for poor women—the masculine work ethic intertwined with poverty discourse—is widely disseminated in public discourse as a means of reinforcing mainstream behaviors and values (Abramovitz 1996, Hays 2003). Ultimately, in addition to financial rewards, the commitment to work schema promises its followers respect and dignity as part of a moral community of productive, independent members of society.

Unquestionably, the normative demands and institutional forces in the work commitment schema differ from the cultural models analyzed by Blair-Loy (2003) in her study of elite women with demanding professional careers married to wage-earning husbands. For example, while the traditionally masculine work commitment schema guiding low-income mothers choices also has roots in capitalism and the expectation for economic success, it does not demand the drive, loyalty to the firm, and long hours expected of women in high-powered careers. It does not promise its adherents, in addition to substantial financial compensation, the feeling of accomplishment, status, and identity as a female making it in a male-dominated profession—hallmarks of the devotion to work schemas shaping elite women's lives. Work commitment, however, *does* promise self-sufficiency, independence and moral worth, connection to others, and the ability to provide for one's family rather than depend on welfare or others to make ends meet.

To carry this further to get a sense of how poor mothers' dedication to work and motherhood appears through the prism of work commitment in the context of workfare welfare policy, imagine the following scenario. Swap out the image of the poor single mother, and put in her place a married middle-class woman. Imagine suggesting to a married middle-class or professionally educated mother of two young children that she should get a job (if she is not employed outside the home) or increase her hours at work in order to be a better mother and instill discipline and routine in her life. Policy makers could also propose legislation to help married middle-class families cope with rising day care costs (a proposal many of us would welcome) which they justify on the grounds that helping more women enter the workplace will build character among stay-at-home mothers, set an example for other women who would otherwise "stay at home and do nothing," and provide role models for their children. Suppose that these same policy makers express concern over the costs to society of the dependency of married mothers on their spouses. Some people may agree. However, in reality policy makers would never publicly proclaim that work at home is not "real" work, the "dependency" of mothers on their spouses is a drain on society, and children do not benefit from their mother's care. Such a proclamation would be seen as an affront to both mothers and a majority of the U.S. population who continue to hold motherhood and caring for children in high regard.

In illustrating the differing moral criteria used to evaluate the work and family choices of married middle-class mothers compared to low-income single mothers, I don't mean to dismiss the strain felt by many women caught in the grasp of competing demands between work and family, from working-class mothers to women at the top of their professions, nor the diminished opportunities confronted by many women whose choices are constantly evaluated through gendered assumptions. Rather, my intent is to bring to light the differing moral and cultural structures—devotional schemas—that shape poor and low-income women's decisions about paid work and family responsibilities obscured in the current work-life debate and public perceptions of poor and low-income single mothers.

I NEVER GIVE UP

Jeanine Sanders, a forty-year-old mother of two—a daughter in middle school and high-school-age son—started a new job three weeks ago at a call center after a long history of on-and-off-again employment and welfare assistance. She attributes her sporadic job history to bouts of anxiety and "I don't know what is wrong with me issues" affecting her for many years, and at the time of the interview was having a difficult time coping with the recent loss of her mother to cancer.

She attended counseling while enrolled in the life skills and employment training programs (which Jeanine says were very helpful), but now with a new job and a bus commute she no longer has time. She has a car but it is not working, and she was waiting for a visit from her father to do the needed repairs she could not afford. During the interview the phone rang twice and Jeanine looked over without answering. "It is probably creditors. They're just trying to get money out of me that I don't have." She liked her new job and how "it was a fun place to work, very fun place to work" and she was hopeful that finally this job would bring her the self-sufficiency that had eluded her for many years. Despite her years on welfare, Jeanine stated,

> I don't ever give up. That is one thing about me I never give up. Yeah, I never give up. I've always been somebody that, you know, if I make a mistake or something like that, then I always go out and try to, you know, get another job. I'm always trying. I don't ever give up and say I'm going to go on SSI.[6] No, no.

Jeanine's story is not unusual among women on welfare moving in and out of low-wage work who face multiple obstacles in finding and keeping a job (Dodson and Bravo 2005, Seefeldt 2008). Most Americans would not be surprised to hear that Jeanine, a poor single mother, is having trouble making ends meet. They may be surprised to hear her determination and characterization of her efforts, or skeptical that she is merely offering excuses for her lack of responsibility. Viewed differently—through the prism of work commitment—Jeanine's efforts in trying to succeed in the workplace provide a powerful source of identity in confirming for others as well as herself the kind of person she is. When Jeanine insists that *one* thing about her is that she never gives up, she affirms the belief that getting a job and going to work demonstrates character even as she faced setbacks in her ability to do so. That is to say, she is somebody who is making an effort to better herself, take care of her family, and, in contrast to others, is not content to rely on public assistance. Defined through the work commitment schema her job is the pathway to self-respect and transformation into an independent, productive member of society.

Further, the cultural model that resonates with Jeanine's description of her efforts to support herself without the help of welfare is widely shared—reaffirmed above in public discourse as a broadly shared aspect of American culture. It is not simply a question of individual values as some characterize the divide between the poor and "mainstream" Americans (Murray 1984, 2012). The work commitment schema has deep roots in capitalism and belief in the American Dream where anyone who works hard can be successful, and those who are not have only themselves to blame (Hochschild 1995). The work commitments schema compels poor and low-income women like Jeanine to keep trying to get ahead in the workplace as a sign of character and not somebody who is supported by welfare assistance.

However, as much as Jeanine is drawn to the promise of self-sufficiency and social esteem gained by having secured a job, she must reconcile the influence of an equally compelling and competing source of identity, the family commitment schema. This powerful gendered cultural model offers a vision of motherhood that demands that mothers be there for their children and portrays children as needing their mother's care. As Jeanine says, "It has been difficult because the kids don't like being away from me. They have a real hard time with it, even now. Even now, they are having a really hard time with it because I have just always been there. I have always been there *with* them and always been there *for* them. Even now that they're older they are still having a struggle with it."

Jeanine's concern for her children may be familiar to mothers who work outside the home and at times are torn between their children's needs and their need to work. At the same time most working mothers are not evaluated in terms of their moral worth by their ability to hold down a job. Jeanine's description of the two competing forces pulling her in opposite directions brings home the point that conflict between work and family, even for the poor, is not simply a matter of balancing too many demands with too few resources but reconciling two powerful cultural models of a life worth living. For Jeanine, this is epitomized by the worker who does not give up, who demonstrates character through earning a paycheck instead of a welfare check—running head on into the moral imperative that she, as a mother, must be there for her children.

As discussed earlier, for middle-class as well as low-income mothers, conflict between work and family is essentially a contradiction between powerful cultural understandings that shape identities as workers and mothers, our most personal desires, and also our aspirations. However, the mothers in the pages throughout this book face a different social and cultural environment than that depicted in popular images of work and motherhood today. Poor mothers who live in low-income neighborhoods where few jobs are likely to be good jobs and jobs overall are scarce also make choices about their commitments to paid work and motherhood, and they do so influenced by broadly shared assumptions about their responsibilities as workers and mothers. In these neighborhoods, dual-career married households are rare, motherhood and children are highly valued (Edin and Kefalas 2005), and paid work provides a positive identity in contrast to welfare dependency.

As women in this study discuss work and family commitments in terms of gender roles and societal expectations, in practice, this does not mean that mothers whose understandings align with the cultural definitions offered through work commitment were not also devoted to their children or that when mothers identify with family commitment they do not value paid work. Instead, these categories reflect the tendency for women in the study to identify more strongly with a particular cultural model. Although many women state that work is meaningful, they often qualify these statements with concern for the welfare of children. As respondents draw upon aspects of these cultural models, there is little straightforward, unequivocal adherence to work commitment. While several mothers in this study find aspects of paid work fulfilling, they identify as workers primarily in the context of fulfilling their responsibility to their children financially and as role models transmitting values of independence, respect, and responsibility.

REWARDS FROM WORKING OUTSIDE THE HOME

Similar to findings from studies on working-class women, most of the women I interviewed characterize their work force participation as "needing to work" in opposition to "choosing" to work, yet this construction masks the variety of meanings attributed to work outside the home aside from the quality of jobs and financial rewards.[7] Paid work is rewarding for several reasons including the ability to put food on the table. It is also a source of self-respect, opportunities for women, and feelings of accomplishment for getting out there in opposition to being stuck at home. Work outside the home provides women a break from the tedium of child care and an opportunity to socialize with other adults. Even low-wage work has rewards in self-esteem, social life at work, relief from the burden of child care and housework, overall pride in doing a job well, and providing for families (Johnson 2002).

Personal Rewards

Getting out of the house and interacting with others was a rewarding aspect of working outside the home. As this mother put it, "I think the self-esteem and just the, being around socially, being around so many people is good for anybody, especially women because we've always been put in the role of being home."

Louise Parker, fifty-three, mother of two grown children and three adopted school-age children, also frames work outside the home as an opportunity for women to pursue other roles. In response to my question about women working outside the home, she explained

> I think [paid work] is a good thing. I don't think that women ought to be sheltered in a home at all times, unless that is what they want to do. I think they should get out and be what they really want to be. That is what I tell my kids. That [paid work] is something to do, not just like cleaning house and that is it. Raising kids, and that's it. There is more to it. . . . They [mothers] need to make money, to earn money, to do something in life instead of sitting at home and doing nothing.

As many stay-at-home mothers will concede, being home and taking care of children can be isolating, and mothers can also feel pressure from the broader culture in characterizing the time spent at home as "doing nothing," compared to the value of paid work (Hays 1996).

Nina Flowers, age twenty-three, former TANF recipient and mother of a two year old, works part-time as a restaurant server. She describes the rewards of paid work as allowing her to do something for herself. "It is nice for the woman to get out and it, it was very nice to get out and to do something for myself and you know to just even just to have a little time away. To be an adult, you know . . . to, to feel like, 'Oh, I'm you know, using my brain again, and I'm not . . . I'm not coloring or talking ABCs."

Working outside the home can provide a counter to the sense of losing one's self found among stay-at-home mothers, a characterization more accurate for middle-class and professional mothers than low-income mothers whose self-identity is not aligned as closely with the workplace (Perry-Jenkins 2012). However, as these mothers tell us, it is a source of adult companionship and a break from the tedium of child care. Moreover, as Sharon Hays (1996) argues, the flip side to the high value assigned to paid work is the portrayal of stay-at-home mothers as mindless and boring, a characterization mothers seek to avoid.

Kari Michaels, a twenty-four-year-old, single mother of two children—a five-year-old boy and seven-month-old infant daughter—stayed home with her baby for six months and just recently left TANF for a full-time job in retail sales. She, like Nina, finds work rewarding in getting her out of the house and allowing her to connect with others and do something for herself.

> Work makes you feel good. You're not cooped up in a house and you're not just talking to kids and you're meeting people and friends. I guess that when I was here with the kids all the time I kind of start going crazy. I was like "oh, I want to go out and I want to do something." I don't know. And so even just working part time, it's better for yourself because you have that time away too. I mean you want to be with your kids but you still need time for yourself even if it is at work. It would be nice if it wasn't at work, but I mean at work I really think of that as my quiet time, comfort time and . . . it gives me a break. It lets me meet new people, and socialize with someone other than a five-year- old.

Another woman expresses a similar view. "It [work] gives you that little time off from home life, what's going on at home. And you are actually around other adults and it's not all kid talk. You can talk about real things— gives you that social life."

Arlie Hochschild's (1997) study on the "time binds" facing contemporary families, found that the workplace rather than home provided many workers relief from the hectic demands of work and family life. In Hochschild's study, employees worked for a family-friendly corporation, which is not the case for any of the mothers in this study. Most jobs held by my respondents were low wage with no or few benefits. They were also not demanding in the way Hochschild described the pressures faced by workers trying to move up the corporate ladder. Rather, the workplace is a refuge from the isolation from home because it provides adult conversation and a break from shoulder-ing the responsibilities of parenthood alone. Respondents find work to be rewarding because it brings them a sense of doing something meaningful, a break from the isolation of home life, and connection to other adults.

Character

Although the sense of "doing something" and forming connections to others was commonly cited as a benefit of working outside the home, the most compelling power emanating from the work commitment schema is the transformational aspect of paid work as a sign of character and responsibility for low-income women on welfare—a masculine model of moral worth (Korteweg 2003).

Staci Morgan, thirty-three, a very outgoing, single mother of a four-year-old, was seven months pregnant, on TANF, and working at a subsidized job as a desk clerk for a nonprofit agency when I met her. She lived in an apartment in an older home on a tree-lined street. She has never married, although she has an off-and-on relationship with the father of her son and the baby she is expecting.

Staci emphasizes the transformational quality of paid work. Paid work, according to Staci, builds character and is a sign of doing something with one's life. "So I know that in myself that working makes me a better person. Just like my dad. When he worked he was a better person. So to me, work is an emotional feed. A good positive feed. I mean, who wants to work when you think about it, who wants to work? If they gave you a money tree! Would you trade that in to work? No! I'll keep my money tree thank you. But you know it's good for me. When I don't work, I feel useless like I'm wasting my life."

The proverbial money tree symbolizes both the practical necessity and more intrinsic merits of paid work. Staci implies if given a choice, most people would be happy to be relieved of the day-to-day burden of working. That is why we describe particular activities as work and others as leisure. But work has far greater meaning than simply a necessary means of providing for day-to-day needs. It also molds someone into a person of character. Her point is that work is not only about financial gains, however important this is in the lives of poor women, but in addition signals identity as a contributing member of society.

Staci's comments echo the views of social conservatives who argue that requiring work in exchange for welfare benefits instills responsibility in welfare recipients and provides the structure and oversight they need to improve their lives (Mead 1997). Staci would agree. Work outside the home has the capacity to make her a "better person."

I was surprised to hear Staci, visibly pregnant with her second child, tell me how when she is not working she is "wasting her life." Moreover, her description of work in such reverent terms stands in stark contrast to the type of jobs she held. Staci recited her long history of work experience. "Fast food, assembly, ummm what else have I done, God there's been a lot . . . dishwashing, prep cook, housekeeping, child care. I think that's about it, that's about it. Mostly fast food."

It may also seem absurd to most readers that with Staci's history of low-wage jobs that she would give such a passionate testimonial to the emotional returns she gets from working outside the home. However, studies of impoverished populations make similar claims about the salience of paid work in the lives of the poor. An example is sociologist Katherine Newman's description of the work ethic of low-wage workers in the inner city. "The nation's working poor continue to seek their salvation in the labor market. That such a commitment persists when the economic rewards are so minimal is testimony to the durability of the work ethic, to the powerful reach of mainstream American culture, which has always placed work at the center of our collective moral existence" (1999, 61).

Staci, like Newman's subjects, finds that work has transformative capacities even if the jobs are ones many would consider to be bad jobs. Staci lays out the publicly shared values that policy makers suggest will be adopted by welfare recipients as a result of entering the workforce. Welfare reform's mantra has since its inception been that any job is a good job, and work commitment promises that this will bring poor mothers dignity and respect. Of course not all mothers spoke of work as giving their life meaning. And many respondents did not express such faith in low-wage jobs. Yet, when some respondents talked about paid work, they did so with great conviction and in doing so indicated themselves as morally responsible persons.

Examples for Children

Mothers frequently cited employment as a source of pride and a positive model for their children. An example is Nadine Tenney, forty-three, a recently separated mother of an eight-year-old son. She lived several miles outside of town in a small, older mobile home park.

> I don't care if it is scrubbing toilets. I've done that before, you know. It's a job. I take pride in any job, even when I did scrub toilets and cleaned offices and stuff. I still took pride in it. . . . It gives me a feeling of accomplishment, I can do this, I know I can do this, and I am going to do the best that I can. And I think it shows David [her son] that "Wow, Mommy, you know, Daddy's not here, Mommy's got to do this and you know she can still be here with me too."

The majority of women leaving welfare for work enter low-wage jobs.[8] Yet as demonstrated, respondents find a great deal of satisfaction in working outside the home beyond economic benefits. They find dignity in work. Although the work commitment schema promises financial rewards and a path to self-sufficiency, it also defines work as a satisfying endeavor that indicates moral worth. Defining and interpreting the work they do outside the home filtered through this particular cultural and moral script allows Nadine and Staci to find meaning in what others characterize as "bad jobs."

Moreover, I found that mothers did not necessarily have to be working to express belief in work commitment's promise of independence and the character-building quality of paid work. The pull of the cultural model extended to others also.

Carol Grant, a Native American woman, divorced, with three elementary-school-age children who were living with her mother, demonstrates this. Carol was not working and received a small General Assistance (GAU) grant available to unemployed women with medical disabilities. When I spoke with her, she was participating in job training and drug and alcohol counseling. Carol, like many others, expressed her dislike for the TANF program. She also saw herself having to rely on TANF sometime in the future when she reunited with her children.

> I don't want to live on welfare . . . I mean, I'm not downing any of the other mothers out there that are on TANF because I'm going to have to be on it too for them [my kids]. But at the same time, I'm not going to be one of those women who are going to depend on the state handout. I want to do this [working] for myself, and I want to do it for my kids and I want to show them a good example you know. I want to show them they don't have to depend on the state or a man, that they could do it for themselves.

Carol's response echoes Nadine's views on how working outside the home provides a good example for children because of the independence it brings. And, similar to findings in Sarah Damaske's (2011) study of work and family attachments, both mothers state their reason for working as "for their families" but in Carol's case it defines her need to be on welfare. She demonstrates the complex contradictions inherent in work and family conflict for low-income mothers and how those are exacerbated by the stigma associated with welfare and demands of work requirements. Carol identifies with self-worth earned through work outside the home even as she acknowledges her current need to rely on TANF to care for her children. Moreover, she expresses belief in work commitment and the positive identity associated with this cultural model in individualist terms. Carol defines herself according to the tenets of work commitment: independence, character, and the promise of self-sufficiency. While she, like other mothers, also either implicitly or explicitly distances herself from other poor women: women who were on TANF, women who refused "bad jobs"—women sitting at home content to rely on the state or a man.

WORKING FOR FAMILY

We met Jane Peterson in the introductory chapter. She is twenty-four, never married, and mother of a two-year-old daughter. She works full-time as a nursing assistant riding the bus to and from work, a routine that takes about an hour each way. Each afternoon on her way to work she drops her little girl off at her sister's and then at night her sister brings her back home until Jane returns from work after 10:00 p.m. Jane received TANF following the birth of her daughter. She told me she did not work for six months after her daughter was born, and she laughed when she said, "I felt bad about it too." I asked her if she meant she felt bad for not working and staying home with her child. She replied, "Yeah. Because, I knew I should be. I should have been working. Because for the first six months of her life I lived with my dad and my stepmom and I didn't have to work."

Jane moved to get away from her baby's abusive father: "I knew that he wouldn't follow me. I left him about five or six times, and he always got me back." Initially she was not able to find a job, so according to Jane, "I didn't have any money. I looked for a job for about three months and didn't find anything. So yeah, then I just had to go onto welfare."

Jane's remarks demonstrate strong allegiance to work commitment and, like others, negative views of welfare assistance. She was the only respondent who indicated that she would like to work more than her current forty hours a week. Jane said that the only drawback to her current work situation was her nonstandard work hours of 2:00 p.m. to 10:00 p.m. Jane's commitment to work can be characterized as remarkably steadfast. She represents the extreme end of the views of the women I talked to, but her account of how she views the role of paid work in women and children's lives illustrates clearly the rewards and demands of the work commitment schema.

> [Children are] better off with their parents, their mothers, working. Then they learn responsibility, that you have responsibilities when you grow up. And then when they grow up and move out of the home then they won't just stay home and clean house and make dinner. You've got a five-year limit why waste it, why waste it when you could you know be taking care of your kids? But also you want a better life for them right? And maybe kind of push yourself out there. You know even if you can't find anything, at least you are out there looking. You are going to feel better about yourself because you are trying; at least you're trying to look for a job.

Jane left little doubt about whether she thought mothers should go to work or be stay-at-home moms. There is also little doubt that her response is influenced by policy changes where women are required to work and may feel forced to work when their preferences are to stay home with children. Although many women might agree with Jane's views on cleaning the house and making dinner, her view that children are better off when their mothers work outside the home is not widely shared. Rather this view aligns with the disdain for welfare mothers *as mothers* codified in welfare reform compared to middle-class or working-class mothers (Mink 1998, 121). Furthermore, she reassigns the moral credit earned through mothers' self-sacrificing, caregiving labor to work outside the home. Even looking for a job is preferable to staying at home, and working outside the home means, "taking care of your kids." For Jane, work and family trade-offs are between a job and self-respect or staying at home in a morally demeaning state of reliance on public assistance. Thus, the stigma surrounding welfare assistance and TANF's insistence on paid work from poor mothers work hand in hand with the moral compulsion of work commitment to redefine work outside the home as mothers' family responsibility.

Moreover, for Jane and others, negative views of welfare assistance push women toward work commitment in defining working for pay as a mother's obligation to her children. Working outside the home provides a better life for children and self-respect. Responsibility to Jane is something learned from her work outside the home, not from duties associated with raising children. As she put it: "They [mothers] show to their children that they can be responsible and they know that, one thing for their daughters, you know that you are not going to have to be stay home, take care of your children, do what your husband, or you know for instance, the man says. I say do your part to earn money. You're bringing home the bread."

Jane insists that working for pay, "bringing home the bread," rather than staying at home and caring for children is how mothers set a good example for children. Jane, as did Carol, also defines a model of responsible motherhood that involves rejection of the two-parent married-family ideal in favor of women's independence from men as well as the state and tacit endorsement of single motherhood. She argues that paid employment frees mothers from "having to" stay at home. Although people sitting at home tend to be women caring for dependent children, moral worth is demonstrated through work outside the home. In this case, the masculine ethic of work commitment defines and affirms deservingness for poor mothers on welfare—good mothers bring home the bread. This understanding of work–family trade-offs and what women should do rarely appears in conservative public discourse that places blame for society's ills at the feet of working mothers, nor does it appear in the public push back by mothers (the so called "mommy wars") who are weary of being made to feel guilty for the work they do outside the home (Douglas and Michaels 2004). It is hard to see much similarity to the opt out debate's examination of women's choices as a privilege available to a small group of advantaged women, or alternately an assault on or critique of feminism's supposedly empty promise that women can "have it all" (Jones 2012).

WORKING MOTHERS ARE NOT WELFARE MOTHERS

Studies on class differences in women's work lives suggest that because working-class women "need" to work they do not experience the gendered opposition between work and family life. In Jennifer Johnson's study on working-class women, she argues that in contrast to middle-class mothers, her subjects saw their work outside the home as work *for* their family, rather than work *or* family (2002, 123). This need-versus-choice divide forms the basis of contemporary cultural evaluation of women's workforce participation. Even today where most mothers work and expect to work outside the home, the cultural imperative demands that mothers frame their paid work in terms of their children's best interest (Hays 1996, Damaske 2011). This particular gendered construct does not adequately consider the meaning of work outside the home in providing for families when it occurs in an environment where women cycle in and out of work and welfare in order to care for their children.

We met Suzanne in the introductory chapter when she explained her work preferences, "the ideal situation would be me not working and taking care of my kid." Yet, she also believes that working outside the home shows children that it is better to work for a living than rely on welfare to take care of your family. Suzanne was currently on TANF after being fired from her job as a nursing assistant. "I slept through a shift and I got fired, and that's what made me go on it." Suzanne told me how difficult it was for her to have to go on welfare, which she refers to as being "on state," a morally degrading situation where she "had to really lower myself to go on state. . . . It was pretty low in my family to have to be on TANF."

When I asked her whether she received any child support from her son's father, she told me, "No, I found him before they [TANF] did. He's sponging off the state himself." If the baby's father provided sufficient support for Suzanne to limit or opt out of paid work she would not feel so harshly judged by her family as "lowering herself" as her dependency on his child support would be evaluated as an appropriate gendered division of labor. Suzanne's negative characterization of receiving public assistance makes sense when defined through the work commitment schema even though it helps her realize her ideal situation of being home with her child. Rather than seeing a job as simply a means of financially caring for one's children, while extremely important, jobs are also morally freighted in ways that transcend economic responsibilities. Work holds moral salience as a means of taking care of kids and allows mothers, who would otherwise stay home supported by the state, to be examples to children. In Suzanne's eyes working outside the home is something she does for her family to meet their practical needs and as an example of the work ethic characterizing U.S. society. Paid work also creates an identity apart from that of welfare mother. "It [working] shows that they are not—if you're on state versus going to work, it shows children that is all right to do that instead of getting a job to be able to take care of their kids. Parents that go to work rather than being on state shows that it's better to do that [go to work] than to get money from the state."

Connie Gleason, a Native American woman in her early thirties, lives with her husband and children in big wood-framed house, surrounded by a large fenced yard with a swing set in the front. She has struggled for years with alcohol and drug dependency, and this is a major factor in her life in terms of her ability to keep a job and care for her children. Connie was seventeen when she first married, has been married three times, and has five children. Connie discussed how her family received welfare for most of her childhood and how she has been on and off welfare as an adult. She ruefully described an incident from her childhood that illustrates the interweaving of poverty and welfare assistance into expectations surrounding paid work.

> I've known welfare since I was, you know—I actually—when I was a little girl, this is very sad (laughs). I was like, we were at the food stamp place and I was like, "Moooom, how I am I gonna remember where all of these places are!" I was really scared. "How am I gonna remember where to go get my food stamps and where to go get . . . ?" And she was just like—her mouth was hanging open. "Well, I pray Connie that you are not going to have to know where these places are!" I've just known that [welfare dependency] since I was a little kid and I thought "whoa! How am I gonna remember all of this stuff," you know. It's just crazy. . . . To me I never had anybody around me that worked. Nobody around me worked! My mom was on welfare till my youngest sister turned eighteen—only twenty-five yeaaaaaaaars!!

Almost every woman in the study had either been reliant on welfare themselves at some point in their lives, either growing up, as an adult, or knew someone who was "on state." The circumstances portrayed above are ones that most Americans have little personal experience or awareness of and would be dismayed at the thought of a young girl concerned that she would not be able to remember where to find food stamps when she was on her own. Connie's mother shared this dismay, as we can see from her reaction, and Connie is not proud of the situation. Her point in telling me this story was to illustrate the downward moral spiral that children can so easily fall into by virtue of welfare dependence in contrast to the redemptive power of paid work. Mothers need to set an example for their children, and this is accomplished through getting a job.

As part of work-readiness preparation, women enrolled in WorkFirst (the name of Washington State's TANF program) are provided with job training including soft skills such as appropriate dress, showing up on time, and so forth. And as demonstrated above, in addition to their own experience growing up, children's response to their work or lack thereof can impact how mothers see themselves and the significance of paid work. Thus reinforcing the salience of working outside the home as an integral aspect of mother's family role.

This becomes clear as Connie tells me about her own children's reaction to her efforts to get back into the workforce, when she appeared dressed in work attire provided by the welfare office.

> This is kind of going off the kids, being a good example or whatever, working, stuff like that. They just loved it "Oh Moooooom, you look so . . . you look like you work at an office or something!" They've never seen me like that. It

just was, you know eye opening, you know, that yeah, I do need to get back to work. I'm not going to just stay home all the time. . . . They just—when I'm fixed up and I leave in the mornings or whatever. They're "you look so nice mom" or whatever, and it makes me feel good and makes them feel good. It's just all around good!

Whether expressed explicitly or implicitly, mothers frequently juxtapose the virtue attached to work outside the home with the indignity of welfare assistance affirming its presence in the lives of these women as they make choices about work and family. Working outside the home confers a positive identity and example for children opposed to the negative image of a welfare mother who stays at home doing nothing.

Nadine whom we heard from above, in contrast to Carol and Connie has never relied on welfare, and she clearly did not want to be thought of as someone who would ever turn to public assistance and the stigma that accompanies it. When I asked her if she was getting TANF benefits she was adamant that she was not! "No. No. Um, for me I want that to be an absolute last resort. I will take any job that I possibly can to avoid that. I know there are some women who need it. But there are also some women who abuse it, and I don't want to get in the system and not be able to get off. So, I want that as a last resort. That's what I will do. I will work two jobs."

Studies on women's work and family decisions argue that women—read working mothers—feel compelled to minimize non-economic rewards such as self-fulfillment when they speak of paid work lest they appear self-centered (Damaske 2011, Garey 1999). This may well be the case for working-class and middle-class women, but it does not take into account the social milieu of poor women's lives where the non-economic rewards from paid work extend beyond self-fulfillment to the establishment of moral identities. Even further removed from the work and family choices of mothers in this study, are the "hard choices" faced by elite professional women driven to devote themselves to lucrative careers by masculine cultural scripts which promise them self-fulfillment and substantial incomes.

In contrast, for many mothers in this study as I explore in greater detail in a later chapter, paid work represents a moral identity opposed to "sponging off the state" and being held in contempt by others. Suzanne, Connie, and Nadine's characterization of welfare and those who rely upon it shows how the stigma of welfare influences how these mothers interpret their options and see themselves in relation to others. It shapes the views of those with firsthand experience and also others like Nadine who never received welfare. Social conservatives and others may chastise higher-earning women in careers for presumably choosing to devote too many hours to their careers at the expense of their family's well-being. However, they do not apply the same moral evaluation to paid work outside the home when caregiving would otherwise be supported by a welfare check. In this instance, both groups of mothers are constrained by the moral dilemmas presented by the cultural opposition of work and family. But for poor mothers, working outside the home filtered through work commitment, establishes an identity as a person of character—providing for and earning the respect of her children and community.

MOTHERS NEED TO WORK

Some mothers do approach welfare assistance and paid work from a purely practical approach based on economic necessity—they need to work. However, discussions of TANF and paid work inevitably invoke moral issues even if mothers are primarily focused on the practical aspects of finding jobs and providing for families. As we have seen above, women frequently criticize others who rely on TANF for their lack of effort. Mothers who rely on welfare or have in the past also resent aspects of the program, however the most damning critique is the requirement that mothers of children under one year of age be required to work.

Angela Michalski, thirty-two, is an unemployed mother of three small children ages three, six, and nine years. When I met her, two of the children were in school and the three-year-old played in the front room while we talked. She lives in a small house in a working-class neighborhood one block from a major commercial street. She suffered a back injury, which resulted in the recent loss of her job. Angela said she was not going to reapply for TANF benefits, because she was close to the sixty-month time limit and wanted to save her remaining months. "I have already been on it fifty-one months. I need those extra months for emergencies. I think in a way it [TANF] is good. In a way it is not. I mean in my opinion welfare should be there to help anybody out only if the people are willing to go get a job instead of not doing nothing staying at home."

In addition to worrying about using up the remaining months of eligibility, she resented the regulations, such as signing in on the computer and reporting her job contacts when she was looking for work "And that is another reason why I got off TANF. I don't want to obey by the rules."

Angela is currently looking for employment and has a long history of low-wage work but was having little success finding another job, as she stated several times that it was very difficult to find a job. Prior to relocating to the Northwest from the East Coast several years ago, she held a steady job working in a warehouse. She said she liked this job for its regular hours and would like to find a similar job the area. The fact that she did not finish high school makes finding a job more difficult, but she is working on completing her GED.

In the job she just left, she worked nights and weekends doing janitorial work at a large shopping center. Her live-in boyfriend was willing to watch the children as long as the state would pay him. When that fell through, Angela could not find day care for her children. I was not aware that he was home at the time of the interview until a man came to the door asking for him. Angela opened the door part way and was very curt in responding that her boyfriend was sleeping. As she closed the door and come back to resume the interview, she muttered, "Loser, get lost."

It should not be surprising that Angela sees working outside the home as something she needs to do in order to take care of the practical needs of her children. She told me "They know I got to work—make money so they can have a good life, clothes on their back, food in their mouth. It's showing the kids that their moms are responsible for working and making the money and raising them and supporting them."

There was nothing in our discussion that led me to believe Angela felt that time spent at work interfered with her ability to care for children. On the contrary, we heard her denigrate full-time home making supported by welfare in opposition to the more responsible choice of working outside the home to care for children. However, in spite of Angela's earlier negative characterization of women who are "not doing nothing staying at home," she resists the idea that mothers should be required to work. "I think you should be able to raise your child until at least one and then go look for a job, in my opinion. . . . I don't think it is fair when a mother's been on welfare and they have a baby and have to put the baby in day care. I think that's unfair."

Angela's remarks mirror those of many Americans who share her concern about mothers working when children are very small. The majority of the U.S. public also agrees that welfare should be for people who try to better themselves (a hand up, not a handout) and that Angela should pursue the promise of paid work to bring her self-sufficiency and independence. However, what troubles Angela is she also believes that mothers should have a choice whether to stay at home with infants under one year of age. The requirement by the welfare office that mothers find a job once infants reach three months of age threatens Angela's work commitment because she sees this as unfair to mothers. In my conversation with Angela, she clearly expected to work and was very frustrated by her inability to get and keep a job. And, in the past, she had worked full-time when her own children were under one year of age. However, the idea that mothers are *required* to do so shifts the moral nexus away from paid work to one of forcing mothers to leave their children in the care of others, violating broadly shared understandings of a mothers' obligation to children. Efforts by the welfare office to move mothers into paid work that appear unfair or coercive can erode the moral authority of work commitment and thus the legitimacy of work requirements— relative to the expectation that children need their mother's care. As I discuss in greater detail later, when question of fairness and choice about working arise, particularly for mothers of small children, respondents resist. They waver in allegiance to work commitment when they believe welfare policies threaten children's well-being.

JOB QUALITY

Paid work, defined through the work commitment schema, promises financial rewards, respect, and dignity. Allegiance for some mothers is tied to the quality of the job. These mothers take a more contingent approach to paid work. If work is not rewarding, then mothers are not bound to keep their commitment.

Donna Wilkins, a divorced mother of three who currently receives TANF, told me, similar to others, that work brought "Self-esteem. It makes me feel good about myself." But when I asked her if the type of job made a difference she replied, "Yeah, because nobody wants to go to work to a job they don't like. Because what's, you know, what's the use in trying to do something you don't want to do?"

Donna stated she wanted to work. She was actively looking for work at the time of the interview, and she had a long work history. She lived some distance from the city in a more rural area and told me that jobs were hard to find. Yet, she also did not want to work at a dead-end job. "Yeah, I don't want to work at McDonald's or anything because I mean, anyone could just walk over there and get a job. I'm just not one for fast foods anyway."

Others share this lack of faith in paid work when the job is not rewarding, and weigh the benefits of work force participation with the quality of a job. Yvette Johnson, a twenty-three-year-old African American, never-married mother of a three-year-old, currently receiving TANF, presents her disdain for low-wage work as a direct challenge to welfare policies that encourage poor women to take any available job including fast food.

> I won't work in a fast food. I refuse to. I told welfare that too. I won't work in fast food. You guys can tell me to go apply, but I won't work there. They are like if that is the only job you can get, you should take it. I won't take it because I worked in fast food too long. I worked for Burger King for a year. I worked for McDonald's for almost two years. No, I am tired of fast food. It is time to go up from fast food, to go up to something else besides fast food.

For Yvette and others, fast food jobs were particularly notable as examples of paid work that breaches the promise of a sense of accomplishment, dignity, and upward mobility. Donna remarks that anyone could get a job in fast food and Yvette indicates that fast food jobs are not a way to move up. Low-wage jobs appear to challenge work commitment for Donna and Yvette, but they do not cause a complete loss of faith. Respondents tell me they still want to work but not in fast food jobs where they don't find the dignity and respect that working outside the home is supposed to bring to poor mothers. Many readers may have little understanding or sympathy for these mothers' perspective and the refusal to take any job no matter the type of work if the alternative is welfare. Their response is at odds with the idea that any job is a good job—central to TANF policy—with the hopes that once connected to the workforce, former welfare clients will gain the skills to move up to better jobs.

Some mothers, as we have seen, manage to find dignity in paid work that others shun. The image of the fast food worker in Newman's (1999) characterization of a collective morality does not resonate with Donna and Yvette. And their resistance is not necessarily based solely on financial rewards. It is based on the lack of respect and the characterization of fast food work as unskilled and the lowest rung of the employment ladder. In their eyes, paid work is supposed to be meaningful, but they cannot be motivated to join the community of workers when they do not find it so.

To summarize, I find that respondents find paid work rewarding in terms of self-esteem, feeling good about themselves, escape from child care and housework, and the opportunity to connect with the outside world. Paid work also carries the power to transform and indicate moral selves. However, the power of paid work may fade in the eyes of some mothers who resent work requirements as unfair when children are small, and who are not willing to work in jobs that do not bring them dignity and self-respect.

WORK AND FAMILY TRADE-OFFS

The biggest challenge to the legitimacy of work commitment's demands is the influence of the family commitment's charge that time spent in the workplace is time that should be spent caring for children. Not surprisingly, most respondents expressed at least some uncertainty and ambivalence in their responses. Quite often when discussion shifted from work and jobs to children, they would contradict themselves or waver between the competing demands of work and family. Many others weighed the trade-offs in terms of the quality of the job and their desire to care for their children. Although the value of paid work is not limited to economic resources, for some mothers material rewards must be sufficient to balance the family commitment's demands that mothers should be home with children.

Jeanie Steele is twenty-four years old, the mother of a one-year-old daughter, and received TANF cash assistance. I spoke with her in her apartment while her baby slept in the next room. Jeanie planned to continue her education and complete a degree in art. The walls of living room of the small apartment were covered with colorful artwork, and there were stacks of children's books on display. When I asked her about working outside the home or staying at home with her daughter she responded: "Yeah, it's just, I don't know. Something that doesn't seem worthwhile to me—it feels like, I feel bad not being with her. 'Cause it's. . . . If it's something I feel I'm doing is important then I can justify it for having her in day care. I know it is important to have wages coming in [laughs], but to sit there and make sandwiches all day in a Subway, I feel like is a waste of my time when I could be spending it with her. I don't know."

One way to interpret these findings is they indicate that many respondents do identify with paid work and find work compatible with raising children. Recall that 78 percent of my survey respondents agree that when mothers work outside the home they provide a good example for children (table 3.1). In interviews, mothers state that work enables them to be good examples, provide for the practical needs of children, demonstrate independence and a strong work ethic, and maintain self-respect. However, 67 percent of my survey respondents also agree with the statement "It is better for everyone if the man in the household has a job outside the home and the woman takes care of the family."

Survey data indicate both positive views on paid work and support for a traditional gendered division of labor. Explanation for these findings may be due to the tendency for working-class women to hold more traditional views on men's and women's work and family roles (Rubin 1994, Deutsch 1999). And as I show below and in the following chapter, the family commitment schema continues to exert considerable influence on women's work and family attachments. Respondents find that paid work brings both economic and non-economic rewards, but many mothers in the sample found it difficult to consider the rewards from work apart from the tradeoff between those rewards and the well-being of children.

Giving Up on June Cleaver

Jeanie, a single mother, is still with the father of her child, but she told me living together was not an option because there was too much fighting in their relationship and she worried about the impact on her daughter. When Jeanie talks about paid work and staying home with her daughter, she struggles with her choices. She did stay home with her baby for seven months after she was born, supported by TANF with some help from the baby's father.

Jeanie says:

> When I was younger I used to think it's just better to have the dad work and the mom stay at home, you know. And that'd be great you know. But as of,

since I've had her mostly, I've started seeing how much benefit it could give her to see me working, and just to be . . . to have more money not to be broke all the time. . . . And so I think, I think it would be better now to see me—to see the mother working and everything. 'Cause eventually I think most women are gonna have to be [working]. Hardly ever are they gonna get like the nice little husband works all day and you get to wear your June Cleaver outfit [we laugh]. You know? And just to not have dependence on someone else. To be able to be independent I think would be a good example too because it [dependence] leads a lot of women into bad situations where they get stuck and they haven't worked. They haven't had to work for that many years and all of a sudden the guy dies or they get divorced or whatever and they're stuck.

The promises of work commitment: financial rewards, examples for children, and independence resonate with Jeanie, but she has difficulty committing herself all together. The pull of family commitment can disrupt or lessen allegiance to work commitment. She jokes somewhat ruefully about the model of June Cleaver but is reluctant to surrender the ideal of stay-at-home motherhood. Jeanie's response sheds light on the seemingly contradictory survey results presented at the beginning of the chapter, where respondents agree that paid work is meaningful, but they also support the cultural ideal of a man working for wages supporting a mother to stay at home and care for a child (table 3.1). This option is not a reality for the overwhelming majority of the women I interviewed, yet continues to influence perceptions of what women and men *should* do according to culturally appropriate gender roles that persist despite the changes in society. Much of Jeanie's desire for independence is due to her wish to provide her daughter with a strong role model, but also because as a practical matter, she believes that dependence on men makes women vulnerable to being "stuck in a bad situation." As Jeanie describes it, the birth of her daughter has drawn her toward work commitment, however ambivalently. Although she states she is torn between paid work or caring for her daughter, it is only since the birth of her daughter that she began to consider how beneficial it would be for her to work outside the home.

Although it may seem counterintuitive that having a child inspires work commitment, prior studies show that poor mothers experience motherhood as a pathway to adulthood and responsibility (Edin and Kefalas 2005). Jeanie states that it would benefit her daughter to see her working, and she desperately wants financial independence. As a never-married single mother on welfare, she cannot depend on a male wage earner and she has seen too many women end up in bad situations when they could not take care of themselves.

Work or Family?

We can find instances of mothers' attempts to bridge the oppositional competing nature of work and family commitments by recasting paid work as a family responsibility. For example, respondents state that work outside the home to financially support children is an important aspect of mothers' care. Mothers also tell me and believe that they are good mothers *because* they work. Jane, the most ardent work-committed respondent, had a hard time responding when I asked if she agreed with the statement that work outside the home is *more important* for women on welfare than time spent caring for children. After a long pause she replied:

> That is hard . . . oh boy. Aaaah.
>
> I: There is no right or wrong answer.
>
> Jane: [Long pause] I am thinking.
>
> I: Let me ask you a different way. Do you think that that is the message sent to moms on welfare?
>
> Jane: Yes. Yeah, that they need to be out working and not being home with their children. And yes, you need to be home with your children, but you also need to be working at a job to support them. If I had the choice of working or staying home with my child, I would have to say I would want to, I would still work because you know, I have to support my child and it's not like I have thousands of dollars, you know. If I was rich and had a rich husband, heck I would stay home. But I don't. And you hafta, you hafta work to support your family.

Jane has trouble forming a response when I pose the question as one of choosing whether child care *or* paid work is more important. When I rephrase the question in terms of the priorities of the welfare office, Jane answers immediately in the affirmative and integrates the work she does outside the home with her responsibility for her child. Jane vacillates some over the issue of choice when she says if she were rich she would stay home, but she uses this scenario to make the point that she is not rich, and neither are the women she knows. Ultimately, she sees herself as doing the right thing by herself and her child.

Today's vision of work and family is one where women are expected to work to support their families and very few women resist the notion of paid work altogether. Moreover, most of the women in the study view paid work as positive for the financial rewards and self-esteem that it provides and relief from the stigma of welfare mother. The issue that creates the tension is belief that devotion to work comes at the expense of children.

CONCLUSION

The discussion in the previous chapters established how attitudes in the United States about mothers' unique role as caretakers of children shaped welfare policy and encouraged poor women to stay home and raise children rather than go to work. As social conditions changed and women moved into the workforce, this, in combination with historical and cultural beliefs about the moral fitness of the poor, led to policies that demanded work of poor women in exchange for continued state support. Yet, policy makers also clearly struggled to implement reforms requiring that welfare recipients work due to longstanding ideas about men and women's work and caregiving roles. The assumptions that women should care for children and that men should provide were for many years so taken for granted that challenging them was to disrupt the "natural" order of things. Of course, we know that this did not apply equally to all men and women, but it was the model of work and family life idealized in American culture. At its core, these are the broad historical, social, and cultural forces that shape the institutions of the family, the workplace, and welfare.

When the welfare system supported poor women to stay home and care for children and at least limit market work it aligned with taken-for-granted cultural structures that were largely unseen and unquestioned—there was no institutionalized contradiction between gendered cultural expectations of men as providers and women's family roles of caring for children. Today, for poor women, staying home with children indicates a lack of personal responsibility and contributes to the stigmatized identity of welfare mother.

The narratives offered by the respondents in this study show that decisions about work and family are ultimately moral decisions based on widely shared cultural models of and for society. I find that poor women embrace the work commitment schema as they demonstrate responsibility for children, character, and positive role models through paid work outside the home. In addition, negative assumptions about welfare recipients reinforce the salience of work commitment as participation in paid work generates moral identities apart from welfare mothers. Fulfillment in paid work outside the home is understood through work commitment's definition of the character building aspect of work and also the moral worth and respect earned through paid work. However, allegiance wavers when jobs do not provide dignity, respect, and the upward mobility promised by this cultural model. Some women resist working in jobs deemed dead end and/or that cannot compensate for the time away from children. Additionally, respondents resent being forced into working outside the home. As we have seen above, the pull of the family commitment schema provides an additional challenge to work commitment. This is the subject I turn to in the next chapter as I explore the competing demands of the family commitment schema.

NOTES

1. See Glenn 1994, Jones 1986, Collins 1996, and Solinger 2001 for discussion of the work and family lives of minority women and how they were excluded from the construction Friedan describes relegating middle-class women to domestic life.

2. Kim Parker (2012) "Findings from Women, Work and Motherhood": A Sampler of Recent Pew Research Survey Findings. Pew Research Center, Washington, DC (April 12), presents results from several Pew Research surveys and reports from 2009 to 2013 on trends in work and family and how the American public views these trends.

3. See Pew Research Survey Report, May 29, 2013 "Breadwinner Moms: Mothers Are the Sole or Primary Provider in Four-in-Ten Households with Children; Public Conflicted about the Growing Trend." In 2012, roughly two-thirds (65 percent) of women with children younger than age six were either employed or looking for work. Compared to 39 percent in 1975. In the Pew Research poll, 51 percent of the adults surveyed said children are better off if their mother stays home and doesn't hold a job, while only 34 percent said children are just as well off if their mother works. 13 percent of respondents say that it "depends" on the circumstances." A 2003 *CBS News/New York Times* survey, 61 percent said children are better off if their mother does not work outside the home, 29 percent said children were just as well off if their mother worked.

4. See Pew Research Report, D'Vera Cohn, Gretchen Livingston, and Wendy Wang, April 2014, "After Decades of Decline, A Rise in Stay-at-Home Mothers." The characterization of professional married mothers as those opting out is misleading in that they make up a very small percent of stay-at-home mothers. Only 5 percent of stay-at-home married mothers have master's degrees and family income of $75,000 or more.

5. Coontz 2013, Peskowitz 2005, Warner 2005 and others criticize much of the debate over women's choices as creating difficulties for women. Some comments from those who responded to Coontz's *New York Times* column suggest that the debate still touches a nerve. One response criticized a group of stay-at-home mothers "educated, intelligent women, choosing—choosing!—to make their worlds smaller and smaller—while the writer's own "daughter has grown up seeing me enjoy work and the distinct, independent identity it can bring." At the other end of spectrum, "Being a stay-at-home mom was more interesting than my time at Harvard, more interesting than my stellar career. It was all passionate, unequivocal, and joyous. I feel desperately sorry for all the working moms who missed out and spend their times and careers trying to pretend they didn't." And finally "I can't believe we are still talking about this." While these responses can only be taken as anecdotal evidence of where we are today, they do provide a snapshot of people's feelings about women's work and family roles. What they also suggest is that the issue is not going away.

6. Jeanine refers to (SSI) the Supplemental Security Income program a federal means tested program that supports low-income persons with disabilities; elderly, children, and adults who are unable to support themselves through employment.

7. Anita Garey's (1999) study on working-class women explores this culturally constructed model of motherhood in which mothers are either working mothers or stay-at-home mothers. Working mothers frame their work force participation as needing to work rather than for selfish reasons of self-fulfillment. She found that even mothers who worked full-time on swing shifts identified as stay-at-home mothers. Sarah Damaske (2011) taking a life course perspective argues in her study of working women that a dichotomous division between need and choice misses the varied meanings women assign to paid work and the influences over the life course that shape how and why women's work is steady, intermittent or interrupted. Class differences matter, but they are not the only factor shaping women's work attachment.

8. A wealth of studies referred to as "leaver" studies in the early days of welfare reform tracked outcomes for mothers who left welfare and consistently show that most mothers who leave welfare for work, work in low-wage jobs. See (Boushey and Gundersen 2001, Cancian et. al 2002, Loprest 2001, Pavetti 2001, Seefeldt 2008).

Chapter Four

Family Commitment

Guilt Is for Mothers with Good Jobs

And, you know that's one of the things that I think I have had the hardest time with ever being a single parent is because my kids are my heart. My kids are my main thing to be concerned about. And I would rather go without things than to jeopardize my children's well-being.

—Gina

FAMILY COMMITMENT SCHEMA

I begin this chapter with an overview of the family commitment schema. I then show how its definition of childhood and intensive motherhood often collide with changing expectations of women's responsibility to provide. Borrowing from family values rhetoric, mothers see the failure of others to abide by the basic mandates of this powerful cultural model as a moral deficiency with dire consequences for children as well as society. Choice emerges as contested moral terrain. Mothers question the priorities of women who purportedly choose work over family and lament the constraints on their own ability to devote themselves to children first and foremost.

FAMILY COMMITMENT DEFINED

Like the work commitment schema, the family commitment schema provides compelling scripts for guiding, evaluating, and shaping what we know as reality (Blair-Loy 2003). It influences how people evaluate themselves and others, their aspirations, and their identities as responsible moral adults. It shapes respondents' views of themselves and others as women and mothers, providing a framework for filtering, understanding, and making sense of one's life. As a powerful gendered cultural model it resonates further as a source of identity and meaning bound up in deeply held, taken-for-granted understandings about men and women internalized as natural and self-evident.

As an abstract model, the family commitment schema assigns primary responsibility for home and family to women. It rests on an idealized notion of motherhood based on the circumstances of the white middle-class woman. Paid work outside the home is not forbidden altogether but must not interfere with a mother's total devotion to her children. Essential elements of the family commitment schema are: caring for one's children trumps all other commitments, children do best when cared for by their mothers, and women should find fulfillment in caring for and raising children.

COMPETING SCHEMAS

The demands of family commitment run head on into those of work commitment. Recall in the last chapter how the benefits of working outside the home—both objective and subjective—draw women toward work commitment. Some mothers proudly explain how they demonstrate independence and self-sufficiency through paid work and contrast their own work ethic with negative assumptions about welfare recipients. Viewed through the lens of work commitment, working outside the home becomes mothers' family responsibility. Therefore working mothers derive status as good mothers through their ability to provide for their children. They also model responsibility and demonstrate character.

However, limited work opportunities present a dilemma for many respondents. We heard Jeanie's ambivalence as she weighed the tradeoffs between low-wage work and spending time with her young daughter. The source of her doubts is a powerful rival vision of family life, which defines children as vulnerable and mandates that mothers be devoted to their care. When the demands of family commitment collide with the independence promised through work outside the home, mothers find themselves in a no-win situation caught between two contradictory definitions of their responsibility as mothers and providing for children's needs. Suzanne poignantly illustrated this dilemma in the introductory chapter when she spoke about the need to get a job and her distress over leaving her small child. "Yeah, if a child is really young, I understand that staying with them makes sense so then they have a really good bond with their children. I think that they should go out and look for a job as soon as they can. Although, it just breaks my heart to have to do it, to leave him at home myself. I had to do it."

Many interviewees believe that mothers should work outside the home, but like many working mothers they are torn between the demands and rewards of paid work and conviction that children need the nurturing and bonding that can only be provided by their mothers (Hays 1996). The double bind for poor mothers results in a moral and emotional struggle to reconcile seemingly conflicting definitions of their obligations as workers and mothers. Suzanne tells us that it "breaks her heart," and Jeanie finds herself "really torn" on the trade-off between nurturing her daughter and modeling success through paid work.

> I'm really torn on that one because I think they are going to get better care from their mother than someone taking care of eight other kids, or seven other kids. It's more individual. I don't know. I think there's more of a security that way if it's their mother taking care of them and more of a bonding and everything like that, but at the same time I think it's important to have. . . . I don't really have any strong woman role models in my life. I've never had that and I wish I did. . . . And we've worked hard on that, because I think I want her to have a strong female role model and I'd like to be that for her . . .
>
> But, I don't know. Maybe until a certain age, up until kindergarten or first grade, and then they're going to be in school and then [I will] be working, you know full-time. Because then they are going to see you out there being successful. You know they are going to be away from you anyway because they are going to be in school. So what else are you going to be doing? You should be out working, you know? 'Cause the baby years it's really good for them to be with their mother, especially under a year. I think it's really important. So, I'm really torn on that because I think it's better for a girl to see a strong woman in her life.

Jeanie vacillates over her desire for her daughter to see her working outside the home—a role model associated with independence and expanded opportunities for women. Yet, she also believes that mothers should be with their children through the preschool years. The cause of her dilemma is feeling forced to choose between two morally compelling definitions of her obligations. Some mothers resolve this by integrating work outside the home as part of their responsibility as mothers. Jeanie struggles to do this. She envisions either a strong woman who works outside the home or the stay-at-home mother. Try as she may, she cannot help but see work and family in opposition, however much this seems out of sync with today's work and family lives.

Jeanie is thus caught between two powerful gendered cultural scripts defining her role in her daughter's life. And, as each demands unswerving devotion, she faces the agonizing dilemma of attempting to reconcile work commitment's masculine definition of self-sufficiency and independence with family commitment's call for mothers to devote themselves to children.

However, for others the opposition between work and family does not result in uncertainty or the feeling of being pulled in two different directions. For example, Amber Wilson, twenty-six, a widowed, stay-at-home mother of two young children, had recently enrolled in college classes. As we discussed her future plans to work full-time when her children were older, I asked whether she thought that mothers who work outside the home are positive role models for children.

Her response: "you have a six-month-old baby, that's not a role model. That's mom being gone. You . . . even a five year old, that's not a role model. He's not gonna be, 'Wow I'm real—geez—my mom is such a good mom because she goes to work all day." In contrast to the ambivalence expressed by Jeanie, Amber ridicules the notion that from a child's point of view a mother working all day would be considered a good role model. Reflected through the family commitment schema, the example mothers provide for children when they work outside the home is no match for a mother's obligation to children in the home, and in turn, the benefits children derive from their mother's care. Amber's remarks underscore the taken-for-granted, self-evident nature of the schema. Even five-year-olds know that working outside the home is not what makes a good mother. Good mothers stay home and care for their children.

PAID WORK AND CARING FOR CHILDREN
ARE TWO OPPOSITE THINGS

Poor and low-income mothers do not form their views and respond to cultural schemas in a vacuum. Nor can we understand their choices as separate from their identities, the social and cultural environment, and communities to which they belong. Chapter 2 demonstrated how changing expectations and social arrangements in U.S. society—where the majority of mothers combine paid work and raising children—contributed to policy changes demanding paid work from poor women in lieu of or in exchange for welfare assistance. Several related issues make this especially problematic for poor and working-class women. One is the dearth of alternative valued identities and the high value poor women place on children where motherhood is the most important, fulfilling role in low-income women's lives (Edin and Kefalas 2005). The second is demanding mothers take a job outside the home competes with the belief that good mothers should physically be there for children. Lastly, many mothers in this study share assumptions about the harmful effects on children when mothers devote themselves to work. Together, these factors contribute to a situation where mandating paid work for poor women is perceived as obstructing their responsibility as mothers to protect and care for their children.

Anna Kelso, a twenty-four-year-old single mother, has never married and receives TANF. Anna has two small children, ages two and four, and lives with her children and disabled mother. She was appealing a sanction from the welfare office for refusing to work when her youngest child was ill and hospitalized for two days. Although many respondents experience some ambivalence in their attempts to reconcile the demands that they work outside the home with their desire to be home with children, few mothers were as adamant as Anna that working outside the home was irreconcilable with meeting children's needs.

As she explains "I mean, a good mom is just basically focused on your children's knowledge, education, and focusing mostly and foremost on them. Putting them first because if you don't put them first they're not going to succeed." I asked her if working could be part of this and she disagreed.

> No. Those are two opposite things. Because being a mom, like my mom always told me, it's a twenty-four hour job. You never stop. I mean if they, if somebody, if they want to look at it as work, then we do have jobs. I mean we have 24-hours-nonstop-365-days-a-year jobs. I mean we don't have breaks. We don't have vacation time. We don't have any of that. We don't. I mean, so . . . I don't consider it a job. I just consider it, you know, doing what we wanted to do. Take care of them.

Others agree with Anna that the work that mothers do is not like other jobs. Validating Anna's views this mother says: "It is not an easy job. It's not. Because it's not an eight-hour day or ten-hour day, it's a twenty-four-hour-a-day job." Anna resists the notion that caring for children is equivalent to paid work. For her, the expectation that a mother should be totally devoted to children is self-evident. Anna notes that "somebody" might want to label what she does as work and call it a job, because caring for children requires around-the-clock, non-stop attention. But she indicates that the requisites of family commitment—that mothers be totally devoted to their children—are not to be confused with the self-interested rational demands of the market.[1] Caring for children, being a mother, is not a "job." It is what mothers want to do. Paid work and family commitment occupy two opposing, separate realms of life.

The broad sweep of this cultural model can be seen as Anna describes the time her four-year-old child was hospitalized. "Welfare wanted me to leave him in the hospital and go up to the class. And I told them there is no way in heck; there was no way I was leaving my child in the hospital! They [welfare office] tried to tell me my mom could go and sit with him. [I told them] That's not my mom's responsibility!"

Anna's response is a mirror image of Sharon Hays's (1996) narrative illustrating the cultural model of intensive motherhood informing the practices and beliefs demanded by the family commitment model. Hays's anguished mother is a professional woman, not a mother on welfare. And in her example, a purportedly cold-hearted boss, not the welfare office, asks why someone else besides a mother cannot stay with a sick child. The point of convergence is that both mothers find it incomprehensible that *anyone* would fail to understand a mother's need to be with her sick child. The cultural logic of the responsibility of mothers to care for children is self-evident, untouchable, and sacred (Hays 1996, 1).

Additionally, Anna's views on paid work and caring for children illustrate that work commitment is no match for family commitment in offering Anna and others a framework for finding self-fulfillment and meaning in their lives. In contrast to others who find that working outside the home provides membership in a moral community, Anna's moral identity lies in motherhood. Moreover, when Anna talks about the demands of motherhood she refers to mothers as a collective, invoking group membership. Motherhood is defined in terms of what *we* do, indicating that others share her understandings of what motherhood entails. The all-encompassing responsibility that mothers have for children emerges as a model of universal motherhood whose adherents are promised a meaningful life in which good mothers devote themselves to children first and foremost.

However, when I note that Anna describes the demands of motherhood as an understanding shared among all mothers, this is not to say that in practice mothers truly share a unified set of beliefs and activities about how they should care for children, or that one objectively exists. In fact, studies of poor mothers show that middle-class mothering practices have a greater influence on working-class and poor mothers than the reverse (Edin and Kefalas 2005, McCormack 2005). And, as Sharon Hays argued in her study on middle-class motherhood, "different social circumstances of mothers shape their interpretations and responses to the dominant model of child rearing in distinct ways" (1996, 76).[2] Anna, like other poor mothers, maintains her standing as a good mother despite her status as a single mother on welfare by insisting that the central tenet of motherhood is "being there" a definition that does not require her to be supermom but to be attentive and devoted to her children, protect them and keep them safe (Edin and Kefalas 2005). This is something that Anna can provide that does not entail the expensive, expert-guided, intensive childrearing model that Hays (1996) describes for middle-class mothers. Anna responds to family commitment's demands that mothers have primary responsibility for children by insisting that mothers should be there for children 24/7. Given the heightened salience of motherhood in poor mothers' lives, it is not surprising to find that Anna's interpretation of the obligations of motherhood are increasingly problematic when "good" mothers are now expected to go to work.

Conflict between the demands of paid work and family life are all too familiar to many mothers. However, Anna's experience demonstrates, that demands by the welfare office help create a unique version of this dilemma for the poor. Instead of taken-for-granted expectations about women's responsibility to care for children, the emphasis on paid work turns the tables on gendered assumptions and defines mothers' responsibility through work commitment demonstrated by paid work outside the home. To borrow from Mimi Abramovitz (1996), policy makers created a new family ethic for poor mothers reflected and codified in PRWORA. However, the challenge to policy makers and the evident contradiction for poor mothers comes from the powerful pull of family commitment where responsibility for children belongs to a mother. Caring for a sick child is the definitive expression of the self-sacrifice and moral obligation expected of motherhood. The contradiction between a mother's responsibility to work outside the home or stay at home to care for a sick child is a test of values in which motherhood almost always wins. Requirements that women work outside the home can leave mothers feeling that they are under attack for fulfilling their moral obligation to their children. As one mother painfully shared, "it is like we have lost the right to be mothers."

Devaluing a mother's calling to care for her children can be interpreted as an affront to mothers everywhere. Of course, the flip side of relegating women's moral obligation to children and interests to home and family is the closing off of opportunities for women in the workplace (Williams 2010). Middle-class, professional, and elite mothers at the center of today's work-life debate face the opposite conundrum when criticized for devoting too much time to their careers and supposedly neglecting their children or conversely being pushed out of the workplace by an environment hostile to family responsibilities (Stone 2007).

There are undoubtedly contradictions in these understandings as women's lives have changed and most women expect to combine paid work with motherhood. However, few people consider how efforts by the welfare office to redefine poor mothers' work and family priorities in promoting paid work over caring for children may intensify these contradictions.

FAMILY COMMITMENT: THE "NATURAL" GENDERED SCHEMA

Although paid work indicates responsibility and membership in a community of upstanding citizens, women's connection to children emerges as a self-defining process tied to roles for women perceived as natural. Thus, adherence to family commitment does not require that respondents embrace a new understanding of what Kathleen Gerson (2002) refers to as the gendered division of moral labor. In contrast to the work commitment schema which defines women's responsibility for children in line with the masculine good provider role (Bernard 1981), the family commitment schema retains the "traditional" cultural mandate that assigns caring for children to women and breadwinning to men. It preserves essentialist notions of connectivity and caring as women's moral domain, whereas work commitment shifts mothers' moral domain to the autonomous independent worker and masculine bread-winner. Moreover, however much social scientists and gender scholars understand men and women's work and family roles as socially constructed, many of the mothers I interviewed maintain that women have a natural capacity for child care. As these mothers express beliefs about work and family obligations through the lens of family commitment, they invoke a cultural model that is commonly understood as based on biological differ-ence between the sexes.

Although some mothers knew of single fathers that were doing a good job in raising children, they believe that women's care-giving responsibilities are based on differences in men and women's biological capacity to bear and care for children. Several interviewees also say it does not matter whether a mother or a father stays home; what is important is that a parent be home with children. However, this did not shake their belief in natural gender differences. In practice, in their own lives, this parent was usually the moth-er, and there were few men who they deemed competent to care for children.

Nancy Owens, a married mother of two children ages ten and thirteen, offered her brother in-law as an example of a man who was any woman's equal in caring for his family. He was the primary caregiver to his children while his wife worked fifty to sixty hours a week. Nancy explained, "You know how women have that extra little momma instinct. Some men have it, some men don't. He has it! But yet he's still a very manly man." However, things differed in her own household where she was the sole wage earner and her husband stayed home. He did not have the "momma instincts" attributed to her brother-in-law. "Bless my husband's heart, but he just is terrible at housekeeping. [laughing] He tells the kids, wait till your mom gets home. I have no clue!" It is also apparent that however much appeal shared childrear-ing practices have in theory, mothers who do not devote themselves to their children are seen as shirking their primary responsibility as mothers and women.

Linda Robinson, a forty-three-year-old African American mother of three children, two grown and one in elementary school, manages her apartment complex and also does housecleaning. She has been the primary wage earner for her family since her children were very small. Linda worked full-time in a management position in retail, a job she enjoyed and took great pride in until she was laid off several years ago. As we discussed her work life she charac-terized single mothers as good role models when they worked outside the home. I then asked her, if a father was around, should a mother stay home to raise children? This elicits a different response. "I don't want to play the sexist role, but I am a very . . . very logical, very reality-based person. I mean come on! The mothers are the ones with the breasts! The mothers are the ones that are the nurturers! The mothers are the ones that kiss the wrongs and hug you and wipe the tears and they're the more emotional ones. That is not a sin! It is the way it has always been!"

Linda turns to biology as well as tradition to assert that there is no question that mothers are best suited to care for children. She dismisses any notion to the contrary, by pointing out that her remarks may appear sexist in light of today's expectations, but she is just stating the obvious. According to Linda, the gendered roles assigned to men and women are natural, the way it has always been and should remain, despite the changes in society where women are expected to work outside the home.

Nadine, introduced in chapter 3, also understands family commitment's definitions of motherhood and women's roles as the primary caregiver of their children as grounded in inherent sex differences between men and women.

> My opinion is a lot of men—not all men—don't bond like a mother does with the child. The mother starts right from conception. And the father just doesn't because he will never feel what we feel. Never experience birth like we experience it, you know. And they're the breadwinners. They go. They don't see the first steps and the first tooth, and the first boo boo and the, "Oh, he ate solid food today, and he's walking or he's rolling instead of crawling." So, I think it's much more important for me.

Although, we have seen greater flexibility in gender roles in the last few decades, with men taking on more responsibility for raising children and women contributing more financially, traditional attitudes on parenting remain strong (Stone 2007). However much men may take part in a child's early development, women are still seen as the primary caretakers. For my respondents, this may be partially explained due to low father involvement among poor and low-income populations where single fathers are not able to support their children financially (Edin and Kefalas 2005, Edin and Nelson 2013). But, as demonstrated in Nadine's narrative, mothers believe that sex differences between men and women explain their different priorities; women's interests cohere with those of children and men's with paid work. Of course, not all mothers explicitly link the expectation that mothers' primary duty is caring for children to biology, but most express belief in distinct gender roles for men and women.

Jeanie, who earlier expressed her ambivalence over work and family demands, frames the naturalness of women's devotion to family in opposition to men's responsibility to provide. Jeanie and others see women's role as the primary caretaker of children. Women do it because they are expected too, and they are also more competent than men.

> I think for a man, they feel that that's [paid work] their primary job, and for a woman, I think you feel that your kid is your primary job. I think that women have more of a feeling that their kids are their main priority than men. You know his job is to go do whatever he does, which is security right now and mine is to take care of her. And sometimes it makes me mad when it comes down to it because I want to go out too, but I am the one that has to take care of her when she's sick. I think I'm better at it though so it's okay [laughs]

Jeanie's resentment that she is the one who always cares for her sick daughter suggests rejection of the family commitment schema's definition of mothers' obligations. However, the fact that it is Jeanie, not the child's father, who puts the child's needs before her own desires reinforces the salience of the schema's demand that it is mothers who must commit themselves to children. And as Jeanie laughingly tells me, she as a mother is better at caring for her daughter. In the end she confirms the powerful gendered assumptions that undergird belief in mothers' inherent competency and responsibility to care for their children.

Many mothers attribute women's responsibilities to inherent differences between men and women, which are then reaffirmed by their own experience. As stated earlier, these views may seem counter to today's trends in family arrangements where fathers perform a greater share of child care and domestic duties than they have in the past. And fathers who provide this care may certainly disagree that mothers are always best at nurturing and caring for children.[3] In spite of this, we see that gendered assumptions continue to shape respondent's understandings of differing expectations for men and women. Defined through the family commitment schema, the gendered division of labor between men and women is seen as a moral obligation, the natural order of things, and the "way it has always been."

My conversation with Marianne Olson, a divorced forty-eight-year-old mother of two grown children and an eight-year-old daughter, further illustrates the persistence of the schema in shaping women's lives. I asked whether she agreed with the idea that today given the changes we have seen in society people would say that paid work is equally important for both men and women. Her response took me by surprise, when she replied "Well, these must be women that have wives then." I would have laughed had Marianne not been so serious, as the desire for a wife is something of a running joke among married heterosexual women as the solution to their own hectic lives in meeting the demands of work and family. Marianne's dismissive reply to my question indicates how ridiculous she believes it is to equate men and women's paid work and family commitments. The only scenario where a woman could be as committed to paid work as a man would be if a woman had the support traditionally provided to men by wives.[4] In Marianne's view, social change of this magnitude is both nonexistent and also contrary to the natural order of things. As she explains: "I think that women have always been the primary caretaker of their children, and it's not only understood among women themselves, but it is understood among all society that we take care of children and that is our job, first and foremost. That's why they consider barren women not as useful as fertile women."

Marianne's comments confirm the social value attached to motherhood although we rarely hear it expressed today in such provocative terms.[5] In fact, Marianne's traditional view of women may be rather shocking to hear and certainly will make feminist readers wonder if not cringe when she states that despite widening opportunities and gains in gender equality, women's value is measured through their capacity as mothers. Whether or not one agrees with her, she affirms the tenacity of this traditional view of women's place in society. Women's primary responsibility is home and children, and as Marianne points out to me, a fact that should be obvious—motherhood remains the standard by which society defines adult women (Ireland 1993,133). As antiquated as this description may be for today's family and work arrangements, it illustrates the depth of the gendered family relations mandated by the schema.

As cultural schemas persist over time, they become naturalized as taken-for-granted understandings so established that no alternatives are considered possible (Blair-Loy 2001, 2003, Epstein 1988). Correspondence with a gender belief system that assigns men and women different work and family roles based on assumed inherent differences between the sexes, renders the demands of the schema as immutable (Lorber 1994). For many women, the naturalization of motherhood in family commitment results in a prescription for interpreting the reality of one's life so compelling and taken-for-granted that one cannot imagine it any other way. Whether derived from biology or social roles, family commitment's mandates result in an almost seamless expression of women's "nature."

THE SOCIAL COSTS OF MOTHERS' WORK OUTSIDE THE HOME

The family commitment's definition of childhood—that children are fragile, vulnerable, and need their mothers' care—works hand in hand with the demands of intensive motherhood to inform respondent's views on the social costs of mothers' paid work. The majority of interviewees believe that children need their mothers at least in the early years. This is when children are most impressionable, the time period when mothers and children bond, and mothers are responsible for the nurturing and caring that will provide the foundation for a child's future. In short, mothers if they are at all able should remain at home "with their babies." As we will see, the failure of others to abide by this broadly shared understanding of childhood and mothers' responsibility represents a moral failing with repercussions for both the welfare of children and all of society.

Linda insists that young children need their mother's care and expresses concerns for the long-term consequences of mothers' paid work. "I think it matters on the age of the kids. Yes, I think that mothers should be with their babies. When they are little, when they are small, yes, yes, I do. Because if they don't get what they need when they are little, from six down, then they're screwed up when they become young kids. Because see, our teenagers are being lost right now."

Mia Reynolds, age thirty, has never married and is the mother of two small children. She lost custody of her children for a year because of domestic violence and her inability to protect them from witnessing abuse by their father in their home. Her children stayed with her mother until she regained custody and she and her children now live in a transitional housing development for families. Although her experience is understandably foreign to most readers, and some may even question her ability to care for her children, she conveys a similar sentiment about the needs of small children and a mother's obligation

> I personally think that a mom should stay home with her kids as much as she can until they are five years old. And the reason I say that is that the first five years are the most important in a child's developmental state. And I think that for the first five years that's when you teach them that you love them. That's when you teach them to trust. That's when you teach them to be who they are and who you are! It is those first five years that are the most important years of their life.

Yvette, introduced in chapter 3, agrees: "from the time they are born to the age of six is the most important years of that child's life. All parents should be there for their children from the time they are born to the time they get older."

The circumstances of the mothers above differ from those of the majority of married mothers of small children who combine paid work and motherhood. And the views as expressed here may well seem out of step with today's expectations for women to combine paid work and motherhood. Recall, however, that a majority of Americans also indicate concern over the impact on small children when mothers work outside the home (Cohn, Livingston, and Wang 2014). Thus, one could argue that Linda, Mia, and Yvette's comments simply affirm what many Americans believe about the workforce participation of mothers of small children; if mothers are able to limit their paid work they should in the best interest of their children particularly when they are young. However, the mothers here are not those featured in discussions of contemporary work-life conflict, torn between the costs of forgoing lucrative or even fulfilling careers and the social benefits of doing the right thing by their children supported by a wage-earning spouse. Rather, they are low-income and poor mothers, whose work and family priorities are obscured in the public work-family debate, responding to broadly shared cultural definitions of children's needs and mothers' moral obligation to "be there for their babies."

Respondent's views on women's nature and family roles put them at odds with progressive feminist arguments in support of paid work for women. Suggestions for helping families cope with the demands of work and family include flexible workplaces and affordable day care, in conjunction with a more egalitarian division of household labor in order to reduce the burden on mothers when combining paid work and child care (Jacobs and Gerson 2004, Coontz 2013). Advocates for stressed-out mothers also argue that traditional views on maternal care create needless anxiety and induce guilt in mothers rather than address the reality of contemporary families (Douglas and Michaels 2004, Peskowitz 2005, Warner 2005). We need look no further than sociologists Jacobs and Gerson's debunking of conservative arguments about the harm to children when mothers work outside the home to appreciate the rift between poor and low-income mothers' understandings of children's needs and their own obligations, and progressive views on solutions for working parents:

> Concerns over replacing full-time maternal care with other forms of childrearing are also based on the dubious, but persisting, belief that biological mothers are uniformly and universally superior to all other caretakers. It is hard to imagine any other form of work for which such a claim could be made or taken seriously. Mothers are an enormously large and varied group. It makes little sense to assume that they are all equally and uniquely prepared to be their child's only or best caretaker. Instead children benefit from having a range of caretakers—including fathers, other relatives and paid professionals. They also benefit from parents who are satisfied with their choices, whether this means working or staying at home. (2004, 195)

As demonstrated earlier, this runs counter to the views of many mothers I interviewed, most of whom believe that mothers are superior caregivers. Undoubtedly, a good share of the U.S. public would agree that if we want to help stressed-out families, the solution is not simply to relegate mothers to the home as full-time child care providers and blame their workforce participation as the problem. In fact, a majority believe the best situation for families is for both parents to share paid work and care giving (Parker 2012). Most would likely also agree that it is ludicrous to lump all mothers together in drawing conclusions about their ability as caregivers.[6] However, many of the mothers in this study share conservative assumptions about the social costs of mothers' paid work and beliefs about the superiority of maternal care, despite the findings of social science researchers.

Louise, age fifty-three, spoke about the importance of paid work in chapter 3, but she worries about its social costs: "Nurturing children's needs is important. That is what makes it rough for me to say. I approve work, but sometimes it is the children that make the decisions for you. Sometimes they need you more. Not being able to tell you, they do other things to show you that they need that attention."

Louise's uncertainty is typical of mothers caught between the contradictory demands work and family, but as she says, the needs of children ultimately lead her to the appropriate choice. However, not all mothers struggle as Louise does between two opposing visions of responsible motherhood. Earlier Anna described the opposition between work and family, but unlike Louise she does not experience ambivalence and makes clear her priorities.

Here Anna explains her views on the significance of a mother's presence and what gets lost when someone else cares for her child:

> I mean, with the way the welfare system works, when your baby's three months old you have to be in the work system. Well, that's three months and then it's your child with somebody else while you're working. You're missing out on all these little tiny milestones that she could be doing during the daytime that you would want to be focused on. And you know, that's my main thing is I wanna be there and I wanna see everything. I don't want somebody else seeing it and then tell me about it. So, it's not the same.

Even if mothers were convinced that paid caregivers were competent in taking care of their children, that would not overcome the problem, as Anna explains it, of her missing out on important markers of a child's development that in her view help shape what it means to be a mother—a job that is not to be equated with any other form of work. Anna understands that her stance holds little moral sway with welfare officials. But their lack of support does not lessen and may even bolster her conviction as to the demands of motherhood. Anna may not strive to be the perfect mother, nor does she hold any illusions about her ability to have it all. She does believe her responsibility, as a mother, is to be there for her child.

Family commitment's capacity to shape respondent's understanding is validated through essentialist notions of women's nature and longstanding ideals about men and women's work and family roles. Mothers frequently refer to traditional gendered family arrangements in warning about the consequences for children when mothers go to work.

Samantha Matthews, a twenty-four-year-old divorced mother of two small children, ages two and three, works in a fast-food restaurant and was laid off temporarily as the restaurant remodels. I asked Samantha whether she thought paid work was as important for women in society as it is for men. Samantha responds:

Yeah, I think that is why we have a lot of problems in society today. I think there is a definite reason why things were set the way they were before. Men are really good physical laborers. We are generally better nurturers. When a child looks at you and cries we're generally better at handling that. Generally men tend to be a bit more irritated more quickly. I honestly think that kids were better off when they had structure at home. When they had moms teaching them, not day care teaching them. When they had mom raising them, not day care raising them. We are not raising them anymore. Somebody else is raising your children while you go out to work. I can't stand that.

Though Samantha initially responds that paid work is as important for men as for women, this is not a marker of success for women on the path to gender equality. Rather, as she sees it, the changes in gender arrangements and mothers' workforce participation disrupt the natural order of things and men and women's roles. Samantha is not alone in her views, as others tell me the proof of the pudding is the impact on children. Many mothers I interviewed are deeply concerned over what they see as an unraveling of society's values spurred by the exodus of women out of the home into the workplace. As one mother said, "I think the real test is watching our kids nowadays. Look at what's gone on. You know you'd never hear of that stuff when I was growing up. You wonder why these kids are getting in trouble. Well, I know why they are getting in trouble; because they don't have any supervision."

Another mother agrees, with a dig at the notion that women can have it all in combining paid work with caring for children. "Yeah, women are expected to do it all. Do I think that in the future when we look at these children that there's going to be probably some big [problems] . . . well you can already see it now. There is no such thing as doing it all, and by doing it all you sacrifice one thing in order to do it all."

And as Samantha tells me, echoing the most conservative rhetoric about the social costs to both women and children from mothers' participation in paid work: "Oh, yeah. Oh, yeah. I would love nothing more than to be home with my kids all the time, and right now I am. . . . It is crazy what the work does to moms. The kids don't like it, and the moms don't like it. Nobody is happy, but we wanted it. I am still trying to understand why we wanted it."

As middle-class and professional women enter the workforce and find their opportunities expanding—even as their family lives become increasingly hectic and they too, struggle with decisions over time spent in paid work and family obligations—poor and low-income women whose vision of a meaningful life centers on motherhood and children find themselves increasingly marginalized. They get little support among married working mothers, who also resent the stresses in their own lives and whose struggles are theirs to sort out privately. Moreover, the American public, much less conservatives are not rallying to assist poor single mothers to stay home with their children, however much they embrace conservative family values. Nonetheless, the lack of support for mothers to stay home with their children does not diminish their commitment. Rather, for some mothers it tends to enhance the salience of "traditional" gender roles and women's identity as mothers.

ACTUALLY IT IS FREEDOM OF CHOICE

A central premise of this book is the significance of the social and cultural context in which poor and low-income mothers face work and family decisions. Although questions about women's workforce participation writ large remain central to the work-family debate in the United States, few are directed toward how the material and moral context differentially shape the way women's choices are evaluated and the consequences of those choices. All too often women's work and family decisions are portrayed as driven by rational economic calculus, whether these women are poor and low-income mothers, married middle-class and professional mothers, or elite wage-earning mothers in dual-earner families. Taken to its logical conclusion, some women work because they have to, others because they want to. This perspective robs poor women of choice and wipes out consideration of the gendered moral and emotional factors we have explored thus far in shaping work and family decisions. As demonstrated earlier, this is too simplistic an explanation of women's choices. Moreover, even those sympathetic to the struggles of poor and working-class women overlook choice as a moral dilemma for poor and low-income women who *need* to work.

According to sociologist Jennifer Johnson, working-class women do not suffer from guilt or feelings of "being torn" between work and family because "working-class women, especially poor working-class women, were often forced to work, motivated by need not preference" (2002,124). Johnson acknowledges that working-class women may experience frustration with lack of flexibility in the workplace and time and money problems but not the opposition between work and family domains characterizing middle-class work and family conflict. As she explains, working-class women perceive paid work in terms of work *for* family, as opposed to work *or* family—the latter model a luxury achievable by women who do have a choice to limit paid work because their spouse has sufficient earnings to support a wife and children (p.123).[7]

Judith Warner, writing on the challenges facing contemporary middle-class and professional women from a progressive feminist standpoint, offers a different perspective on the issue of choice. In *Motherhood in the Age of Anxiety*, she describes the toll exacted on contemporary mothers in the constant barrage of media attention to women's work and family arrangements and the second-guessing of mothers who feel they can't get it right no matter what they choose. She writes:

> Choice is the fetish word of our generation, perhaps the most sacred of all our articles of faith. We all know the reasons why working mothers work, money, above all, but secondarily satisfaction, adult companionship, intellectual stimulation, a sense of security and independence and status—the ability, in short to provide for their families and remain true to themselves. But from talking to women, I've found that the reasons that stay-at-home moms stay home are not all that different, in that at base, they spring both from a psychological need for self-fulfillment and an effort to meet the material needs for their families. (And *not*, as many commentators would have us think, from a moralistic idea of what was the right thing to do.) (2005,147)

Many Americans, myself included, would agree with Warner's defense of mothers' ability to make choices in their own best interest and that of their families without all the pressure and second-guessing as to the appropriateness of their choices. She writes of the disillusionment faced by women who completed college, married, and entered careers expecting that things would be different from their parent's generation in that they could manage both fulfilling careers and motherhood. However, whether referring to middle-class or working-class and poor women, Warner too easily dismisses the moral salience of work and family choices on the grounds that all decisions arise from necessity (2005).

Her book provides a welcome push back against conservative attempts to undermine feminist progress in expanding choices for women. And, as much as I share Warner's desire to relieve mothers of unnecessary stress, I argue that work and family choices are wrenching because whether out of need or desire they always involve decisions over the "right thing to do." Moreover, the cultural and social context within which middle-class and professional mothers, and also working-class and poor mothers make decisions has a huge bearing on how mothers' choices are evaluated and the consequences. The conservative moralizing Warner warns about sanctifies middle-class mothers who choose to opt out of paid work as doing the right thing by their children at the same time insisting poor women get a job as punishment for daring to have children outside of marriage (Hays 2003, 19).[8] The significance of this distinction is seen below in Vera's description of the choices facing poor single mothers.

Vera Kelly, a married, forty-nine-year-old mother of three, whose youngest daughter is seventeen years old, works full-time as a home health care aide, and her daughter lives at home helping her to care for her disabled husband. We were discussing the changes that had taken place under TANF (as a young mother she had relied on welfare), and I asked her if she thought single mothers should have to work.

> Actually it is freedom of choice. Some parents were made to stay home and take care of their kids. There's a lot of parents out there it would drive them

crazy to stay home and take care of their kids all the time. . . . But if a certain
person does not want to work, I don't think she should be forced to have to go
to work. If your choice is to stay home and be a *good mother*, take care of your
baby, then that should be your choice. And you don't have that choice anymore. It's gone. If you go to work we [welfare office] will give you money to
help take care of your baby. If you don't go to work, you are on your own. I
mean you don't have a lot of choice.

Although Vera acknowledges that not everyone is suited to be a stay-at-
home mother and should be able to make their own choices, she clearly
indicates that in her eyes mothers should have the choice to stay home and
take care of children—and good mothers choose to stay home. Moreover, the
choices she describes are not those facing middle-class women and professional working mothers who also feel caught between the competing demands of paid work and motherhood. The American public would agree in
principle with Vera that if someone wants to stay home and take care of their
baby they should be able to. If this were a married mother supported by a
wage-earning husband we would certainly understand if not cheer her decision. The difference, obviously, is the disappearance of support in the case of
a poor single mother who would rely on welfare to limit her paid work in
order to be a "good mother." In fact she would be viewed as irresponsible,
shirking her obligation to provide for her family, seen as lazy, blamed for
having children she cannot afford, and ultimately accountable for much of
society's ills for her failure to marry (Hays 2003, Sidel 2006).

Douglas and Michaels in the *Mommy Myth* took up the issue of choice for
poor mothers in a lively and sometimes derisive critique of contemporary
motherhood labeled "the new momism." They share Warner's view that
motherhood, idealized in the media and by conservative moralizing, places
an unrealistic burden on women who could never hope to live up to its
demands. They also pointed out the contradiction between idealized versions
of motherhood and child care, and TANF's requirements that poor mothers
find jobs outside the home. According to Douglas and Michaels, attacks on
poor mothers through media stereotypes of welfare mothers served to make
married, white, working mothers feel good about themselves in the face of an
onslaught of conflicting prescriptions about how to be a good mom. They
also noted that in addition to making working mothers less sympathetic to the
struggles of the poor, the most damaging media narrative about welfare
mothers came from the idea that they had the same options from which to
choose as other mothers and instead chose to rely on welfare. Douglas and
Michaels found this notion absurd and ask whether we really believe that
poor women *choose* to be poor (2004, 201–2).

However, the thrust of their argument was not that poor mothers on
welfare might also face anxiety and grapple with their identities as workers
and mothers. It was to chastise American society in general, and middle-class

mothers in particular, for equating their own choices with those of poor mothers, who had none, and, further, for using poor women to feel better about their own inadequacies regarding motherhood. Although they rightfully pointed out the hardships of poor mothers, morality was reduced to the supposedly irresponsible choices of welfare mothers.

Kathleen Gerson (2002) shifted the moral lens to gender relations in characterizing work and family decisions as moral dilemmas and asserting that the choices of *all* mothers were vulnerable to judgment. Gerson cited changes in taken-for-granted, gendered work, and family roles in contemporary society as the basis for men and women's difficulty in reconciling how to provide and care for their families when traditional rules no longer applied. Women cannot avoid ambivalence and second-guessing when they seek to balance caring and connection in intimate family relationships with the independence and autonomy derived through paid work. However, as demonstrated throughout this chapter, for a significant number of women in my study the choice that holds the greatest moral currency is that of a "good mother" who puts her child first and foremost. Autonomy and independence associated with paid work outside the home, however desirable, are not morally equivalent to mothers' main job, which is taking care of their children.

I think many would agree with the proposition that poor and working-class women *and* middle-class and upper middle-class women when faced with choices regarding paid work and family care are often doing the best they can in a situation where all decisions involve second-guessing. However, it is also clear that the ability to make a choice without the oversight of the welfare office and the consequences for mothers who make the wrong choice—refusing to get a job—is an important consideration in the social conditions, both material and moral, that differentiate the work and family experience of impoverished and low-income mothers from others. Choices regarding work and family differ starkly when the only (however limited) option is welfare or a combination of paid work and public assistance to care for one's family. There is also no doubt that many women in this study believe that the morally superior choice is made by the mother who stays home with children, or limits her workforce activity to properly care for her family. This choice demonstrates that she is a person of worth, fulfilling her responsibility to her children and society.

In this context, choice and/or lack of choice serve as focal points for establishing moral self-definitions where decisions about work and motherhood function as symbolic resources in affirming moral identities. For many respondents fault lines emerge in alignment with the oppositional model of work and family where poor mothers embrace a family values ideal as a reflection of their commitment to children. Whatever ones' position along this divide, it is rare to find the choices of poor women taken seriously, much less championed, in the ongoing concern over paid work and motherhood in today's society. Limiting morality to conservative family values ideology, and choices as non-existent for the poor, obscures how economic constraints, demands from the welfare office, and broadly shared moral structures work hand-in-glove to shape mothers' choices.

"MOMMY WARS"

The gist of the enduring public debate characterized by popular media psychologist Dr. Phil as the "Debate That Never Dies" (Guilty Moms 2009) between stay-at-home and working mothers illustrates the continued influence of the cultural opposition between women's work and family roles which many gender and family scholars (as well as many working parents) wish that we could put to rest (Allen 2012).[9] Critics of the "mommy wars" view them as a media-driven construction that exaggerates difference among women and obscures the important dilemma facing families—a lack of real options for today's parents (Allen 2012). One solution to ending what Leslie Morgan Steiner refers to as "this catfight" among women is for mothers to stop the criticism and support all choices as valid, whether that means work outside the home, full-time, part-time, or full-time motherhood (2005, x). Clearly, we are not there yet.

Whether we use terms *mommy wars, opt-out revolution,* or debate whether it is possible to have it all, the mommies in this study who describe their resentment over the choices they face inhabit a different social environment than the women whom they frequently criticize for choosing careers over motherhood. These mothers have few material resources and limited job opportunities. What they do have is a moral resource in their position as good mothers who put their children first.

Readers met Gina, a forty-nine-year-old mother of four children in the introductory chapter. We sat at the kitchen table in her rambling two-story house in an older low-income neighborhood and talked about the changes in society for women. Gina insists that despite these changes women's first priority should be children and was harshly critical of mothers whom she perceives as not putting their children's needs first. While striking the table with her hand to emphasize her point, she declared, "If a woman wants to, you know, make a career, and go out there and work and have a career, which I am not against, I have no grudges with that. But if that is more important to her, why have kids? Why does she even bother to have kids? You know what are they, just another possession? [laughs] But you know, I am not against women working or having a career, but put your kids first."

Although she repeatedly insisted she was not against women working outside the home, she makes a clear distinction between devotion to careers and devotion to children—setting up the opposition between work and family in very similar terms to the media-driven mommy wars featured on *Dr. Phil*. It would be easy to dismiss these views as a caricature of the cultural wars pitting mothers against each other. And at least one influential study shows that mothers have a great deal more empathy for each other than the media hype leads us to believe (Hays 1996). However the striking similarity in language from the assumption that mothers in careers do not sufficiently value their children to the insulting "why have kids?" suggests that something more profound drives this debate. This is not to say Gina's position is valid or more legitimate than others. Rather, it reveals the objective, broadly shared structure of these understandings. Our conversation took place at the kitchen table, not in front of a televised audience set up to be deliberately provocative. And there is no reason to doubt that mothers sincerely believe that children's needs trump any other obligations. The widely available, broadly shared character of these cultural models provides powerful normative scripts to guide mother's understandings including their evaluation of mothers who would choose to work full-time when they do not have to.

Gina continues:

> I think for the most part, most parents or women are motherly and to have to be away—now some women I know prefer to be away from their kids—but I don't know why they have kids then. But I find most women I have ever talked to—it tears them up, it tears them up to be away from their kids, let somebody else raise them. And I think most women would prefer if they have to work, work part-time or something so they don't have to be away from their kids that many hours.

According to Gina, to be motherly is to be moral. Although, she agrees that women should have the choice to work and raise children, like others we heard from earlier, she believes that women who devote too much time and attention to work do so at the expense of children. Professional women are suspected of putting their careers first—a choice that puts them in clear violation of culturally prescribed expectations of work and family. Thus, Gina's embrace of family commitment assigns poor and low-income women who limit paid work to spend time with children to a clearly superior moral status compared to professional working mothers.

Gina also turns the tables on stigmatized depictions of mothers on welfare. Earlier she stated that given the choices they face, she views women on welfare caring for their children as having their children's best interest at heart. In fact, when I asked her what she thought of the idea that it was better for mothers on welfare to work than stay home with their children, she looked incredulous and replied "mothers work all the time." Moreover, in her view, poor mothers are viewed as morally worthy as a *group* demonstrated by putting their kids first in contrast to the valorization of paid work over raising children. A mother's willingness to place her child's welfare above material gain becomes the criteria for evaluating moral worth.

It is apparent that Gina, like other respondents, holds a vision of mother-hood defined through the mandates of the family commitment schema. If women must work outside the home and place their children in day care, this is understood as a choice that generates considerable anguish. Given a choice, according to Gina, good mothers would not choose to work full-time and mothers who *have to* work must strive to place a child's needs above theirs.

FAMILY VALUES

Many readers may be surprised at the frequency with which poor and low-income mothers turn to social conservative's traditional family values arguments about men and women's roles, particularly those pertaining to mother-hood (used to demonize poor women on welfare) in asserting their right to mother their children and remain at home (Limoncelli 2002).

As demonstrated earlier, some respondents' views about changes in work and family life match outdated conservative cultural rhetoric that attributed problems in society to mothers' increased work force attachment (Blanken-horn 1995). It was striking to hear mothers interpret and understand their obligations as mothers and workers through the lens of an idealized past where children and families were thought to be more highly valued than they are in contemporary society (Coontz 1997). For some family-committed mothers, the lack of support for mothers to stay home with their own children further illustrates how far astray U.S. society has gone and symbolizes a much broader moral decline in the institution of family and society.

Samantha, who spoke earlier about her opposition to the changes occurring in society and the consequences for children, feels her status as a mother is currently under siege from requirements by the welfare office for women to work outside the home.

She says:

> I don't want to be a full-time worker. I absolutely don't like the idea. I want to be a part-time worker. I want to be there part-time so I can still be a mom. I'm kind of sexist and I'm kind of not, and I'm kind of old-fashioned, and I really, really, really wish we could fight to be mothers again. I feel that women have lost that. We've lost the right to be at home with our children and raise them, *unless we're rich. We've lost the right to be moms.*

Optimal preferences, in her view are to limit work and spend more time with her children, an activity that in the past would be possible due to wide-spread belief and acceptance of a traditional gendered division of labor. As

Samantha sees them, the stakes in the changes occurring in society and playing out in the welfare office not only are about limiting the time she has for her children but an assault on her core identity. Moreover, the consequences of the changes extend to less privileged mothers as a group who find their right to care for children—to be mothers—usurped by social changes they are powerless to control.

Her sweeping generalization of stay-at-home mothers as rich is sure to dismay many readers both those who combine work outside the home with caring for small children and also those who stay at home full-time as far removed from the reality of their own lives. However troubling, it does illustrate the divisions among women in understandings of work and family obligations and the differing moral and cultural context shaping their decisions.

Laura, thirty-nine and mother of a thirteen-year-old daughter, is one of only two women in this study who was a full-time homemaker supported by a husband. She is by no means rich (despite the characterization by Samantha). In her view self-sacrificing stay-at-home mothers (good mothers) like herself are under siege for their choices leaving selfish career women free to enjoy their luxurious lives despite the costs to their children and others.

> I hear that a lot. "I work, you stay home. I am a better mother." I don't think it is fair. I am being judged for staying home. I get it everywhere, the market, church, wherever, all over the place. If you can do it [have a career and family] and there are no consequences—and I know there will be—there will be backlash because your kids will let you know. You know you were not around when this and this happened. The women that are off on a great cruise, well, good for them. I hope they are happy, but they don't need to make the rest of us who stay home and do what we believe is right for our families, feel like crap or guilty just trying to be a good person.

Laura's remarks do sound very much like the "catfight" among women that many mothers would like to put behind them. But her defensiveness also serves to highlight the meaning of work and family choices. As Laura tells us, mothers who stay home with children are good persons guided by family commitment's model of children's needs and her responsibility as a mother. She not only indicts other mothers for behaviors that violate the family commitment schema's demands by putting their own interests before their children's, she also reaffirms her own identity as a mother under attack for her devotion to children.

For some respondents, paid work is a way that mothers fulfill their family obligations. But devotion to work that supercedes devotion to family indicates a moral failing in one's obligation to her children as a mother. Although limited by financial constraints, respondents insist that there are choices that can be made, and morally superior choices *place children's needs first* and demonstrate competency as good mothers. The strongest advocates for the belief that a mother's primary responsibility is to her children condemned other mothers for devoting themselves to work at the expense of their children, and society for its lack of support for mothers and children.

I JUST THOUGHT I WOULD TAKE CARE OF THE CHILDREN

Many divorced mothers convey disillusionment and resentment over their need to work outside the home. They felt that they had done the right thing and lived up to their end of the bargain as they devoted themselves to children. Their choice was to marry and stay at home to raise children. Their subsequent divorces and inability to remain stay-at-home mothers weigh heavily on them. Though some of their anger and resentment was directed at ex-spouses, they also condemned trends in society where families and children were no longer valued.

Tamara Mardston, a thirty-four–year-old mother of two children, ages nine and thirteen, is a stay-at-home mother. She and her children live in a small, well-kept home owned by her uncle overlooking a stream in a rural area on the outskirts of town. Tamara supports her family by providing twenty-four-hour care for her disabled nephew. She and her ex-husband divorced, remarried, and subsequently divorced again. We were discussing how this left her in a precarious financial position and how she was determined to be home with her children. Tamara described her relief that she did not have to cope with the welfare office demanding that she get a job. She explains: "The TANF thing came through just as I was getting off [welfare], and so I was grateful for that—that I did not have to be forced to get a job because I wanted to be there for my babies. I mean it has nothing to do with laziness whatsoever. It has everything to do with priorities which were the kids for me."

A phrase that Tamara used several times in our interview when she discussed her and other mothers' responsibility for children was that it is not fair. "Yeah, I needed to work, we weren't making it. It is still very hard with living on just what I get with him. But I was bound and determined to be here for my children and my primary focus is my kids. I feel like I had them, why should I have somebody else raise them? You know it's not fair."

Tamara's ability to take over her nephew's care resolved a "bad situation" for the family who was not happy with his nursing home and also allowed Tamara to stay home with her children. Although it may sound odd given Tamara's poverty, few respondents have comparable options. And certainly Tamara's choice has not come without considerable material sacrifice. Yet she considers herself extremely fortunate as she describes the situation as "heaven sent." "Otherwise, I would have been forced to take a job. Not wanting to, but forced to. Having my nephew here was better because I could be at home. So that way I was fine with it all, but it was heaven sent." The sense of unfairness that Tamara describes is the lack of support for poor women who feel threatened in their ability to care for their children. Many like Tamara believe that raising children is their primary job. As she told me, "because it is the hardest job in the world but yet you don't get paid for it. It's so unfair." For many women the breadwinner/homemaker model still resonates as a cultural family ideal—this is what most women want and ought to do as a mother. As Tamara says, "I would love to be married to a good man who had a great job, and then I could stay home with my children till they're gone. Then I could do something. That is my ideal."

I interviewed Lisa Davis, a forty-year-old mother of three who had been divorced for almost a year, in the home she shares with her mother. Two of her children were at school and the youngest, a sleepy two year old, spent most of the interview on his mother's lap. Lisa was having a difficult time adjusting to her need to find a job and support herself and her children. She was extremely grateful for the help from her mother who watched the youngest while she attended the job skills training program.

She mentioned several times that she never could envision her life taking the turn it did and felt frustrated with the lack of support and changing expectations for her responsibility to care and provide for the children. "I have been very happy to be able to stay home with this one [little boy]. That was my whole plan when I got pregnant with him, is that it would be that I would be staying home with him. Unfortunately, things have gone another direction so we're—we'll see how it goes."

Lisa worked part-time while she was married before the birth of her youngest child, making phone calls from home—rising early in the morning before she got the children off to school and for a few hours while they were in school. "I've never been one that actively sought a career. So I basically just thought that we would, that I would take care of the children. And you know if I had to work, just work a little bit. Be a mom. That's what I thought I would be doing."

Lisa refrained from judging other mothers' work and family choices. Her remarks reflect the shattering of her vision of a life ordered through family commitment's mandates. She did not condemn other mothers for working but rather expressed great sadness and frustration at the constraints on her own ability to live up to expectations that had been turned upside down. When speaking of day care she responded "I know there are people out there that are very good caregivers and that there are very good daycares. However for myself, I just had always wanted to do all the first things with my kids. And so that's where I saw myself going. You know if you had to work, you had to work. So I don't say that moms that work and do whatever is a bad thing. But I would prefer that probably taking care of the kids is my priority."

It is hard to miss the similarity in Lisa's definition of the expectations of motherhood with those of other mothers. And also the emotional toll from her inability to live up to her vision of marriage and motherhood.

> I think they get more out of having their mother at home than having to go to a day care. You know even leaving them with my mom all the time feels funny to me, because you know, its just, it's not mom I guess. I just think there's some things they need from their mother. You know my mom worked all the time. And I was basically a latch key kid. Came home after school, was home alone, or home with a babysitter, whatever, and I didn't like it. So, it's not something I wanted to do with my children.

Christi Williams, age thirty, also emphasizes the now familiar concern, that mothers may work outside the home, even want to work outside the home, but work that interferes with children's needs threatens one's ability to live up to the demands of motherhood. A recently divorced mother of two elementary-school-age children, who home schooled her children prior to her divorce, Christi told me she wanted to be a stay-at-home mom, but since her divorce has no choice but to go to work.

> If I didn't have children it wouldn't matter either way. I enjoy both. But I feel like I'm cheating my children. I feel like I am short-changing them. Because I'm supposed to be the one that's there when they need me. You know if they don't feel like I'm there for them, it, that's what contributes to—it's not like it's the parent's fault—but that's what contributes to delinquent children. They've got to know that you are there. And for me it's hard in my mind to deal with that because I feel like I'm cheating them. You know, I think that every mother wants that ideal job, be home with their kids and do a little work. Um, my situation I can't do that anymore. I have to go to work. And you know, I have to find someone to watch him. And I've been talking with him. Ideally I would like to stay home, but realistically I can't. It really bothers me that my children are in day care before and after school. Um. It drives me nuts in fact, but there is really nothing I can do about it. If I had my choice, I would be at home with my kids because I feel like they are my responsibility over anything else. So it's been really hard with me to deal with that, that I can't be here.

Christi's description of her situation summarizes many of the concerns voiced by other mothers as they face constraints on their ability to live up to the demands of the family commitment schema. Mothers experience personal angst, but they also see their choices and their responsibility to devote themselves to children as reflective of a world view they share with other mothers—revealing the widely recognized cultural mandate imposed by the family commitment schema and how it remains influential in the lives of women.

CONCLUSION

Thus far, we have seen that contemporary portrayals of mothers' paid work and family responsibilities look quite different from the vantage point of poor women who claim the moral high ground by insisting on taking responsibility for their children. The moral dilemma at the heart of work-family conflict for mothers in this study arises from societal expectations that mothers put their children in day care and find a job—an expectation in violation of the mandates of a competing powerful cultural model demanding that mothers stay home with their children. Perceived as such, work outside the home prevents women from fulfilling their obligations as mothers.

Importantly, we gain little understanding of the choices of mothers whether to work or not by considering them solely through the logic of rational economic costs and benefits. In this study, women do face significant challenges in their ability to provide and care for children. Yet as demonstrated above, women's work and family choices are not wholly self-sacrificing or wholly self-interested. Even mothers who need to work find their choices shaped by the realities of limited resources and responsibility for children, in addition to broadly shared understandings of what women *should* do as mothers and workers. Some respondents creatively manage ways to remain at home and care for children when paid work outside the home would be the optimal financial decision. And, this is not simply a rejection of the value of work outside the home; rather, paid work competes with their duty to care for children.

Family commitment demands that children's needs trump all other obligations; paid work is not forbidden altogether but must never interfere with mothers' obligation to her children (Hays 1996). Thus, if women must engage in work outside the home, paid work must be secondary to children's needs and undertaken *for the family* rather than for personal fulfillment or otherwise "selfish" reasons (Damaske 2011, Garey 1999). Echoing the divisive language of the "mommy wars," some respondents criticize the choices of more advantaged women as putting their own needs before those of their children in clear violation of the demands of family commitment and practices required of good mothers.

Moreover, motherhood is a powerful social identity for both middle-class and working-class women (Hays 1996, McMahon 1995), but it is particularly salient for poor women who have few alternative valued identities (Edin and Kefalas 2005). Thus, it is not surprising to find respondents whose world views are defined by family commitment's demand that a mothers' first responsibility is to her children, fiercely defending their right to mother their children against pressure to work outside the home.

Moral dilemmas are most acute for women who hold traditional views on caring for children and face the elimination of public support to do so.

Though a significant number of mothers who identify with the family-commitment schema also find paid work to be morally pleasing, belief in family commitment provides moral and emotional resources with which to resist demands that they leave children with others and work outside the home. The taken-for-granted nature and emotional grip wielded by this powerful cultural model helps mothers see their situation not as the result of individual failings but the failure of institutions to understand the moral obligations demanded of mothers struggling to raise children on low-wage jobs and public assistance. In the next chapter we consider these contradictions reflected through the prism of public assistance and the stigma of welfare mother.

NOTES

1. See Nancy Folbre (1994, 2001), and Paula England (2005) for discussion of the lack of economic value assigned to of the unpaid work that mothers do in the home and different economic assumptions attached to carework more generally as a "labor of love" performed primarily by women, devalued because women (and minorities) do it. Sharon Hays (1996) argues that the cultural logic of intensive motherhood is a counter to the rational self-interested logic of the market in capitalism.

2. Annette Lareau's (2003) study *Unequal Childhoods* shows how parenting practices differ markedly by class. Middle-class parents engage in a model labeled concerted cultivation where children are seen as projects. In this model parents are very involved in their children's lives and shaping their future success. Poor and low-income parents in contrast engage in parenting practices labeled natural growth. This style of parenting involves less oversight and involvement, fewer scheduled activities and greater freedom. The result is the reproduction of class where lower class children acquire fewer skills to navigate important institutions thus blocking opportunities necessary for success as adults.

3. Scott Coltrane argues in *Family Man* (1996) that as men care for children they acquire some of the "instincts" associated with women in anticipating children's needs. See also Jennifer Senior's (2014) *All Joy and No Fun: The Paradox of Modern Parenthood*. Senior interviewed middle-class families about the impact on parenthood in their lives including differing parenting styles of fathers and mothers who shared child care and paid work demands. She describes a more intuitive emotional style for mothers and a more utilitarian approach for fathers. This tends to leave mothers feeling more stressed and at least perceiving they to do more of the child care (79–81).

4. A December 8, 2013, *New York Times* article, "Wall Street Mothers, Stay-at-Home Fathers," by Jodi Kantor and Jessica Silver-Greenberg reported on a small but growing trend of high achieving women whose success is facilitated by the presence of a full-time stay-at-home father who takes care of children and domestic responsibilities. The gist of the article is that the expanded opportunities for women in positions of power has been accompanied by a reversal of gender roles where male spouses are taking over the duties formerly associated with wives, allowing women to achieve in areas where child care responsibilities made having a two-career marriage impossible because of the demands of high powered professions such as Wall Street investment firms.

5. See (McMahon 1995, Glenn, Chang, and Forcey 1994) for discussions of the social construction of mothering and motherhood. See (Ireland 1993, Morrell 1995) for a discussion of childless women and motherhood.

6. The historical record also shows that this is not a new phenomena as poor women, women of color, and their children were not protected from working outside the home by

separate spheres ideology as were middle-class married mothers. (See Gordon 1994, Mink 1995, and Abramovitz 1996.)

7. Hays (1996) finds that middle-class working mothers also justify their work force partic-ipation in terms of working for their families in accordance with appropriate childrearing practices mandated by the ideology of intensive motherhood.

8. As Pamela Stone (2007) argues, when professional women quit work to return home, they were always praised for making the right choice, even if their choice was the result of failed attempts to alter their working conditions, find support at home, and otherwise overcome obstacles to their choice which was maintain careers while raising children.

9. The Dr. Phil show titled "Guilty Moms" features stay-at-home vs. career mothers. Al-though the show is characterized as trying to find middle ground and support for all views—in support of women, it serves to stir up the "mommy wars" and pit women against one another. http://drphil.com/shows/show/1327/.

Chapter Five

Work and Family at the Welfare Office

They're probably just trying to send the message that, you know, they want them to get a job, they want them to become somebody. You know, if you're gonna sit home on welfare all your life, you're just not gonna get nowhere.

—Tricia

The denigration and stereotyping of single mothers—a regular fixture in U.S. culture since colonial times—works hand in hand with portrayal of "welfare mothers" as lazy, unwilling to work, and "choosing" to remain on welfare, thereby transmitting their lack of initiative and motivation to children.[1] As Sharon Hays suggests, the cultural demonization of welfare mothers "is so ubiquitous in our society that it tends to seep into one's consciousness almost unnoticed" (2003, 121). Not surprisingly, low regard for women on welfare, and by extension poor and low-income mothers, spills over into their work and family lives differentially shaping their choices, the evaluation of those choices, and the consequences.

This chapter considers the intersection of welfare policy practices and work-family conflict as they are filtered through widely shared assumptions about poor women on welfare. It reveals a social and cultural environment in which poor and low-income mothers respond to competing work and family demands far removed from the contemporary work-family debate among the U.S. public. Put starkly by Mechthild Hart, welfare policies seek to turn bad mothers into good workers (2002,171). The work and family paradox in welfare polices—telling women they *must* work and that they and their children are better off if they do—marks a profound shift. Our culture's gendered opposition between work and family is transformed from unconscious taken-for-granted understandings operating behind the scenes to a perceptible, discernable force given shape by the demands of the welfare office. This is not to say that women suddenly *see* the ideological forces behind their struggles, but that contradictions are felt more keenly as conflicting demands are codified in requirements and practices.

The mother who would stay home supported by a welfare check does not reap society's blessing for her devotion to children. We need only compare cultural images. On the one hand, the stay-at-home educated, professional mom opting out of her career is sanctified as doing the right thing for her children. On the other hand, welfare moms, who depend on public assistance to limit paid work and spend more time at home are vilified as lazy, abusing the system, and shirking their duty to children and society.

As discussed earlier, both groups face contradictions, but different moral, institutional and material forces shape the contours of the struggle. The lives of the women I study differ from mothers featured in articles about the high cost of day care for dual-earner professional families (Quartz 2013) or the difficulties facing mothers as they try to resume careers after opting out (Warner 2013). No one is sharing Sheryl Sandberg's (2013) advice about how to "lean in" or cautioning poor mothers about the folly of expecting to "have it all" as they wait in the food bank line. The distance can be seen clearly from the interaction that takes place inside of the walls of the welfare office.

NOBODY LIKES WELFARE

Few people in the United States actually know any "welfare mothers." The majority of people form their views of the welfare population not from personal interaction but from the wider culture through information from media, television, newspapers, and magazines (Weaver 2000, 9). Over the past thirty years, people in the United States are also increasingly likely to live in neighborhoods with people of similar income status—high-income families live and interact with individuals of similar means; lower-income families are more likely to live among and interact with other low-income families (Fry and Taylor 2012). Thus, in contrast to most Americans, low-income and poor mothers form their views of welfare through more intimate contact in combination with the media images and stereotypes that inform the American public's knowledge of the poor. They are also are more likely to personally interact with social welfare organizations.

Welfare, broadly defined, refers to a variety of social assistance programs. However, the term *welfare* is most closely associated with TANF and AFDC, programs which primarily support poor women and their children (Karger and Stoesz 2010). These among other means-tested benefit programs are associated with assumptions about welfare as a moral hazard and the moral failure of poor single mothers who depend upon it. Poor mothers as a group are seen as the "takers" in society despite skimpy TANF cash benefits—quite

to other income-support programs and the more generous
﹍nefitting middle-class families (Karger and Stoesz 2010).[2]

﹍s meagerness, welfare assistance provides crucial resources for
﹍ies—housing, food assistance, income support, and so forth. It also
﹍s ideal resources mirroring changes in women's work and family lives
﹍ an important distinction for poor women: deservingness depends upon a
﹍other's willingness to provide financially for her children. The broadly
shared ideological underpinnings of welfare provision—the independent,
self-sufficient worker moving up in the work force, and mothers caring for
dependent children—mirror the opposition at the heart of work-family conflict. Mothers respond to this paradox in varied ways as they interpret their
options—filtered through conflicting values. On the one hand, our culture
purports to cherish family commitment and preaches "family values." On the
other hand, there is strong social pressure to conform to the work ethic and
strive for upward mobility.

Mothers currently receiving welfare, those who have in the past, and
those who have never turned to welfare share assumptions about "welfare
people" and resent being lumped together with all the accompanying negative attributes associated with welfare assistance. Poor mothers who do receive assistance state they need it—whether to fulfill their immediate needs
(food, shelter) while caring for children in the home—or for longer-term
goals of reaching self-sufficiency with a good job after completing an education. Despite their own reasons, however morally justified, this does not
spare them from internalizing and sharing stereotypes about welfare recipients. They believe similar to the majority of the U.S. public that welfare
recipients should work but also believe there should be social assistance
programs to help those who are trying to better themselves (Mead 1997,
Watkins-Hayes 2009).

Mothers on and off welfare tend to separate their own need for assistance
as different from others, at times expressed in harsh condemnation of those
deemed less deserving. Frequently, criticism of welfare extends to caseworkers and "the system" for preventing mothers from fulfilling their basic responsibilities to provide and care for their children. Recall that welfare policy
aligns in practice with the work ethic defined by the work commitment
schema. Thus, conflict is most severe for mothers whose definition of mothers' responsibility aligns closely with that found in the competing family
commitment schema. Further compounding the moral dilemmas surrounding
their choices is the problem that although respondents themselves report that
many on welfare "just sit at home and do nothing," they resent the assumptions of caseworkers that include them within this stigmatized circle of those
who take advantage of the system.

WELFARE MOTHERS

The more proximate experience of poor women to welfare organizations and individuals on welfare ties broadly shared assumptions about welfare and poverty more closely to their own moral identities and conceptions of self-worth. There were few mothers in this study who had never been to the welfare office. Almost all either currently receive or have received public assistance—food stamps, Medicaid, or housing assistance if not TANF (or AFDC) at some point in their lives. As is typical of families on public assistance, they are likely to have moved in and out of low-wage jobs relying on assistance as a temporary means of support and/or turn to welfare following the birth of a child, illness, divorce, or other family transition (Karger and Stoesz 2010).

In this section, Becky and Nadine, two divorced mothers introduced earlier as they discussed meeting the demands of work and family as single mothers, describe their experience with social service agencies. In doing so they compare their own choices with disparaging characterizations of women on welfare, joining many Americans who share their views (Hays 2003).[3] I asked whether single mothers on welfare should be required to work.

Becky declared, "If anybody should be getting help from the government it should be the elderly people who have no family and they are stuck in horrible situations, or mothers or widows with small children. Not these young girls that are getting pregnant at fifteen and their mom's been on welfare, their grandma's been on welfare, and they just go right on to it."

It is hard to overlook how readily Becky weaves stereotypes about women on welfare into her response to my question. Her comments underscore the pervasiveness of myths about welfare and its recipients. Although these beliefs are widely shared, they are far from empirical reality. Consider these myth-busting facts: the average age of a woman on welfare was thirty-four in 2005 and relatively few are teen mothers. Most recipients cycle between welfare and low-wage work, and the most common cause of beginning a spell on welfare is divorce or separation—triggering Becky's own trip to the welfare office related below. Even before TANF made welfare support temporary, more than half of recipients left within one year of going on welfare, rising to 70 percent before two years (Karger and Stoesz 2010, 278–79). Yet, despite evidence to the contrary, assumptions about welfare persist and powerfully shape attitudes toward poor women.

Becky demonstrates this again through her own experience at the welfare office.

> I was never so mortified as when I signed up for food stamps. I went in there and I did not know anything about anything. In the office up here, they didn't have any signs telling anything. So I asked this lady and she said, well you

need to sign up on the computer screen. They called my number and then they said, well, I'm sorry we don't take new applications. I left in tears. All these people were coming streaming in. All these young teenage girls who just come be bopping in know exactly where to go, exactly what to do and, it was horrific for me, I felt humiliated. And, and I'm not sure why.

I: You're not sure why you felt humiliated?

I just felt like, because I never wanted to ask for help from people. I know that when I was a child there was always a stigma about welfare people. And when I was stretching my pennies when my kids were babies, and I would have my little list, and I would have my little amount of money I would get and we would have plenty of food. I would get my stuff and then I would pass a big, fat woman who's got her little thing with her, her [EBT] card. And she's got the cart just loaded with things that I couldn't afford to buy; you know convenience foods.[4] She's got cash on the side that she uses to pay for her alcohol and things that don't fall under the thing. But it would just make me so mad. Because I felt like, you know, I could be on welfare right now, but I'm not because I can make my pennies stretch.

It was not unusual to hear mothers characterize people who depend on welfare in negative terms. It happened so frequently I began to expect it. However, Becky's statement stands out for its litany of stereotypes of welfare recipients including categories of deserving and undeserving—the elderly deserving poor vs. teen mothers. These comments illustrate clearly that my question tapped into something deeper than moving poor mothers into jobs. Becky carefully distances herself from the stigma and shame associated with welfare assistance. She portrays her own choices as those of a self-sacrificing responsible mother, scraping together her meager resources to do the right thing in contrast to the stereotypical assumptions she holds about the overweight, lazy woman squandering the taxpayers' money on convenience foods and spending her cash on booze.

Becky concluded her account of her humiliating experience by telling me it ended well. In a decidedly more upbeat manner, she describes her return to the welfare office. "But I put my big girl boots on and I went back that next morning really early. And the lady that I ended up talking to was just really nice. And the last time I went in to take myself off. I will not take when I shouldn't—in my mind. You know, to me it's ethics."

Becky was obviously embarrassed and also angry after her initial trip to the welfare office. The recounting of her trip back, however, was not one of humiliation but an opportunity to demonstrate determination and maturity by rising early (certainly not what lazy welfare mothers would do) and "putting her big girl boots on." She was rewarded for her resolve by the nice treatment by welfare office staff. She distinguishes herself from other welfare mothers again by "taking herself off" welfare.

Douglas and Michaels argue that media depictions of poor welfare mothers in the 1980s and 1990s helped middle-class mothers feel better about themselves as they dealt with their own pressures to meet expectations of idealized motherhood (2004). Becky experiences something similar. But a crucial difference is that her presence in the welfare office and need for assistance puts her at risk for being mistaken for the mothers she criticizes. The middle-class mothers Douglas and Michaels critique for their lack of compassion for mothers on welfare never face this threat. Becky makes clear she is someone who takes only what she absolutely needs, all the while reinforcing stereotypes of others who abuse the system.

Nadine, also divorced, and mother of a young boy, had earlier described her desire to show her son independence and that he could count on her to support the family. In response to the question I asked Becky about requiring mothers on welfare to look for work, Nadine replies: "Well [pause], they keep having children and they don't stop. And then her and all her little youngins running around on welfare, I think they should be cut off." And those children should be taken away and be put into homes. These people that live on welfare and just have baby, after baby, after baby, after baby. No, I think they should be 'pshhhh' [as in cut off]."

Nadine then relates her own trip to the welfare office and reminiscent of Becky's account describes her personal humiliation.

> I had my gall bladder out when I had a job with no insurance. I had to have it out. . . . I had to go to the state for help. And I was crying because I didn't want to do that. But I couldn't work. I needed medical coverage. And then I'm sitting there [at the DSHS office] and this woman comes in, in socks with three or four little children trailing behind her like little ducks, no shoes, filthier than dirt. And I'm thinking, "Oh my God." And it made it so much more difficult to get that.

> I: Difficult for you to

> For me to go. Because [pause] I needed it! I had no other choice!

> She [the woman] in my opinion is lazy. All you have to do is be a baby machine and "give me my money and my food stamps and let me go." And it was so hard for me to take that. I had nothing until I filled that [application for public assistance] out, and they paid the hospital and everything. I think that is where it becomes very strong for me. I'm gonna do whatever it takes so I don't have to be there again because I didn't like it [being] in the needy situation. I didn't like that. It hurt for a long, long time. Years. It still bothers me now, and that's why I say I will do whatever it takes.

Someone unfamiliar with sitting in the welfare office waiting for their name to be called may have a hard time understanding Becky and Nadine's feeling of humiliation and characterization of others. Their experience is particularly painful because they find their circumstances blur the boundaries distinguishing them from the "welfare people." Sitting in the welfare office looks from the outside as if they are just like those other mothers on welfare. Additionally, like most mothers I interviewed, those on TANF included, they state that they *need* assistance, that "they had no choice" compared to others whom they assume to be less deserving. My position is not to judge Becky and Nadine as more deserving than others or the legitimacy of their views but to present the context within which my subjects make choices and how this impacts those choices and their evaluation by others. Their narratives illustrate how cultural assumptions shaping welfare policy work hand in glove with gendered cultural models shaping work and family decisions, thus influencing the choices of women in starkly different ways. The mothers in the work-family debate familiar to most Americans do not fear being mistaken for welfare mothers.

Becky and Nadine's depiction of women on welfare mirrors the most degrading images of poor mothers on welfare found in public discourse. But their views differ more in degree than in kind from how most respondents talk about "welfare people." Invariably when respondents discuss welfare, and why welfare requires mothers to work, they tell me that they believe that a reason for welfare reform was because people abuse the system. However much their own circumstances—relying on welfare only when they really needed it—counter this narrative, this does little to convince mothers that *they* are more representative of typical welfare mothers and thus closer to the rule than the exception demonstrated again as Nancy explains the circumstances under which she has relied on welfare.

Nancy is a married mother of two and the major breadwinner in her family. She discusses her reliance on food stamps when she was without work. She interprets and explains her action as necessary to provide for her family's needs, occasionally under circumstances out of her control—the "oopsies" in life that all people experience from time to time.

> Families should be first. But yet you have to also remember that you have to be responsible for them. So for me, I'm not a milker. I have had to have some food stamps to help me out every once and while in between [jobs], and I'm glad it was there. I had to really swallow my pride at first. And then I realized it's there for oopsies. And I'm not abusing it. I'm appreciating it. And I only take it when I really, really have to. And then when I'm doing really good, I'll help out at the food bank. Because, been there done that, and we all need help. So I try to give back, I appreciate it. I don't want to abuse it. I know another person who milks it. And it kind of makes me a little ill to my stomach. It's wrong. It's not there to be milked.

Nancy, in contrast to Becky and Nadine, expresses greater understanding of the need for women to get help from time to time for their families. At the same time, she also distances herself from the "milkers" who abuse the system. Similar to other mothers, applying for food stamps entailed swallowing her pride and convincing herself that she was deserving because she "really, really" needed the help. These accounts illustrate the pervasiveness of the stigma of welfare and its influence on mothers' own sense of worth compared to others who purportedly abuse the system. Nancy resists inclusion in this stigmatized group by indicating her appreciation for the help and the revulsion she feels for her acquaintance who "milks" the system. She makes amends for her transgression by giving back to other poor families when she can.

It is tempting to consider these comments as simply ad hoc explanations that mothers employ to salvage their own self-esteem. But the ubiquity of these narratives in the broader culture points to the structural character of these understandings. Widely shared cultural models such as these condemning the poor and single mothers for their disadvantage require continual reinforcement to sustain them over time otherwise they risk replacement by new understandings (Sewell 1992). As mothers use these cultural models they create symbolic boundaries separating themselves from others and establishing their own moral identities apart from stigmatized identities as welfare mothers (Lamont 2000). In doing so they legitimize and reproduce these models which are further reinforced and validated in the wider culture and interaction within their communities.

WE'LL GIVE YOU HELP, BUT NOT A GRAVY TRAIN

The question of whether poor women should be required to work outside the home in exchange for welfare benefits has been answered affirmatively by the U.S. public and institutionalized in public policy. But as these comments demonstrate, work requirements are not simply a means to replace welfare support with market work. Respondents' views on welfare in general and changes brought about by welfare reform are shaped by a complex assortment of social factors. Personal biography, experience within the welfare system, and the publicly shared cultural models that define moral identities and criteria for deserving and undeserving poor influence views on welfare and whether poor mothers should be required to work outside the home.

Mothers in the study who favor requiring welfare recipients to work believe that work requirements enforce the work ethic in the poor and can help women get jobs to take care of their families. Some also suggest that the policies are helpful in that they will no longer reward immoral behavior of individuals who abuse the system. In contrast, lack of support for the changes is due to fears that the changes will hurt individuals who "really" need help and are trying to better themselves, the lack of good jobs, and belief that mothers should be allowed to stay at home to care for children. Many respondents hold these conflicting views simultaneously echoing the American public who in general, resent helping those who abuse the system, but worry about those who truly need assistance (Reese 2005, Watkins-Hayes 2009) and the consequences for children.[5]

Laura, a married stay-at-home mother, has never received welfare. When I spoke with Laura, she alternates between sympathy for children's needs and those she deems actually needy and anger at those whom she believes take advantage of welfare. As we spoke she grew increasingly agitated when I asked her whether she supported work requirements for mothers on welfare.

> He [Laura's husband] doesn't just work so that someone can just sit home and produce babies so they just sit on the gravy train. "Let's do that, honey. Let's have lots of babies." That isn't fair. But, let's take care of the kids, too. . . . Balance. There needs to be a limit. People will eat it up like candy, and they will get their cousins into it, too. They think it is their God-given right to be on welfare. Need help? We'll give you help, but not a gravy train. Have a little pride and self-esteem. Say, "Nope! I can pull myself up by my bootstraps." . . . I do know people that have three or four generations of it, and it makes me sick. How can you do that? For those who severely need it, fine, help them. What about the people that get the welfare, and they are on dope all the time?

No doubt Laura's is an emotional response. It gets to the heart of the controversy over work, family, and welfare policy. Yet, as angry as Laura is about what she perceives to be the widespread abuse by people who think it is their "God given right to be on welfare," she also feels that there are people that need help and deserve to be helped. Similar to others, she articulates the moral and ethical concerns shaping welfare assistance that spill over to work and family conflict. She indicates, as do many mothers, that she worries about the well-being of children. And her inability to reconcile the conflict is apparent again when she remarks later "I hate for moms to go out and work when you have children." Laura's struggle is her inability to reconcile cultural models of individualism and assumptions about people on welfare with traditional gender roles. As we saw with others, part of this is personal. She sees her own husband working hard to provide for the family in contrast to others whom she sees as taking advantage of the system. Further, her reliance on her husband's wage to be a full-time homemaker is certainly not regarded in the same light as a woman on welfare. Yet despite this, as much as she abhors those who take advantage of welfare, Laura cannot avoid feeling caught between the conflict inherent in work requirements for poor mothers that clash with family commitment's priorities and concern for children when mothers go out to work.

Rarely do questions about welfare fail to elicit a reference to the "fact" that there are those who take advantage of the system. Kathie Moro, thirty-four, a divorced mother with two children, age five and fifteen years, lost her job due to a work-related injury. She currently receives TANF, having been denied Worker's Compensation benefits until she gets another full-time job. She frames the issue this way. "Due to certain circumstances, to stay at home with your kids and be on welfare for a certain length of time is okay for those who need it. But those who are able to go to work and not rely on the state, that's what they should do. They should not rely on someone else to pick up where they can fill in."

Kathie's support of TANF as a temporary measure for those who need it describes her own situation and aligns closely with the views of policy makers. She notes that circumstances might deem it necessary for women to rely on welfare for a limited amount of time, but anyone that can work should be required to do so. In keeping with the goals of TANF, welfare assistance should be a temporary form of support to allow mothers to get a job and reach self-sufficiency. At first glance it would seem that moral evaluations have taken a backseat in this response—certainly compared to the views expressed earlier. But it is impossible to avoid moral evaluations altogether in response to questions about paid work, family responsibilities, and welfare assistance. If we were to replace the mother on welfare with the mother supported by a spouse's wage, Kathie's response would read like this. "Due to certain circumstances, to stay at home with your kids and let your husband support you for a certain length of time is okay for those who need to. But those who are able to go to work and not rely on their *husband*, that's what they should do. They should not rely on someone else to pick up where they can fill in."

Though this narrative reflects an increasing number of many married heterosexual families' work and family arrangements today, we have yet to fully embrace ideologically and morally this prescription for men and women's work and family commitments. In spite of the changes in women's roles, many Americans do not view stay-at-home married mothers as refusing to pull their own weight.[6] The exception is the welfare mother. Though less apparent in Kathie's narrative than Laura's, the work commitment and family commitment schemas in conjunction with cultural assumptions about "people on welfare" help shape who is considered worthy of support to stay home and care for children and who will learn personal responsibility and develop a work ethic from labor outside the home.

THEY'RE NOT THERE TO HELP YOU

Just as many mothers hold negative views about welfare recipients, many also hold negative views about the welfare system. Unlike the stereotypes we heard earlier, mothers also offer a variety of other reasons for their dislike of welfare that are less familiar to those who have not had to interact with "the system." They resent how it stigmatizes all single mothers, the failure of welfare to help poor women, rigid rules and restrictions, and insensitivity to the needs of mothers and children.

Amber, a widowed mother of two small children, like Laura, has never relied on TANF benefits, but she did apply for subsidized housing assistance. Her account of her experience at the DSHS (Department of Social and Health Services) focuses not on others who abuse the system but on her treatment by caseworkers.

> The caseworkers don't look at it by case by case. They look at everybody as the same. I'm on housing right now. . . . And going through that system is awful. And if I wasn't confident, and if I wasn't educated, they're awful. And they treat you awful, and they make you feel like you are worthless. And they make you feel like you are stupid, and they're not there to help you. Just the way they speak to you. They process you through like you're a number. The whole, the . . . it's just really backwards. Housing was the most awful experience I've ever had in my life. They give you this big packet, and you have to fill it out, and they tell you if you miss one thing and you don't bring everything filled out completely correctly then, you're off for a year. You get put at the back of the waiting list.

Up to this point her description is similar to others—applying for welfare is an awful experience—but rather than characterize people on welfare as the problem, Amber directs her anger toward "the system."

> And it was awful, awful, I mean. So I don't know. Women who do it on a daily basis, either they become so beaten down that they're not even affected by it anymore or they just get used to it. And that is something that no woman or anybody should ever get used to, being belittled or being talked to like that. Everything that I've experienced is that they look at everybody like they are using the system. And when they make you feel that way, and they put that on you, you're not going to have the motivation to want to get out there.

Negative reactions from caseworkers and also the "hassles" and red tape involved in applying for assistance signal to mothers that they are not competent or deserving. The source of Amber's unhappiness is the sense that the welfare office instead of helping mothers deal with practical problems such as housing, contributes to their difficulties through the demeaning treatment, paperwork, bureaucratic hassles, and threats if they do not get it right. Mothers believe that the welfare office *should* help them. Amber blames the system for beating women down and destroying any motivation they may have "to get out there." When caseworkers and other personnel appear to judge or belittle mothers rather than helping, the system appears as an adversary.

I did not analyze the interaction from the caseworker's perspective on helping mothers get assistance, so I cannot accurately assess Amber's portrayal of their willingness or unwillingness to help. In Hay's (2003) study of welfare reform, some caseworkers' views of their clientele echo those reported by Amber, and not surprisingly others tried very hard to find solutions to their client's problems, at times bending the rules, acting as counselors, lending a sympathetic ear or shoulder to cry on, and doing their best to move mothers into jobs.[7] It is worth noting that caseworkers must cope with the same contradictions facing mothers, in requiring that mothers work and at the same time protecting children's welfare (Hays 2003). But the enforcement of work rules and perceived indifference to the needs of children indicates to many mothers that caseworkers are not there to help.

Among mothers resentful of their treatment was Jolene Lester, twenty-six, a never-married mother of two young boys, recently on welfare but no longer receiving benefits. Jolene offers suggestions for welfare office staff to ease the humiliation described above.

> If they start threatening "well, we're going to start sanctioning you if you don't go into work." I think that's the wrong way to go about it. If they said, "well what can we do to help you get to this point?" that kind of thing. If they did something like that, I think it would help a lot more. Because when they say it like "well if you don't we're going to . . . it's kind of like uuurrrrr. . . . Please don't punish me for the choices that I have made, be they good or bad. But don't punish me for them. You know, I don't consider having my children a mistake. But they will treat you like it was.

Mothers go to the welfare office when they have exhausted other options and it is frequently a demeaning and humiliating experience (Hays 2003, Morgen, Acker, and Weigt 2009). This is not to say that mothers are never helped or that they always encounter unwelcome or belittling treatment on the part of welfare office staff and caseworkers. But welfare policy is both about helping the poor and also shaping the behavior of the poor, and these sometimes-contradictory goals play out every day in the practices of providing assistance contingent on eliciting certain behaviors on the part of recipients.[8] Moreover, caseworkers have a great deal of discretion in their ability to offer information and assistance and also withhold information and levy sanctions or punishment for not following the rules (Watkins-Hayes 2009). Jolene interprets the sanction as not only evaluating her work ethic as lacking but also judging her choice to have children. Sanctions serve as a stark example of the judgment and moral evaluation poor women face as they seek help in addressing the conflict in their own lives between providing and caring for children.

The practice of sanctions creates a confrontation pitting the merits of work versus motherhood in a manner not seen in the day-to-day experiences of most Americans. However, one could argue that women who fear losing a job to care for a sick child experience a similar confrontation and this obviously causes terrible anxiety and stress. But these mothers however justifiably upset and frustrated, do not face denigration as mothers in the same manner Jolene describes. Certainly, studies on women's work and family lives show that the workplace penalizes mothers through lower wages and discrimination in hiring and promotion (Williams 2010, Budig and England 2001), but they are not subject to sanctions for their choice to have children and rarely questioned as to their *fitness* to be mothers.[9] When the demands of the welfare office seem like punishment for having children, interactions increasingly feel like a battle pitting children's interests against the demands of the system.

Welfare today relies on market forces to instill personal responsibility in mothers by encouraging/requiring them to work outside the home. Additionally, policy makers insist that welfare recipients will be better off by doing so, hence the slogans used to promote TANF, "work is always better than welfare" and "any job is a good job." The support provided by the welfare office is supposed to motivate clients to this end. Child care, transportation vouchers, work training, and transitional Medicaid support welfare policy's goals of moving women off the welfare rolls into employment. Moreover, according to rational economic logic most mothers *would* be better off working. There is however a catch.

"No one is better off on $440 a month!" exclaimed the director of the welfare office when I mentioned several mothers told me that they were torn over their inability to stay home and mother their children.[10] I saw this as emblematic of the tension we've seen in mothers' attempts at reconciling paid work and caring for children, and welfare policy requirements. That is, while there is no denying that economic criteria play an important role in respondents' work and family decisions, policy makers err in dismissing how mothers feel about their responsibility to provide and care for children. The logic of rational economic calculation competes with mothers' understanding of a life privileging full time motherhood and devotion to children.

PAYING THE DAY CARE BUT NOT THE MOMS?

According to economist Nancy Folbre (2001), cultural understandings about the value of care work obscure the economic value of the work that family members do in caring for others. This helps explain the American public's reluctance to put a price tag on the value to society for the unpaid work parents perform in raising children. Additionally, people who are paid for care work (day care, elementary school teachers, home health aids), primarily women, earn less than others because women do it and also because the job is seen as intrinsically rewarding—that is to say a labor of love (England 2005). Rational economic logic falls apart, however, when assessing the cost of supporting a poor mother to work outside the home instead of caring for her children and the cost of funding for day care.

As many working mothers know the cost of day care is a burden on working families both for the working poor and for middle-class families. Alissa Quartz's *New York Times* (2013) article, "Crushed by the Costs of Child Care," noted that in thirty-five states and Washington, DC, the cost of center-based care was more than college tuition at a public college. In fact the high cost of day care contributes to working-class families' greater likelihood of having a stay-at-home parent than middle-class or professionals (busting the opt-out revolution myth) (Cohn, Livingston and Wang 2014).[11] This fact comes with an important caveat—choices for working-class mothers are not solely driven by costs, but also influenced by gendered expectations of women's work and family roles.

When payment for child care exceeds the cost of supporting a mother on TANF, and the welfare office is willing to pay the day care to free a mother to work or look for a job, mothers use the economic rationality argument to assail welfare policy makers. Why would the welfare system pay *more* for a child to go to day care than it pays for a poor mother to stay home with her child? This signals just how out of touch the welfare system is with family values. Marianne posed it this way. "Now you have to work, you know, instead of being able just, just be able to take care of your kids. And the thing is, if they're so willing to pay for child care you know. Why not just give you the child care money so you can take care of the children?"

Marianne's question makes perfect sense if support for poor women is driven by economic rationality. But that requires disregarding the normative context of welfare policy, as observed by Sanford Schram, "welfare reform with its cutbacks may be about saving money, but it is also about saving the cultural values of work and family" narrowly construed to ignore the reality of single motherhood (2000, 34). Marianne is making a normative claim based on economic logic, reinterpreting it through her vision of a mother's duty to care for her children. Requiring a mother to work outside the home in exchange for continued welfare assistance, while paying a day care *more* to care for her children, allows her to see with laser-like clarity the mismatch in widely shared values. The stated policy goals of TANF support both family values and employment for welfare recipients in opposition to welfare dependency. But the rhetoric, money, policy programs, and practices promote the culturally defined masculine work ethic as filtered through the work commitment schema.

Amber repeats Marianne's challenge by referring to an example, which to her indicates how far the system has gone off track.

I think it was crazy. In one case they made this mom work twenty hours to receive TANF. And the only job she was able to get was like at Burger King. And she had 5 kids. So welfare was paying a day care, like $2500 a month and her $400 a month, because they wanted her to work 20 hours. I mean, in that respect, you know what? Something is wrong with society when we want to remove the kids from their mom, so that mom can work at Burger King.

Paying a day care such a large sum of money to care for children so that their mother can work at a low-wage job violates the basic tenets of family commitment and further erodes the legitimacy of workfare policies. Amber's response is triggered by the noticeable almost palpable incongruity between two cultural models offering starkly different visions of appropriate work and motherhood for low-income and poor mothers. She knows intuitively that this makes no sense. Just as the inefficient use of financial resources is not the main issue, the anger and dismay expressed by Amber is due to the apparent mismatch in elevating the value of a low-wage job over a mother's care of her own children. The discrepancy in payments to a caregiver compared to a mother exposes the gendered cultural paradox underlying welfare reform. Amber's response reflects that of others who link the requirements of the welfare office to a moral failure within the system.

THEY WANT YOU TO WORK

To most Americans the notion that people on welfare should be required to work seems appropriate. And some respondents do gain job skills and the type of support they need to be able to leave welfare. Although not what policy makers had in mind, one mother reported had she known she could get help with child care once she found a job, she would have left her abusive marriage years ago. However, many also report that they are unhappy with welfare policies due to the difficulty of supporting their children with work in low-wage jobs. Much of their resentment comes from what they describe as pressure from the welfare office to take low-paying jobs without sufficient consideration of the circumstances of low-income mothers trying to make it on their own.

Julie Perez, a twenty-one-year-old Latina mother of a twenty-two-month-old child, was receiving TANF benefits when I spoke with her. Julie moved away to another state for several months to escape her baby's abusive father. She now lives with relatives on the outskirts of town, who help with her daughter while she attends a work-readiness basic skills class. Living out of town is also due to her fear that her former partner will find her but entails an hour drive each way into the city. She reported that she was unhappy initially with the way she was treated when she signed up for benefits, but she now has a new caseworker that is more sympathetic to her domestic-violence situation. Julie relates the "hassles" related to finding a job and child care prior to her current arrangements.

> If you don't have a job by the twelfth week they go "first job that comes." It does not matter if it is 4:00 a.m in the morning. You take it. They tell you there is twenty-four-hour child care. Put 'em [your child] in that. They don't care. They don't care. They say make sure you have back up day care, and if you have to work nights make sure that you have twenty-four-hour day care. That is when they bring the twenty-four-hour day care. I don't think they really care. They want you to work.

Kari, who now has twenty-four-hour day care for her children, described a similar experience when she enrolled in the WorkFirst program. "When they tell you that you have to do the WorkFirst class, you have like two days to find day care. And you want to take your time to find day care. And it's just like, you have these two days to find day care and if you're not here Monday morning at eight o'clock then you get sanctioned. I think that's kind of weird." Another mother reported being upset with the short time period she was given to find day care for her children. "It was less than twenty-four hours that I was informed when the class was gonna start and I had to be there. So I had twenty-four hours to run around and get my children into the day care."

Despite the scramble for day care and other hassles, Kari earlier described how working outside the home provides an opportunity to socialize with other women. She also reported dissatisfaction with the immediate reduction in benefits when she started working.

> There's a lot about welfare that isn't fair. Just like them cutting me off food stamps. That really made me mad. . . . I think they should be happier that you got a job and give you a month to still have food stamps and pay your bills, you know? But they, they don't want you to have any extra money . . . they just cut you off on everything, and they raise everything just all in the same month. You know, my rent will go up and my co-pays for day care. But yeah, you get a job and you lose everything, everything goes up.

Kari does not like losing other benefits so quickly but is happy to be free from the oversight that comes with welfare assistance. "I mean, all the people, that's why they're like 'I basically get the same if I just get welfare and food stamps.' . . . So you are basically in the same money position as when you're on. But I'd rather be working than getting welfare because then they don't have you by the neck. I hate how they control you."

From Kari's vantage point, the immediate reduction or elimination of benefits is a disincentive for some mothers to get a job, and when she weighs the costs and benefits, she does not gain much. Her net gain is the freedom that paid work brings her from the oversight and supervision of the welfare office. Kari's complaint was repeated by others who told me that cutting off benefits so quickly eroded the financial rewards from moving into a job. Jodi who had recently landed a job and was very happy to be working told me, "I had to wait for three weeks to get my first paycheck. I still got some food stamps, a very small amount, but I did not get a grant. I wish I would have, because it would have been a lot easier to catch up on my bills."

Unhappy with the lack of recognition that she has done the right thing by going to work, Kari, instead of rewarded, feels punished for taking responsibility for herself and her children. On the one hand, the pressure to get a job is effective in encouraging women to find employment. But it also creates resentment when the system appears to punish rather than reward mothers by pressuring them into taking jobs and withdrawing support so quickly. In a work and family context where women and children's interest are closely linked, perceived failure to help mothers threatens children's well-being.

YOU CAN'T JUST THROW SOMEBODY INTO A JOB

Mia, introduced in the previous chapter, has been on welfare for the past four years, and as she explained to me, her ideal situation is to be a stay-at-home mother for her children. I interviewed Mia while she was attending the basic skills class at the women's center at the direction of her caseworker. From her perspective, TANF is not geared toward helping mothers and children. Mia told me, "I think their goals are to kick you off and be done with you." I asked Mia if kicking someone off meant getting a job, and she responded by telling me how much she resented the welfare office's emphasis on finding a job.

> You know what? You can't just throw somebody into a job . . . 'cause they're gonna quit. You know? And then wow, somebody is going to be stuck in a job they hate. And if you are a single mom you're not going to quit because you can't quit and pay the bills. So you know what are you going to do? You are going to work to a job that you HATE! And you are going to dread it and it is going to wear you down, and you are going to get depressed. And then what kind of mom are you going to be for your kids? A crap mom!
> That's my opinion.

Few respondents were as forceful as Mia in expressing their resentment of the WorkFirst program and the employment options for women leaving welfare. Yet Mia's evident dislike of the welfare system echoes others' feelings of being pushed into a low-wage job. Her response reflects the widely shared characterization of welfare as a program that does not help but exacerbates the problems of poor women in their ability to support and care for their children.

Although they base their critique on reasons other than Mia's, social conservatives also argue that welfare assistance does more harm than good for poor families, with some proposing eliminating it altogether (Murray 1984). Other less draconian remedies are stricter enforcement of the work requirements that Mia and others resent. Political scientist Lawrence Mead, an architect of the U.S. welfare reform, argues that work requirements not only bring financial support but also are a means of enforcing the responsibility of the poor to live up to their end of the social contract (1997). Thus, requiring paid employment restores a basic obligation of the poor to demonstrate personal responsibility through paid work. As demonstrated earlier, mothers state they share these values but resist efforts to push them into low-wage jobs. Mia's indignation at welfare requirements shoehorning poor women into bad jobs is ultimately tied to a mother's responsibility for children. In the end, a bad job constrains a woman's ability to be a good mother.

In pointing out that a single mother bears a heavier burden when "stuck in a job" because she is the sole support of her family, Mia illustrates the gendered character of welfare assistance and the constraints on women. Kicking poor women off the welfare rolls into low-wage jobs does not improve their lives nor teach them responsibility. As Mia sees it, efforts to teach responsibility to poor mothers harm poor women and children more than they help them. The jobs all too frequently occupied by mothers who leave welfare are the "crap jobs" described by Mia that according to a 2012 study by sociologist Margaret Usdansky and others are associated with higher relative rates of depression among working mothers.

On the surface, Mia's response simply reflects an empirical reality: insisting that women take the first job they find, often a low-wage, poor-quality job, is not enough to move poor women and children to self-sufficiency (Collins and Mayer 2010, Hennessy 2005, O'Connor 2000). In contrast to the promise of work commitment, low-wage labor traps women in jobs hindering them from fulfillment of their family responsibilities and generating more stress for mothers and children. A one-size-fits-all approach does not correspond to the needs of families. Mothers understand this, as do social science researchers.

SUPPORT FOR EDUCATIONAL GOALS

The dilemma facing poor and low-income women is a familiar one for today's families: How does one reconcile the need to provide financially with family responsibilities? One solution to this dilemma is to structure welfare assistance so that poor women receive sufficient support to get and retain good jobs rather than the low-wage jobs available to most welfare leavers. This includes support for education, training for additional job skills, and continued support by the state for mothers to work part-time with hours spent in the classroom counted toward work requirements. None of these solutions is new. However, they were eliminated when TANF replaced AFDC and ended the JOBS program (Pearson 2007, Shaw et al. 2006). Most mothers express bewilderment (if not anger) over what they see as a contradiction in expectations for self-sufficiency on the one hand and the lack of support for educational attainment on the other. Visions of meaningful work and family lives refracted through the lens of the work commitment schema include a job that allows low-income mothers to move up in the world and support their children.

Charla Andrews, a twenty-four-year-old single mother of a three-year-old daughter, lives in a homeless shelter for families after being evicted from an apartment she shared with her brother. On her own since the age of sixteen, she spent several years in foster care as a young child and then lived with her father during her early teens. She attended the six-week life-skills training course and wonders why if women on welfare are to be independent there was not more support for education. "But, the thing I don't understand is, you want them [welfare recipients] to be strong and independent, but do you want them to make eight dollars an hour, or would fifteen dollars an hour be better, just from the little bit of schooling they do have to do? So, why not support a woman who wants to make more money and go to school to get that?"

Why not support women trying to get ahead through going to school? This question spurred my own interest in research on welfare reform policies as they were implemented.[12] It is a question that resonates with most mothers; why not help mothers who are *trying* to get ahead? Achieving the American Dream of self-reliance and financial success is the reward for adherence our strong work ethic, a belief widely accepted by the broader culture and legitimized by conviction that success is available to all. Its ideological foundation is the U.S. educational system (Hochschild 1995). Mothers in this study express faith in educational attainment as the path to the kind of job where they can accomplish the goal of independence and autonomy promised by work commitment.

Restrictive work requirements in welfare are obstacles to mothers' aspirations—and their obligations. As Charla explains, "The way it is now, they don't support it. They would rather have you go out and get a job rather than go to school and get a better-paying job. If they want you to take care of your children—and getting a job is a better way to take care of your children—then going to school and getting a better job would be a better way of taking care of your children."

Included in this group of mothers trying to improve their odds for achieving self-sufficiency is Sandra Morris, a divorced forty-seven-year-old mother of four children. Sandra was enrolled in classes at the local community college when the welfare office called and told her and they expected her to begin working. "We want you in our office at eight o'clock in the morning, and you need to plan to be in here from eight to four to do a two-week training." According to Sandra, this meant she would have to quit school, a situation she found unreasonable. Sandra believes she has the more compelling argument in privileging long-range goals of self-sufficiency and family responsibility over welfare policy work requirements.

> Do you want me working at minimum wage and still living on housing assistance, and still needing child care and medical and dental, and all these things until my kids are eighteen and out of the home? Or do you want me to spend the next two years getting an education that's going to allow me to work for a decent wage—an above-poverty wage—and really give my kids a good example of work ethic and school ethic? You know education is going to be the key to your success, your financial success in these United States. You know, what am I really modeling for my kids? Yeah we're on welfare and it's hard. We live on $540 a month.

She pits family responsibility and a strong "work ethic and school ethic" against welfare's demand that she take a low-wage job. The latter choice in her eyes results in continued scraping by on public assistance. Sandra maps out her clearly superior course of action usurping the moral position of welfare policy makers, and questioning their demands as counter to mainstream values. Viewed though the cultural models of work commitment and family commitment, and the economic realities of the lives of poor mothers, welfare policymakers are seen as out of touch with the needs of mothers and children, or alternatively adversaries to be challenged and resisted.

Jolene, introduced earlier, agrees with Sandra about restrictions on her decision to attend college rather than get a job. Jolene attends school full time, five days a week, in a culinary arts vocational program at the community college. TANF does not support her educational program, which is a contentious issue for her.[13] She resents the fact that she cannot get support for child care while she is in class, although it would be covered if she were working.

> I feel bad for working moms I really do. But you know what? Working moms can get help with child care and I can't because I'm in school. And I would think taking twenty-one credits would count for something. I go to school and I'm there all day and I have two children. But I'm not working hard enough to get help with my child care.
>
> They [welfare] say you should just get a job, even if it is a burger-flipping job because if you're working full-time but still not making enough to make ends meet, welfare will help you. But I'm of less worth than a mother who's out working forty hours a week.

Jolene, similar to others, questions the logic behind support for mothers to take a low-wage job rather than go to school. She is troubled by what she sees as less regard for her because of this choice.

> Because I'm going to school. Because I won't go out to work, and I want to take care of my kids, and I want to go school. I want to go to school and take care of my children. I didn't want to go to work, school, and take care of my children. I can't do it. I wouldn't have time in the day. You know, not without cutting something out. And I'm not willing to cut the time with my kids. I've already cut it enough to go to school. And I'm not cutting any more out. I mean if it ever came down to it, I will quit school if it comes down to it for my kids. But I hope it never comes to that point.

Jolene resents the welfare office's failure to recognize and support her choice of school and time with her children over a low-wage job. She also resents the implication that her choice means she lacks a strong work ethic compared to mothers who work for wages. Furthermore, if Jolene were not a poor single mother, her decisions would be judged by mainstream standards as admirable. In opposition to priorities of the welfare office that low-income women perceive—fairly or unfairly—as work first, then family, and school a distant third. Jolene's priorities are: kids, then school geared toward a meaningful job in the future that will support her family. Either choice, it should be obvious (to Jolene), is superior to getting a low-wage, low-skilled job.

Jolene's response demonstrates again how contradictions in widely shared cultural models create conflict as they play out in the intersection of work and family and welfare policies. Work requirements are supposed to motivate women to enter the work force. But a particularly egregious betrayal of both the work-commitment and family-commitment schemas occurs when work requirements preclude or constrain educational attainment perceived as the path to self-sufficiency that will benefit mothers and children.

Educational achievement corresponds to work commitment's promise of upward mobility and demonstration of responsibility through paid work. Mothers view education as the path to a meaningful job that will support children. Jolene challenges the imposition of work requirements, which ignore her commitment to her children and deny her work ethic. She and others see the contradiction inherent in requiring women to enter low-wage jobs that do not promise upward mobility or allow them to care for children. Why can't policy makers and caseworkers? Barriers to educational attainment reflect a moral failure on the part of the "system" to recognize these shared ideals and obstruct the efforts of mothers to take care of their families.

PENALTIES FOR WORK AND FAMILY CHOICES

Throughout the pages of this book the women in this study demonstrate that choices surrounding work and family are morally freighted and tied to deep cultural structures that help shape self understandings and definitions of a meaningful life (Blair-Loy, 2003). When mothers interact with the welfare system they confront the contradictions inherent in competing cultural expectations. Case workers define and interpret their responsibilities to children in line with the cultural model of work commitment where providing for children through work outside the home takes priority over the caring for children in the home. In contrast to others, poor mothers on welfare who "choose" to stay home face sanctions for doing so.

Yvette was angry about restrictions on her choices and the impact on her little girl. The welfare office notified her that it was imposing a sanction—penalizing her for not working by reducing her monthly cash benefit—in her view unfairly.

Her response:

> You can't just work twenty hours a week at one place and then work twenty hours at this place. It just doesn't work that way. There is no time for my kid at all. It seems like welfare doesn't understand that. I have a child; she is three years old. She is going to need her mom. Her dad ain't in her life. I am the only person now, so I have to be there for her. . . . They [welfare] just don't get the picture. I got a three-year-old child I got to attend to. God is not going to judge me for not getting a job! But, you guys are going to judge me for not getting a job? Isn't it a job being a parent? Isn't a job taking care of your child? Isn't it a job trying to see what the best education is for your child? I think it would be.

Emphasis on paid market work looks different when it is interpreted—as is frequently the case—as an obstacle to mothers' obligation to children. Yvette sees the reduction in her cash grant as punishment for making a choice in the best interest of her child by devoting herself to a job she finds more meaningful than wage work. As she declares above, Yvette has little respect for welfare policy requirements as she bases her decisions on a higher authority.

Yvette's dilemma does point out a difference between her work and family choices and those of more advantaged women. The financial penalties in the form of a sanction by the welfare office for not meeting work requirements are a concrete reminder of the distance between poor mothers' work and family lives and others.

Anna, who earlier described the circumstances that led to her financial sanction by the welfare office when her child was ill, explains the difference.

It's completely different because the people that aren't on welfare, I mean they have *choices*. They got things they can choose to do. And if they want to do it, they can. People on welfare, they choose to do something they get sanctioned.

See that's different. People that have money, the opportunities, they don't have to deal with welfare if they don't want to. They can do what they want to do. If they want to stop working for six months because they want to take care of their kids, more power to them.

Both Anna and Yvette interpret the welfare office's policy of sanctioning women who do not comply with the rules as a violation of their right to make decisions in the best interest of their child—a right extended to others. Both were visibly upset and angry when describing what they viewed as punishment for doing what anyone would agree is what mothers are supposed to do. From this perspective, they hold the moral high ground and are only asking to be given the same rights and opportunities as others who make choices in the best interest of their children.

It may be difficult for an outside observer to understand much less support Yvette and Anna's position. In the United States a question asked frequently in discussions about the high poverty rates of families headed by single mothers is "Why do these mothers have children if they cannot support them?"

Often overlooked in these discussions is the high value of children in U.S. society and the particularly high value placed on family attachments in impoverished communities, where "parenting is the most important role mothers expect to play" (Edin and Kefalas 2005, 174). Given the opportunities for earnings that would support a family, postponement of motherhood until one could afford children would consign most poor women to going to their graves childfree.[14] Forgoing children altogether remains a choice that most women today are unwilling to make whether or not they can afford them. As noted by Jennifer Senior (2014) in *All Joy and No Fun: The Paradox of Modern Parenthood*, the high cost of raising children causes anxiety for middle-class parents where estimates range from over $200,000 at the low end to almost $500,000 per child for upper-middle-income families, not including the cost of college. Few parents are aware of the *real* cost of children when deciding to start a family.

What If Your Kid Gets Sick?

Jolene, in contrast to Anna, finds common ground among poor mothers and other working mothers. "Even working moms have it tough. If they don't I'm amazed. I want to know what their secret is. I mean they've got to go to work. They've got the same problems we have. You know they've got somebody telling them what to do, their paycheck is dependent on them showing up, or them doing a specific thing, and if your kid gets sick then what?"

She notes the heart-wrenching, guilt-inducing dilemma for all mothers, "what if your kid gets sick?" but suggests that the welfare office is even less understanding than the workplace when mothers need flexibility to care for a sick child. "I mean it's the same thing. Work will let you get away with a little bit more. They understand. Welfare does not. They don't play games. They start getting snippy and start threatening to pull money and put you in sanction and start cutting your benefits and they'll all out stop them. If your child gets sick for a week or something and you miss a week in WorkFirst, you get sanctioned."

Her characterization of the workplace—"they understand"—is one that many working mothers might challenge. But Jolene's point is that the welfare office does not care about children and punishes mothers for making choices that any working mother would make in the best interest of her children. Accordingly, a major source of conflict arises from the belief that the welfare office does not share mothers' values about the importance of children nor understand the obligations of motherhood. This, from the perspective of many mothers, is equivalent to drawing a line in the sand. Several respondents locate themselves along this particular moral divide among a community of mothers who share understandings of what good motherhood entails. Women who do not get this—which from the vantage point of the mothers I interviewed, include many of the caseworkers they encountered at the welfare office—are clearly on the wrong side of a battle over taken-for-granted understandings of the collective moral domain assigned to women as mothers. Paradoxically, given the widespread stigma associated with welfare mothers, women in my study frequently invoke a collective moral identity as mothers to discredit the moral authority of the welfare office and caseworkers in general.

Kathie, whom we heard from earlier when she suggested that women should work as soon as they are able, recounts how angry she was with the welfare system because of the stress and anxiety she witnessed in another woman in her basic skills class.

> On a regular basis she was getting called by the day care that there was something else wrong with her child to come pick them up. But then welfare was getting mad because she was missing so much school. It made me so angry that *I* wanted to call her caseworker! You know, I really did. Because she was so torn up on the days that she was there, and from the time that she was there she was so worried. She was so worried that they were okay. And you know all moms think that they can take care of their children better than anyone else. And especially if they are sick or you know. I just thought that was so . . . that was terrible. It was just terrible.

Kathie's anger results from the apparent violation of family commitment's definition of children and mothers. The obligation of mothers to work clearly pales in comparison to a mother's obligation to her child. How could the welfare office not understand a mother's anguish over this situation?

Jolene's account below of the message sent by the welfare office again places the welfare office on the wrong side of a division between the desires of "every mother" to care for her children and undue pressure to get a job. According to Jolene, the message delivered to mothers by the welfare office is "Work first, kids second."

> I think it [welfare] minimizes what *every mother* really wants to do. *Every mother* wants to be there for her children day in and day out. That's what we want to do. Okay? We want to be home all the time. When they come home from school we want to be here. When they leave to school, we want to take them. If you've got somebody pushing you into a job, you can't do that! You know "don't worry your kids are going to be fine without you. Let's put them in a day care, put them in a school do whatever you need to do. But then you need to get out and work, or you need to come to these classes. Oh, your child got sick and you missed a week. Oh, you're in sanction."

Anna, Jolene, and Kathie refer to a shared vision of motherhood where it is understood that being a mother requires attending to children's needs above all else. To punish women for doing so violates basic understandings of what it means to be a mother. When the system appears to undermine this most basic obligation of *all* mothers, family commitment emerges the clear moral victor in opposition to welfare's work requirement.

If mothers perceive that work requirements force them to choose between work and family, few will choose work. As even the most work-committed mothers tell me, "jobs come and go, children are my life." Punishing mothers for caring for children represents a moral failing beyond lack of understanding of their particular circumstances, but rather a betrayal of the deeply held moral responsibility of mothers everywhere.

Samantha's exchange with her caseworker makes this explicit as she delivers the ultimate insult in response to a sanction. Samantha's three-year-old son is a special needs child, and she recounted several instances when she moved him in and out of various daycares because he was not being cared for adequately. "I had a falling-out with my caseworker when it came down to I did not want to be working my work experience (skills training) when my son started acting up, and I said I have to quit. When she put me in sanctions I actually lost complete respect for her as a mother."

Samantha's response affirms the significance of motherhood in her life. In response to her sanction for missing work, she uses the most damaging characterization of all by challenging her caseworker's competency as a mother, in effect labeling her a bad mother. Samantha's comment illustrates once again that motherhood comes with a set of moral obligations that are widely shared and understood by all (good) mothers. How could any mother punish another mother for putting her child's needs first? For some women in my study, the welfare system's attempts to redirect mother's priorities toward work and away from children through sanctions actually intensifies conflict and reinforces client's moral identities as mothers. When seemingly threatened by welfare office policies, motherhood gains increasing salience as a counter to negative evaluations of welfare mothers' choices.

Sending Three-Month-Old Infants to Day Care

For many respondents, requiring a mother to put her three-month-old infant in day care so that she can work is a particularly egregious betrayal of the family commitment's demand that children's needs come first and foremost. It serves as yet another instance of how misguided and out of touch welfare policy is with core family values.

Gina stated in the previous chapter that she does not necessarily believe mothers should rely on welfare. Yet she is also very concerned about the impact on young children when the welfare office demands that mothers work full-time outside the home. Children should be the number-one priority for both welfare policy makers and mothers. Gina speaks not only for herself but also for many mothers when she warns of the danger of "sticking" a three-month-old infant in day care.

> When you stick a three-month-old [in day care] I think you are asking for a loooot of problems, a whole lot. Because that baby is going to get neglected, I don't care. You know maybe you might find a really good day care, but they are few and far between, and they don't have enough daycares to even take care of the women I know. Because I've talked to these women. I hear it all the time! You know women that are just freaking out because they don't want to leave their kids in a home, or they don't want to leave their kids in a day care that young! I see it all the time.

Insistence by the welfare office that mothers of very small infants go to work elicits responses reaffirming collective identities as mothers. Anguish over being forced to leave their infants in day care is a sentiment that all mothers understand and share.

Samantha's comment parallels Gina's concerns about the well-being of babies. "Three-month-old babies need security. If they are bouncing around to a day care and back home, they are not learning anything except for life is crazy. So, when they need nurturing and structure, they're not getting that. . . . I honestly think that is the worst thing for a three month old. At three months old, no, no, I didn't do that when my children were three months old, and I wouldn't do it to another mother."

From Samantha's perspective, the common bond women share as mothers should elicit greater sympathy and compassion and override the priority placed on paid work. There is no clearer violation of taken-for-granted understandings than insistence that mothers leave infants as young as three months of age in day care. Samantha's response reaffirms the taken-for-granted understandings shared by all *good* mothers and justifies her resistance to work requirements.

CONCLUSION

Vera sums up the sentiment of many respondents that TANF punishes mothers who are trying to do what is best for their families. "I remember a few years ago they used to say women had babies just so they would not have to work. Then they would go on welfare. And there's two sides to every story, I'm sure there are a lot people who did that. But unfortunately we all live with the risk that what the bad people do and what the good people do, sooner or later they clash. The bad people make it bad for the good people."

The good people, in Vera's eyes and the eyes of many respondents, are mothers who are taking responsibility and trying to better their own lives and the lives of their children. When welfare policies threaten their ability to do so instead of helping them, it creates resentment on the part of recipients. Mothers resist attempts by caseworkers and the demands of the welfare office to impose moral definitions that group them with the "bad people."

The welfare policy that arose as a result of the clash between the good people and the bad people finds poor mothers in a contest over widely shared values guiding paid work and family decisions. Most mothers characterize this struggle as simply coping with the "hassles" imposed by the welfare office. They respond by getting jobs, creatively finance education through loans and grants, or find other ways to make ends meet and care for children through continued welfare assistance, boyfriends, families, or friends. Few mothers explicitly recognize the contradictory moral forces that make up the gendered cultural models structuring the work and family domains of low-income women.

Some women in my study, embracing work commitment, interpret work outside the home as part of a mother's obligation to children. Others see work requirements as a threat to their status as mothers. Bolstered by a separate spheres ideology that continues to hold greater moral salience for women in their capacity as mothers and wives, and men in their capacity as workers and providers, respondents valorize caring for children. Mothers' accounts above paint a vivid portrait of the moral ideological context in which poor women make work and family decisions and how morality reflected in broadly shared cultural models of work and family life, plays out in the practices and policies of the welfare office.

NOTES

1. See Gordon (1994), *Pitied But Not Entitled*, Mink (1995), *The Wages of Motherhood*, and Abramovitz (1996), *Regulating the Lives of Women*, for examples of how poor women, as single mothers, have been stigmatized since the origins of poor support.

2. Government spending on TANF in FY 2012 was approximately 31 billion dollars—with one-third of that spent on cash benefits. U.S. Department of Health and Human Services, ACF (2013). Harris and Shakin's (2013) CBO report estimates that ten of the most common tax expenditures are far more generous, costing the taxpayers 900 billion dollars in 2013 and disproportionately benefit households in the top percentile of the income distribution. These include the home mortgage deduction (141 billion dollars), and the value of employer provided health insurance (185 billion).

3. An example of this animosity appeared in response to Nicholas Kristopf's (2014) *New York Times* column about the impacts of poverty. Kristopf wrote about a three-year-old boy whose hearing impairment had gone undetected, leading him to suffer speech and development problems that may impact him for the rest of his life. A photo of the boy and his mother, accompanied the column and readers responded by focusing on the mother's tattoos and weight and criticizing her poor choices rather than responding to the issue addressed by Kristopf—the disparities in opportunities for poor children and their consequences.

4. EBT Electronic Benefits Transfer is the debit card issued for (SNAP) the Supplemental Nutrition Assistance Program, commonly referred to as food stamps.

5. See Parker 2012 for results of an April 2012 Pew Research Center survey and report, "Where The Public Stands on Government Assistance, Taxes and the Presidential Candidates," showing that 59 percent of those surveyed agreed that the government should guarantee every citizen enough to eat and a place to sleep. Fifty-nine percent also agreed it is the responsibility of the government to take care of people who can't take care of themselves.

6. Family historian Stephanie Coontz (2013) argues that solutions to work-family conflict that promote traditional family arrangements and/or support for part-time work or reducing the hours of women place greater responsibility on men and decrease their options to work less or spend more time on leisure or child involvement. Increasingly women are expected to contribute to family income and share the responsibility to provide. According to a 2014 Pew Research report 40 percent of all households with children under the age of eighteen include mothers who are the primary source of income for the family, compared to 11 percent in 1960. Thirty-seven percent of this group are married mothers earning more than their spouses, 63 percent are single mothers (Wang et al. 2014).

7. Sharon Hays (2003) devotes a chapter of her book to the hassles experienced by mothers and the difficulties of caseworkers. See also Morgen, Acker and Weigt (2010) for a discussion of client experience with the welfare office; also Celeste Watkins-Hayes (2009) for discussion of the power of caseworkers and variation in implementation of welfare policy on the ground.

8. The history of welfare chronicles attempts to shape the behavior of the poor. Seminal works include Piven and Cloward's (1971), *Regulating the Poor: The Functions of Public Welfare*, Katz (1986) *In The Shadow of the Poorhouse*, Abramovitz (1996) *Regulating the Lives of Women,* and policy prescriptions for changing the behavior of the poor in Mead's (1997) *The New Paternalism: Supervisory Approaches to Poverty*.

9. The idea that women on welfare should not have children is codified in TANF through a provision in the law that allows states to withhold additional funding for children conceived while the family was receiving TANF/AFDC welfare benefits. Seventeen states currently have some form of family cap policy. See *Welfare Rules Databook State TANF Policies as of July 2012*. Office of Planning Research and Evaluation, Administration for Children and Families. U.S. Department of Health and Human Services. Table L10 Family Cap Policies, 1992-2012 (July).

10. $478 is the amount of a cash grant for a single parent and two children with no earnings in the state of Washington in 2012.

11. See Williams (2010), Child Trends (2013). Working-class women today are the most likely to be stay-at-home mothers because the high cost of day care erodes the financial and psychological benefits of working versus staying at home. Earnings are too high for eligibility

for subsidies provided for the poor, and family income is lower than women married to higher-earning spouses. These families are more likely to rely on relatives for their child care needs.

12. See Shaw, Goldrick-Rab, Mazzeo, and Jacobs (2006) for a discussion of TANF's impact in limiting support for educational attainment. See Pearson (2007) for the role of case managers in limiting welfare clients' access to education.

13. WorkFirst supports limited educational training and job skills programs. Vocational training is supported in select programs tied directly to employment, including short-term basic skills and job training tied to work readiness.

14. See Sylvia Hewlett's (2002), *Creating a Life: Professional Women and the Quest for Children* for a discussion of professional women and the crisis of fertility. For a discussion of the significance of children see Hays (1996), *The Cultural Contradictions of Motherhood.* McMahon (1995), *Engendering Motherhood: Identity and Self-Transformation in Women's Lives.* See Edin and Kefalas (2005), *Promises I Can Keep* for discussion of the value of children in poor mothers' lives.

Chapter Six

Survey Findings

This chapter presents results from the larger sample of survey respondents. In chapter 3, readers were introduced to select responses to survey questions corresponding to mothers' beliefs about paid work and family responsibilities. This chapter expands upon the initial presentation of that survey data with quantitative analyses of factors affecting the work and family decisions of the poor and low-income women in this study.

In shifting to quantitative analysis after focusing mostly on qualitative data, recall, an advantage of the mixed method strategy of combining findings in the quantitative analysis with the context derived from the lived experience of mothers in the interviews is that: (1) the larger sample in the survey allows for identification of patterns in responses, and (2) quantitative techniques can be used to test the strength of relationships among variables. The survey data also allows for comparisons between groups. In short, quantitative analyses are able to more precisely identify patterns in factors predicting work and family commitments, whereas the interview data answers the "why" and "how" questions through accounts of the experience of women in this study.

Descriptive statistics of the survey sample and measures used in the analysis are provided in a methodological appendix.

VARIATION BY WELFARE ASSISTANCE

A question I was interested in more fully exploring is variation among women who received welfare assistance under TANF in views on work and family responsibilities. I have argued that demands that mothers go to work in exchange for welfare assistance under TANF bring to light the taken-for-granted assumptions about gendered work and family arrangements. Mothers in my study who are/were subject to work requirements experience the competing contradictions between work and family as they are institutionalized in TANF making them tangible, rather than abstract, unconscious, taken-for-granted cultural mandates.

In addition, in the last chapter we heard from mothers who were dissatisfied with various aspects of work requirements. Some felt constrained in pursuing educational goals and reaching self-sufficiency through paid employment, others because of the time away from home, which they saw as hindering their ability to care for children. We also heard some mothers describe welfare recipients as lazy and undeserving, insisting that they should get jobs rather than sit at home "doing nothing." Given the paradox in the work-family debate underlined in TANF policy as it relates to paid work and child care, I wanted to more closely examine the association of receiving TANF benefits with respondent's views on women's responsibilities as workers and mothers; that is, to see if mothers who experienced firsthand the message that they should go to work rather than stay home with children, respond differently from others in beliefs about mother's paid work and family responsibilities.

To answer this question, I begin by dividing the sample into two groups: mothers who received welfare after TANF went into effect and others. (When referring to TANF, I use the terms TANF and WorkFirst interchangeably, as WorkFirst is the name of Washington's TANF program.) Keep in mind, this distinction does not necessarily indicate that this group of mothers was enrolled in WorkFirst at the time they completed the survey; rather it indicates that they have received TANF benefits at any time (whether presently or in the past). This group of respondents differs from other former welfare recipients in that they received welfare after implementation of changes in the program that required recipients to work, look for work, and/or prepare for work through job skills training as a condition of receiving support for their families through TANF. Importantly, mothers in the group having never received TANF may have received welfare under AFDC or never relied on AFDC in the past. They differ in that they did not receive welfare under the welfare-to-work system implemented by TANF making welfare support contingent on working outside the home.

The first part of the analysis shows results from the survey questionnaire asking respondents whether they agree or disagree with a set of statements about men and women's paid work and responsibility for children and welfare assistance. This section addresses the initial question as to whether the two groups differ. The second part presents regression analysis to pinpoint specific factors; for example, education, employment, and/or age, as predictors of poor and low-income mothers' priorities related to work and family commitments.

The first three tables (tables 6.1–6.3) present results of survey responses categorized into groups corresponding with the major themes explored in the interview data. Results shown are the percent of survey respondents agreeing with statements about work and family compatibility, traditional family gender roles, and welfare by whether respondents received TANF welfare benefits at some point as an adult. T-tests (comparison of means) were used to determine whether differences shown between the groups are statistically significant.[1]

DESCRIPTIVE FINDINGS

Upon initial inspection, it appears that a substantial number of survey respondents indicate support for the compatibility of paid work with caring for children and its importance in mother's lives. At the same time, similar to the majority of the American public, they also express concern over mothers spending time working outside the home when children are small (Wang, Parker, and Taylor 2014) and believe in a traditional gendered division of labor.

Results in table 6.1 present the proportion of respondents agreeing with statements on the compatibility of paid work with caring for children. Although 51 percent of all mothers surveyed agree with the statement "Working for pay is one of the most important things a mother does for her family," a greater proportion (61 percent) of mothers who received welfare in the WorkFirst program agree compared to 43 percent of mothers in the sample who did not. In addition, although a substantial majority (78 percent) of all survey respondents agree with the statement "When a mother works outside the home, she sets a good example for her children," a greater proportion of mothers ever on TANF agree (86 percent), compared to 72 percent of others. In response to the statement, "A working mother can establish just as warm and secure relationship with her children as a mother who does not work," there was no difference between the two groups in their support for this statement. Both groups are also quite similar in their views on the importance of working outside the home for women. Over 80 percent of mothers in each group agree, "Working outside the home is just as important for women as it is for men." Respondents who received TANF do differ from others in agreeing that paid work is tied to mothers' responsibility for children and that mothers set a good example through paid work—a message delivered and supported through the WorkFirst program.

Survey respondents do not differ by TANF group when responding to statements associated with traditional family roles. Table 6.2 indicates that respondents strongly support a gendered division of labor and the importance of domestic responsibilities and raising children for women.

Table 6.1.   Percent agreeing to statements about paid work and family compatibility by TANF

Work-Family Compatibility	Received TANF	Not TANF	Total
Working for pay is one of the most important things a mother can do for her family	60.66*	42.75	51.0
When a mother works outside the home, she sets a good example for her children	85.59*	71.76	78.31
A working mother can establish just as warm and secure relationship with her children as a mother who does not work	78.81	72.18	75.10
Working outside the home is just as important for women as it is for men	83.47	81.34	82.28
Number of cases	122	134	256

* Indicates p-value <. 05

The TANF group and others differ when asked whether they agree or disagree with statements about welfare use. Underscoring the widespread dislike of welfare programs, note that a majority of all respondents (57 percent) agree that welfare undermines people's work ethic. However, the proportion of mothers who agree, "Welfare makes people work less than they would if there was not a welfare system," is lower (47 percent) for those who received TANF compared to 66 percent for survey respondents never supported by TANF welfare assistance. A substantial majority also see the welfare system as helpful (76 percent) with little difference between the groups. When asked to agree or disagree with the statement "Women with young children who receive welfare should be required to work for pay," less than half (45 percent) of respondents overall agree, but among these mothers, a smaller proportion of mothers who received TANF benefits agree (37 percent) compared to greater support among mothers who had not received

Table 6.2. Percent agreeing to statements about traditional family roles by TANF

Traditional Family	Received TANF	Not TANF	Total
Taking care of the home and raising children is the most important job for a woman	78.81	72.87	75.20
When children are born, mothers should not work outside the home	64.75	64.93	64.57
It is better for everyone if a single mother goes to work instead of stay at home and care for her children	38.52	39.23	39.20
It is better for everyone if the man in the household has a job outside the home and the woman takes care of the family	65.25	68.18	66.94
Preschool children suffer when their mothers work outside the home	63.56	63.85	63.83
Mothers should not work full time when their youngest child is under age five	71.43	75.76	74.30
Number of cases	122	134	256

TANF (52 percent). Likewise, a majority (67 percent) agree, "Women with young children who receive welfare should be able to stay home and care for their children." However, an even greater proportion of those who ever received TANF are more likely to support mothers on welfare to stay home with children (73 percent) compared to 60 percent of mothers who did not receive welfare under WorkFirst.

Results in these tables are consistent with the narratives of respondents presented earlier where many expressed traditional views on a gendered division of labor and mothers' primary responsibility for children. The ma-

Table 6.3.   Percent agreeing to statements about welfare assistance by TANF

Welfare	Received TANF	Not TANF	Total
Welfare makes people work less than they would if there was not a welfare system	47.11**	66.41	56.80
Welfare helps people get on their feet when facing situations such as unemployment, a divorce or death in the family	75.00	77.61	76.19
Women with young children on welfare should be required to work	36.67*	51.88	44.62
Women on welfare should be able to stay home with their children	73.11*	60.45	66.53
Number of cases	122	134	256

* Indicates p-value <. 05, **p-value <01

jority of survey respondents agree that an ideal work and family division of labor consists of a male breadwinner and female homemaker arrangement. They also agree that some combination of paid work and child care is the best option for families. The areas where there are significant differences between respondents who have received welfare more recently and others are that post-TANF welfare recipients are more likely to agree that working outside the home sets a good example for children and that paid work is part of a mother's family responsibility. The greater coherence among women in this study in response to statements related to traditional family roles under-scores the persistence of gendered cultural definitions of the needs of children and mother's obligations for their care. Similar to the findings in the interview data, many respondents in this sample hold traditional gendered views on men and women's work and family roles at the same time they also value a strong work ethic in setting examples and providing for children.

REGRESSION ANALYSIS

The remainder of the quantitative analysis expands on descriptive statistics with regression analysis to identify factors predicting greater or lesser convergence among respondents on measures of traditional "family values" and work attachment.

Analyses evaluate the relationship of having ever received TANF on mothers' work and family orientations including the effect of additional factors that shape women's work and family attachments: marital status, age, the age of children, employment and education and a measure of the salience of paid work. I anticipate that having ever received TANF would lead to more inclusive views about the compatibility of paid work and motherhood. Respondents in the WorkFirst program received material resources, institutional support, and encouragement to get a job as part of their family responsibility. TANF is geared toward moving poor mothers into the workforce as financial providers for their children and supports them to that end. It also sanctions poor mothers who do not or will not abide by program requirements that they get a job. At the same time due to gendered expectations, I expect that receiving TANF is less influential as a predictor of traditional family views among this group of low-income and poor mothers, net of other factors.

Independent Variables

In this analysis, *marital status* measures the relationship of married, never-married, cohabiting, and widowed marital status compared to divorced and separated marital status as a predictor of views on work and family obligations and welfare assistance.[2] Single mothers cannot count on a spouse's wage for financial support, and child support from absent fathers among mothers in this study was rare. As we learned in the interview data, divorced mothers frequently expressed dismay over the disruption in their lives and family roles, which included constraints in their ability to stay home with children. Many believe in traditional family arrangements, thus I would expect to find these beliefs reflected in the survey data in comparison to never-married single motherhood. In all likelihood having never married would predict greater alignment with views supporting paid work as part of mothers' family role compared to divorced and separated mothers.

Poor and low-income women tend to have lower educational attainment than others and education, in turn, impacts employment opportunity. I include education and employment as predictors of mothers' views on work and family obligations. *Education* indicates whether one has a high school degree or more years of education, and *employment* indicates participation in paid work whether that is full- or part-time paid work outside the home.

Although few mothers have obtained education beyond a high school diploma the association of higher levels of education with good jobs and the ability to support a family would be expected to increase support for the compatibility of paid work and family responsibilities. Conversely, low-educational attainment is associated with few good options in the labor market, and bad jobs, thus, would be more likely to be negatively associated with work commitment. Mothers expressed these views as they spoke of restrictions on their own ability to pursue educational credentials beyond a high school diploma, which hindered their ability to get a good job to support their children.

Because few mothers in this group of low-income women can count on support from a wage-earning spouse, their views undoubtedly are influenced by the practical necessity to work outside the home in addition to more ideal rewards from paid work, and the stigma surrounding reliance on welfare. I anticipate that employment is associated with greater support for working outside the home. Additionally, some mothers also see paid work as a means of providing strong role models for their children and demonstrating independence. Related to this, I also anticipate that having a job is more closely associated with expectations that mothers on welfare should work and therefore is a predictor of support for TANF policies.

As observed in the interview data, mothers in my study experience conflict in meeting the demands of competing cultural models of their responsibilities as workers and mothers. Much of the ambivalence expressed in previous chapters comes from the meaning mothers derive from paid work and motherhood. The *work satisfaction* variable, "The work I do outside the home is one of the most satisfying parts of my life," measures the salience of paid work. I expect that the more work outside the home resonates as a fulfilling aspect of one's life, the more mothers will see paid work as compatible with caring for children. Conversely, the greater satisfaction found in work outside the home, the less support we would expect to find for a gendered division of labor and primary responsibility for women to child care and domestic responsibilities.

Dependent Variables

I constructed outcome measures based on survey responses in tables 6.1–6.3. Factor analysis was used to determine categories measuring concepts of interest related to work and family, and welfare from responses to items in the survey questionnaire, resulting in three outcome variables. The first dependent variable (column two, table 6.4) indicates orientation toward the *work commitment* schema's definitions of the compatibility of mothers' paid work and child care. Higher values indicate favorable views on combining paid work outside the home with child care.

The second outcome (column three, table 6.4) variable denotes orientation toward *family commitment's* definition of children and mothers obligations. Higher values indicate more traditional views on mothers' family responsibilities.

The final and third dependent variable (column four in table 6.4) measures support for *workfare welfare policy*. Higher values on this measure indicate support for workfare welfare policies requiring paid work in exchange for welfare benefits.

OLS REGRESSION FINDINGS

Table 6.4 presents results of regression analysis predicting orientation toward work commitment and family commitment and views on welfare assistance.

When interpreting the regression results, positive values indicate that higher values on the independent variables are associated with higher values on the outcome variable. Negative values, on the other hand, indicate an inverse relationship, where higher values on the independent variable predict lower values on the outcome variable. Positive or negative values on the coefficient in the regression models can then be interpreted as indicating the direction of the effect as a predictor of the outcomes of interest.

Table 6.4. Regression Models Predicting Views on Work, Family, and Welfare Assistance

Independent Variables	Work	Family	Welfare
TANF (dummy coded, TANF = 1)	.232*	.027	−.366**
Marital Status			
Married	−.073	−.019	−.093
Never married	.370 *	−.489 **	.176
Cohabiting	.173	−.197	.122
Widowed	.083	−.242	.056
Preschool child at home	−.020	.124	.090
Education (dummy coded, high school diploma or higher = 1)	−.007	-.204	−.282*
Employment	.232*	−139	.227*
Age	−.011	.010	.003 -
Work satisfaction	.373***	−.297***	.081
R²	.294	.216	.126

* Indicates p-value <. 05, **<.01, ***<.001

Compatibility of Paid Work and Childrearing

Results in column two show that receiving welfare under TANF predicts more inclusive views of paid work as compatible with childrearing, b = .232, p ≤ .05, net of other factors. Stated differently, mothers who received welfare under TANF's welfare-to-work program are more likely to see work outside the home as compatible with family roles. Also predicting the likelihood of holding more inclusive views on paid work and its compatibility with family demands are having never married compared to divorce and separation, working outside the home, and satisfaction with working outside the home.

The majority of women in this study are single mothers, with divorced or separated mothers making up 45 percent of the survey sample. Having never married is positively associated with views supporting work commitment compared to divorced and separated mothers. In other words, compared to mothers who are divorced or separated, having never married predicts the greater likelihood of seeing paid work as compatible with childrearing responsibilities, b = .370, p ≤ .05.

Employment indicates a mother is working outside the home for wages, either full-time or part-time. Column two shows that mothers' work outside the home for pay, as anticipated, predicts more inclusive views on the compatibility of paid work and family responsibilities, b = .233, p ≤ .05. Although we also heard some mothers express dissatisfaction over low-wage jobs, most mothers expected to work. Also, the role model mothers provide for children in this community when they work outside the home allows them to set an example for children.

Work satisfaction is the strongest predictor of both views on the compatibility of paid work with caring for children and traditional gendered family and work roles. This can be interpreted in line with the pushes and pulls evident in the interview data, and as anticipated, the direction of the association of work satisfaction to the compatibility of work outside the home with caring for children is positive. In short, mothers who find fulfillment in work outside the home also hold more inclusive views on the compatibility of paid work and family responsibilities, b =. 373, p. ≤ .001. To reiterate, many mothers expressed pride in working outside the home and their desire for good jobs. The rub is the competing salience of family commitment.

Traditional Family Values

Column three in table 6.4 shows that having ever received TANF is not a predictor of traditional gendered family arrangements. However, other factors do impact the salience of traditional family values. Never having married predicts a decrease in the likelihood of holding views in line with traditional gendered cultural models, b = −.489, p ≤ .01, compared to divorced and/or separated respondents.

Other than marital status, the salience of paid work was the only other factor influencing greater or lesser accord with traditional family arrangements. Notably, it is also the strongest predictor in pulling mothers away from traditional family roles. Work satisfaction is associated with decreased support for traditional gender roles in that greater satisfaction with work outside the home decreases the likelihood of holding more traditional views on men and women's work and family attachments, b = −.297, p. ≤ .001. As discussed above, understanding paid work as a meaningful and satisfying part of one's life predicts support for mothers' work outside the home. Alternately, finding greater meaning in work outside the home competes with the traditional gender roles found in family commitment and predicts decreased support on this measure.

However, in calling attention to the effect of work satisfaction, it is worth noting that as a predictor of work and family commitments what is being measured is the *meaning* of paid work outside the home as distinct from employment. Work satisfaction was not associated with views on welfare assistance and whether mothers on welfare should be required to work outside the home.

Welfare to Work

Underscoring the resistance we saw from women in this study over what they felt was excessive pressure to get a job, receiving welfare under TANF (column four) predicts an erosion of support for work requirements b = −.366, p ≤ .01. Receiving TANF is associated with support for paid work (shown earlier in column two) but also with decreased support for workfare policies. As we learned in the interviews, this was often expressed as dislike for a program believed to push mothers into dead-end jobs or that appeared to threaten children's well-being. We can interpret these findings as consistent with mothers' accounts and the ambivalence that is woven throughout many responses. Paid work is increasingly expected of mothers, and TANF policy reinforces this with skills training, financial support, and a message that paid work is important in providing for families.

The mothers in this study have relatively significant levels of educational attainment with almost 85 percent earning a high school diploma, although fewer than 10 percent had earned an Associates degree or higher. Although we would not as a general rule consider a high school diploma a high level of educational attainment, it is worth noting that these mothers are not representative of samples of impoverished mothers characterized by severe obstacles to employment that have not graduated from high school or obtained GEDs.

In this sense they are among the most employable of mothers within the welfare population.

Educational attainment of a high school diploma or obtaining more years of education negatively impacts support for workfare welfare policy requirements, b = −.282, p. ≤ .05. In other words, earning a high school diploma or more years of education predicts lack of support for requiring mothers to work outside the home. Mothers in this study are well aware of the lack of good jobs for women with limited education (Corcoran et al 2000, Seefeldt 2008). This response may also reflect a desire for achieving additional educational attainment beyond a high school diploma to increase employment opportunities.

Employment on this outcome in contrast to education is positively related to support for mothers on welfare to work outside the home, b = .222, p ≤ .05. One of the most pervasive myths about people on welfare is that they do not want to work and are content to remain on welfare supported by hard working taxpayers. Although the empirical evidence belies the assumptions behind this myth, it continues to stigmatize the poor and also to keep benefits very low so as to further discourage individuals from reliance on welfare .

To summarize: receiving welfare after the implementation of TANF is associated with increased support for the compatibility of paid work with caring for children but decreased support for workfare policies which require this of poor women, net of other factors. It is not associated with views on traditional family arrangements. Having a job, as expected, predicts greater support for paid work outside the home and is also associated with support for mothers on welfare to go to work. Having never married is associated with greater support for the compatibility of paid work with caring for children and less support for traditional gendered family arrangements. Graduating from high school or attaining more years of schooling is inversely associated with workfare policies, predicting decreased support for requiring mothers on welfare to work outside the home when children are small. Work satisfaction is the most powerful predictor of seeing paid work as compatible with caring for children and incompatible with traditional gender roles. To place these findings in context in terms of the tension between work commitment and family commitment, salience in work outside the home predicts greater support for paid work as women's responsibility—today's expectations reflected in WorkFirst policies—and less support for traditional gendered family roles. However, support for paid work coexists with strong support for traditional views on mothers' responsibility for young children. The implications for these findings are discussed in the following chapter.

NOTES

1. For readers that may be unfamiliar with *t*-tests, p-values and statistical significance, p-values indicate the probability that the observed relationship is simply one of chance, for example a p-value of .05 indicates that there is a 1 in 20 chance that the null hypothesis (no difference between groups) is true. Although we could use a more conservative test, a p-value of less than .01 (1 in 100 chance) for example, it is generally agreed upon that anything less than .05 is a sufficiently stringent statistical test to indicate observed differences to be unlikely due to chance.

2. Marital status is a strong predictor of poverty in family households and thus decisions about paid work and child care. Married family's poverty rates for 2012 were 6.3 percent compared to 31 percent for single female headed families (U.S. Census 2013).

Chapter Seven

Conclusion

It's almost like we need to work if we're poor, but we need to feel guilty if we are successful in what we do. Yeah, guilt is for women that have good jobs. Yeah.

—Marianne

Not too long ago, work and family were seen as separate things even by social scientists. An ideal relationship between work and family relegated them to separate but complementary spheres. The work that women did in the home did not count as work, and paid work was the domain of men. Unquestionably, women's work and family lives have undergone remarkable changes. Today the majority of Americans see ideal family life as a balance between work and family demands in response to droves of married mothers' entry into the paid workforce (Parker 2012). Yet the meaning of these demands, the gendered division of labor, and the moral significance of paid work for women, particularly mothers, has been slower to change (Blair-Loy 2003, Hochschild 1989).

Adults in the United States view work and family as important to both men and women but worry about the social costs of *mothers'* paid work on outcomes for small children (Wang, Parker, and Taylor 2013). However, their concern centers on the amount of time mothers in married dual-earner families spend working outside the home when children are small. In fact, for poor single mothers, the reverse is true. Apprehension over mothers devoting too many hours to paid work ends at the welfare office. Accountability to the masculine provider role continues to be more closely associated with men's employment unless one is a mother on public assistance.

WORK AND FAMILY PARADOX

I began this book by describing a paradox in work-family relations: the differing moral and ideological forces shaping expectations for low-income and poor mothers' devotion to paid work and caring for children in contrast to married middle-class and professional mothers. Working outside the home while raising small children is now what most women do, yet they do so under different conditions, armed with different resources and confront an array of different options. That is to say, elite professional mothers in careers married to spouses with substantial earnings and married middle-class mothers in dual-earning families go to work and care for children within a social and cultural context that differs from that of poor and low-income mothers. Yet, it is too simplistic to dismiss this divide solely as between mothers who choose to work and those who "need" to work. Despite the fact that we now expect mothers to combine paid work with caring for children, gender and class bias surrounding work and family generates guilt on the part of mothers with good jobs for leaving their children with others, at the same time pushing poor mothers into market work in order to fulfill their responsibility to children.[1]

Understanding this paradox rests on awareness of the taken-for-granted widely shared cultural models shaping work-family decisions and welfare policy—in particular their salience in the lives of low-income women. The women in this study make decisions about work and family armed with few material resources. They face greater constraints in their ability to act on their preferences regarding work and family choices compared to middle-class mothers. By including the voices of women from the margins rather than the center of debates over paid work and family caregiving responsibilities, I seek to broaden understandings of the moral and normative forces guiding work and family decisions. As this study demonstrates, explanations dividing mothers into those who choose to work or those who have to work are too simplistic to capture the complexity of women's work and family lives whether married middle-class professional mothers or poor and low-income women reliant on low-wage jobs and/or public assistance.

Tina's story and comments in this final chapter bring home the differing context in which gendered expectations for paid work and motherhood play out under the shadow of welfare assistance for poor and low-income mothers. Tina, thirty-two, a divorced mother of four children whose work history includes short stints at a pizza restaurant and cashier work, is about to start a temporary job setting up events at a local stadium. Her children have alternated living with her and her ex-husband. Currently, the youngest child, her five-year-old daughter, lives with her. The older children, an eight-year-old son, and fifteen-year-old daughter, live with their father and stepmother. The oldest son, age eighteen, lives on his own. Tina became a mother as a teenager, did not complete high school, and has yet to finish her GED.

She spoke about her own childhood.

> I lived with my mom. My mom and my dad divorced when I was two. We did go and spend every other weekend with my dad. My dad was in my life all the time. Yeah, life for me was hard growing up. As my sister put it, I got, excuse the expression, the shit end of the deal just the way I was raised by my mom. Basically whenever there was a new guy in my mom's life, I'm the one that got the crap beat out of them. They basically used me for a punching bag. Oh yeah. And you know it's amazing how I ended up having four kids. You know my kids are my life. They come first before anything.

Tina's statement about the importance of her children, offered without any prompting, was something I heard often in mothers' accounts. Tina also does not trust daycares, a characteristic she shares with other low-income mothers and a reason she gave for limiting her work hours until her little girl enters kindergarten in the fall. "I don't trust daycares in this town. I only look to my family for help in taking care of my kids."[2]

There were other reasons Tina gave for why she was not working in addition to her lack of trust in day care and wanting to wait until her little girl was older. One was simply the difficulty of finding a job in a bad economy. However, her comments on her prospects for working outside the home bring up an issue that few women can avoid—the moral evaluation of mothers' choices whether they work at home or outside the home for pay, albeit with an important twist that gets to the heart of the experience of the mothers in this book. As Tina explains, "Women who work think they're being judged because they are not at home with their kids. And women who don't work and stay home [think they are being judged] because people think they are too lazy to go out and find work. You know. And it's not like that. I'm sorry have you looked at the job economy in this town? There ain't much here! I mean it's hard for me to find a job."

Tina's statement that women are judged for not spending enough time with their children when they work outside the home rings true for many working parents. However, her view that mothers who stay home are judged as lazy is the sort of statement that sets the mommy wars raging anew and calls attention to the distance between the lives of women like Tina and those who are the face of the contemporary work-life debate.

To take this further, poor mothers' choices related to working outside the home and caring for children cannot be understood without consideration of the welfare system and the ideologies that undergird it. One need only listen to Tina's comments below about paid work and women supported by public assistance to see how this plays out in the lives of mothers in this study. As she explains,

> Well, people who work, they look at people on welfare as people who are
> sponging off the state. And some of these people do. I am not one of them
> people. . . . There are women out there who don't want to get off their butt and
> get out there and go work. They'd rather sponge off the state, get the grant, get
> the food stamps, and get the medical. And [pause] I don't want it. But if I can't
> get a job that's gonna give me benefits, I got to do something. If they are not
> going to pay me enough to put food on my table for my kids, I'm going to ask
> for help.

Central to understanding the material and moral context shaping Tina's choices and those of the mothers we have heard from thus far are assumptions about "people on welfare." All of those people "sponging off the state" are mothers raising children. Mothers with good jobs are never characterized this way, as this does not describe their work and family struggles. Tina's account of the economic constraints shaping her work and family responsibilities and the moral evaluations that create a no-win situation for making the right choice epitomize the paradox for poor women in today's work-family debate. Work and family choices shaped by changing understandings of women's work and family responsibilities and cultural definitions of a worthwhile life look quite different from the unique angle of vision provided through the contours of welfare policy and differing expectations for poor and low-income women.

Why Study Low-income Mothers?

The majority of the mothers in this study are single mothers. A significant number of women have a history of abusive relationships with partners or spouses and have overcome or continue to struggle with obstacles to work-family responsibilities such as alcohol and drug dependencies and mental and physical disabilities. For a few women in this study, conflict between work and family responsibilities involves interaction with social service agencies including Child Protective Services (CPS) to keep a child in the home or to "get a child back" after a child has been removed from the home. Explanations of work and family life based on middle-class, dual-earner families do not include work and family issues such as the need to arrange work schedules around supervised visitation of children or daily bus rides from home to day care to work and back again. Home life for middle-class families is unlikely to be found in transitional housing. Nor are there suggestions that mothers raising children "get off their butts and go to work," a taken-for-granted way of describing what welfare mothers *should* do.

An extreme example of work and family conflict experienced by one mother was when her caseworker suggested that she consider terminating her pregnancy when my respondent mentioned she did not think anyone would hire a pregnant woman. These aspects of women's lives are not considered part of mainstream concerns over "work-family balance." In pointing out the distance between my subject's lives and others, I do not mean to imply that married dual-earner families never undergo stress or problems regarding work and family, or that middle-class and professional mothers in careers never experience family hardship or serious setbacks in their ability to deal with the obligations of work and motherhood. Instead, these examples illustrate how the inclusion of poor and low-income women's lives reveals facets of work and family decisions obscured in today's contemporary work-family debate.

Most observers are familiar with the *mommy wars, opting out, leaning in* and discussions over the purported folly of married middle-class and professional mothers wanting to *have it all* in pursuing satisfying careers and family life—terms epitomizing perceptions of work-family conflict in the United States. And a few notable studies do address the struggles of poor mothers to provide and care for children as welfare reform took effect. [3] Thus, neglect of poor women's lives cannot be attributed to a general lack of attention to work-life issues by academics, journalists, and the media and the vast trove of studies and information about men and women's paid work and family attachments. Yet, for all the interest in work and family relations, we know less about mothers who "choose" low-wage jobs and/or public assistance to care for their families and even less about the moral and cultural foundation of the constraints and opportunities shaping poor and working-class mothers' work and family choices.

This omission occurs in some of the best studies analyzing low-income women's work and family choices. Key insights from this literature are that structural constraints rather than individual preferences shape the ability of low-income women to provide and care for children. Jane Collins and Victoria Mayer's (2010) study of poor women's work and family lives after welfare reform demonstrates, using the analogy of "both hands tied," that the deteriorating structure of low-wage labor with few benefits constrains mothers in the market while TANF eviscerated public support for families (read poor mothers). They describe how the solitary wage replaced the family wage, with the burden falling on the shoulders of poor women. The retraction of public support for poor women coincides with the rise of the service sector, erosion of good jobs, and a weakened economy, leaving poor mothers to labor for solitary wages in bad jobs with little support for the reproductive labor necessary to raise children.

In a similar vein, sociologist Jill Weigt's (2006) study of poor mothers' efforts to meet the demands of work and family after TANF examines the intersection of dominant ideology and the material conditions of poverty and low-wage work. She shows how capitalist economic structures work hand in hand with individualist gendered ideology to create a no-win situation for poor mothers who blame themselves for their failure to live up to American family values ideals rather than see the deck is stacked against them by the structural origin of the constraints that make this unattainable. She sheds light on how the double bind for women of being accountable to two competing discourses—intensive mothering and the work ethic—helps subordinate mothers by diverting attention away from structural conditions and back to individual mother's ability to fulfill roles as good workers or good mothers. Both of these studies address crucial factors in understanding the lives of poor women and the structural constraints—both material and ideal—shaping work and family obligations for poor mothers after welfare reform. I agree that structural disadvantage is a major causal factor in outcomes for low-income women and see this work as essential in addressing the intersection of public discourse and powerful interests in poor women's lives. My work builds on this framework to include the moral dimension of social structural constraints and opportunities including the affective, emotional facets of choices about work and family and how these are tied to mothers' most cherished identities.

GENDERED SCHEMAS

Sarah Damaske's (2011) study of working women, similar to my study, analyzes how gendered schema continue to weigh heavily in shaping women's accounts of their family obligations even as most women work outside the home. In her analysis of women's accounts of their work force participation she finds that almost all state they work *for* their families. The *for the family* rhetoric used to explain women's growing participation in paid work frees women from being considered selfish for working outside the home for reasons of personal fulfillment. This conceptualization of gendered cultural schema portrays women across race and class as still accountable to gendered ideology in framing their work attachments whether they work continuously, take time off to raise families, or cycle in and out of paid work. As Damaske argues "The extraordinary entrance of women into the labor market need not undermine cultural expectations that women's work should be connected to family obligations, because ideals of caregiving have been expanded to include financial provisions" (2011, 162). Damaske shows the persistence of gender in shaping women's work and family choices, even as the practical activities of going to work and raising children undergo change. But her subjects appear to use *for the family* strategically in a retrospective accounting of their actions to align with their preferences. I see gendered schemas taking a more powerful role in guiding and shaping mother's preferences. Central to the context in which the low-income and poor women in my study make work and family choices post-welfare reform, women's paid work is associated with moral character, respect, and personal responsibility—masculine constructs of moral worth. Many mothers in my study also state they need to work to provide *for their families*. However, both paid work and the obligation to be there for children offer compelling visions of moral adult lives—exacerbating the tension for poor mothers to reconcile their commitments.

My understanding builds on sociologist Mary Blair-Loy's (2003) formulation of gendered schemas as powerful cultural structures or "devotional schemas" that guide work and family decisions. In addition to moral scripts, schemas are partially internalized shaping identities, desires, and emotions. Yet Blair-Loy studies women with tremendous resources—high-powered elite professional women—a strategy that provides a window into the gendered cultural structures guiding choices about work and family lives unexplained by financial need. Her study illustrates how even women who are presumed to have an unlimited array of choices are still bound by competing gendered definitions of a life worth living tied to identities as workers and/or mothers. Drawn to professional careers by powerful definitions of success and status, Blair-Loy's sample of women confront a set of culturally defined expectations that rule out motherhood's compatibility with undivided loyalty to the firm. Women within this elite group pulled in the direction of marriage, motherhood, and children soon discovered that the demands of careers were at odds (often painfully) with the call to intensive motherhood. Highly successful professional women may be able to contract out much of their daily family tasks and be relieved of the burden of economic uncertainty, but they could not escape being caught between competing gendered devotional schemas.

I find that the choices of less advantaged mothers, which by definition are more constrained, are also bounded by gendered cultural schemas shaping perceptions of the desirable, moral, and attainable, and assumptions about poor single mothers and welfare assistance. However, the cultural models defining poor and low-income women's paid work attachments differ from women who have made it by blasting through cultural barriers and achieving success in formerly male dominated professions. For example, mothers who "opt out" or are pushed out of demanding careers by workplace demands may suffer a loss of identity and experience conflict and disappointment in their inability to satisfy the demands of work and family, yet they are still lauded by society as good mothers for their self-sacrificing devotion to children. In contrast, for poor mothers today who would otherwise rely on public assistance, good mothers arrange for day care and go to work. For the women I study, moral dilemmas arise out of contradictions in enduring gendered cultural structures exacerbated by the conditions of poverty and demands of the welfare office. Moral dilemmas are most acute for women who hold traditional views on caring for children and face the elimination of public support to do so. Moral currency is earned through devotion to work rather than devotion to children.

THE END OF WELFARE

In relating the history of welfare, I focused on the moral and ideological foundations to illustrate how closely they are intertwined with gendered cultural structures shaping work and family attachments. As I frequently tell my students, you cannot understand U.S. welfare policy without considering how gender has been an integral factor in determining who is deserving of support and who is not. As we have seen throughout the book, today's welfare policy continues to provide a reflected image of gendered family and work relations.

When policy makers overhauled welfare, they argued that supporting poor women to remain at home and care for children was no longer feasible given the changing work and family attachments of the majority of mothers (Weaver 2000). We are now approaching the twentieth anniversary of the 1996 PRWORA which ended any entitlement or claim to cash assistance for poor mothers and children by abolishing AFDC and in its stead offering Temporary Assistance to Needy Families. TANF requires that recipients work, engage in approved activities to prepare for work, and/or actively look for work in exchange for cash benefits and services to support paid work. It transformed what Abramovitz (1996) termed a patriarchal "family ethic" for poor women where cash assistance replaced an absent male breadwinner. In the past, poor women were supported to stay at home and care for children in keeping with the gendered expectations of separate spheres which relegated men to providing and women to caregiving. PRWORA established a new family ethic for poor women who are unable or unwilling to marry their way into a family wage and out of poverty. The reformed family ethic mandates paid work, and mothers who refuse face a reduction in cash assistance in the form of sanctions. Thus, today as in the past welfare policy shapes both the material conditions under which poor women go to work and raise their families and reflects and reinforces dominant understandings of paid work and caregiving.

Today we can observe changes in work and family expectations in society as they are crystallized through work requirements in the implementation of TANF. Poor women's eligibility for cash assistance is now based on their participation in paid work *and* their responsibility for dependent children. Reflecting the salience of gender in the tension resulting from these changes, attempts to instill a universal "female breadwinner" ideology (Limoncelli 2002) compete with a universalized model of motherhood.

WORK COMMITMENT

The work commitment schema associates paid work with moral character, personal responsibility, and respect as a productive member of society. Work commitment defines a particular moral vision for poor women who rely on public assistance. We do not find the moral dimension of work commitment as a sign of character in gendered assumptions about middle-class work and motherhood—only poor single mothers are encouraged to pursue salvation in personal responsibility obtained through paid work.

A recurrent theme throughout the stories presented in this book is high regard for traditional family values coexisting with support for engaging in both paid work and childrearing—and the ambivalence that accompanies holding two competing views simultaneously. Most mothers agree with the majority of the U.S. public who also favor combining paid work with caring for children as the best decision for family life today (Parker 2012). Many mothers value work force participation for the benefits it brings to their families. They find work rewarding in providing positive examples to children and identity as productive members of society. For some women, paid work signals industriousness—aligning with the work ethic as a sign of virtue and recasting gendered assumptions about women's responsibility for childrearing. In this case, poor women reconfigure motherhood to include breadwinning in the definition of good mothering, thus reconciling the opposition between the demands of work and family commitment by redefining their responsibility to children via working outside the home. Yet challenges to work commitment's vision of self-sufficiency and the welfare office's promise of a better life, arise from dead-end jobs that do not bring independence nor compensate for time spent away from children (Lein, Schexnayder et al. 2007, Collins and Mayer 2010).

However, I also found similarities in how women perceive the non-economic rewards of paid work with studies of women's work and family lives (Damaske 2011, Hays 1996). Mothers report that paid work brought them self-esteem, opportunities for socialization, and relief from the tedium of child care. In short, the women in my study state that they derive many of the same benefits from paid work as others. A major point of departure however, is that for many of the poor and low-income mothers whose stories I share in this book, working outside the home provides a moral identity distinct from assumptions about welfare mothers.

Most interviewees report that working outside the home is something mothers *should* do and expressed a desire to engage in meaningful work as long as it does not threaten their obligation as mothers. The rub for poor mothers is demands from the welfare office in promoting paid work over child care clash head on with their primary duty to care for children "first and foremost" in their capacity as women and mothers. Thus, work outside the home, particularly for mothers of small children, appears to threaten the well-being of children and contradict the most powerful source of meaning in the majority of mothers' lives: motherhood and the ability to "be there" for children. The dilemma for mothers is reconciling these contradictions.

FAMILY COMMITMENT

The family commitment schema demands that mothers devote themselves to their precious children, and children's interest must trump all other commitments. Family commitment emerges as a particularly gripping and stable cultural model. With its deep ties to naturalized understandings of women's competency to care and nurture it preserves essentialist understandings of biological differences between men and women. The family commitment schema thus reinforces the gendered division of labor between men and women as a moral imperative, the natural order of things and the "way it has always been." This seemingly unassailable correspondence with the gendered social order seamlessly knits family commitment's vision of a meaningful life to individual's sense of identity and self-worth (Lorber 1994).

Mothers who embrace traditional gendered norms while resisting the practices of the welfare office claim a moral resource in their status as mothers and obligation to children. In contrast to welfare policy's emphasis on working outside the home as transforming women into responsible citizens, respondents say that they could not justify leaving children in someone else's care, because they were *responsible* for their children. Prioritizing paid work would contradict mothers' and the U.S. public's deeply held conviction that motherhood and caring for children *are* the most important jobs in the world

Yet to say that women find moral resources in their identities as mothers is not to suggest that defining one's life through family commitment's demands necessarily benefits poor mothers. To the contrary, women who resist welfare office demands find a shrinking social safety net to support their families, and even though as Collins and Mayer (2010) remind us, mothers enter the workforce with "both hands tied," their well-being depends increasingly on market work. The alternatives, as women defend their right to mother their children in challenging workfare welfare policies, are limited; options include reliance on families, child support, and male partners. Contrary to conventional wisdom, poor women may find their chances for self-sufficiency further compromised through partnering with men when relationships devolve into traditional gendered roles. A study by sociologist Jill Weigt (2010) on women's outcomes several years after leaving welfare found that heterosexual partnerships while at times beneficial, also negatively impacted women's health, investment in work and educational goals, as well as their own safety and that of their children. Rather than bring stability, a return to traditional relationships could potentially undermine poor mother's ability to reach and maintain self-sufficiency and independence. The solution then is not a return to dependence of mothers on male providers—both undesirable in today's society for both men and women and as a practical matter out of reach for most families.

AT THE WELFARE OFFICE

Belief that welfare assistance has a negative effect on the work ethic of the poor has endured for centuries (Katz 1996, Somers and Block 2005). Conservatives believe it rewards the lazy and erodes the work ethic, liberals see it as punitive and inadequate, and the women who rely upon it find it degrading and demoralizing (Katz 1996). Respondents in general, share these views—albeit with important caveats. Many characterize welfare recipients as lazy and undeserving of support; others are more sympathetic, but almost all distinguish their own needs as justified and not comparable to others who continue to "sponge off the state."

As mothers' stories indicate, the "problem" with welfare is not erosion of the work ethic or a lack of family values. Respondents in general share the valorization of the work ethic, yet at the same time they challenge the legitimacy of work requirements that push women into low-paying jobs. Working outside the home, for some respondents, distinguishes them from others who are not trying to better themselves. However, the divide between ideals of independence and autonomy and respondent's ability to achieve this through paid work is a major point of contention and resistance to welfare policy.

Some mothers employ alternative resources to resist welfare policy demands that they enter low-wage jobs. Educational attainment secures immediate financial resources in the form of loans and, in rare instances, grants. The future these mothers envision once they complete their educational goals offers self-sufficiency and the dignity of a job that will support their children. Responsibility to children includes attending college with long-range goals of supporting children financially and becoming responsible members of society. Welfare policies that promote independence and self-sufficiency but thwart mothers efforts to accomplish this through increased education seem punitive, contributing to resistance by mothers to caseworkers' attempts to send them into the paid work force.

The most intense expression of resistance comes not unexpectedly when the opposition between work and family manifests itself in work requirements that mothers see as hampering their ability to care for children. Survey data affirm mothers' lack of faith in the system, showing that mothers who received TANF are less likely to support work requirements for single mothers of small children. When mothers enter the welfare office and seek assistance for their families, they confront the paradox explored in this book as a real, tangible component of their ability to provide for and care for children—shaping their experience in ways that differ starkly from the day-to-day lives of most mothers. Only mothers on welfare hear regularly that their children would be better off if they got a job, thus indicating their paid work outside the home holds greater value to their children than the unpaid work women are called upon to do in their capacity as mothers. However, the ultimate betrayal comes from demands that mothers go to work when infants reach three months of age, providing the starkest example that the welfare office does not share mothers' understanding of their obligations and is not there to help them or their families. It places the welfare office on the wrong side of a moral debate over widely shared values recognized by all of society.

The requirements of the welfare system align with the responsibility and demonstration of character in work commitment but compete with the deeply gendered provisions of family commitment. When mothers feel caught between conflicting demands, *requiring* paid work outside the home from the perspective of poor mothers can be interpreted as obstructing women's ability to fulfill their obligation as mothers. Rather than motivating women to work in the best interests of their children, work requirements, when defined through family commitment, become an assault on responsibility as mothers.

PUBLIC POLICY

Judith Levine brings an important issue to light for policy makers in her book, *Ain't No Trust* (2013). She argues that distrust impacts low-income mothers' work and family choices, and widespread distrust among low-income mothers influences their actions in ways counter to the goals of welfare reform. As Levine argues, "If we really want to understand low-income mothers' welfare, employment, and family choices and outcomes, we need to look beyond the mothers themselves to the social context in which mothers find themselves" (2013, 10). Levine sees distrust as largely constraining as she details the different social and cultural environment in which mothers develop distrust. Distrust—exacerbated by the contexts shaping poor women's lives including interaction with caseworkers—hamstrings the goals of welfare-reform policies. Focusing on changing individuals rather than the structural constraints that cause distrust in the lives of the poor limits the effectiveness of policies. Thus distrust may emerge when low-income mothers do not see caseworkers as understanding or taking their interests to heart, or in the case of existing (preemptive distrust) resulting from past experience in disadvantaged communities. I focus on gendered cultural models, rather than distrust, but I find Levine's argument compelling in pointing out the unintended consequences for policy makers when they ignore the social cultural forces that shape low-income mothers' understandings in choices about work, family, and welfare. Levine argues that distrust hampers welfare agencies' ability to move mothers into jobs, because among other factors poor mothers do not see evidence (either from their own experience of that of others) that welfare office personnel share their interests.

Many others have written extensively on public policy suggestions to alleviate the difficulty of low-income and poor women in meeting work and family responsibilities. Improving the economic conditions under which low-income women work and raise their families is an important component in assisting low-income families. Most women leaving welfare exit into low-wage jobs where conflict between work and family is further exacerbated by jobs that are less likely to have "family friendly" polices such as paid sick days and vacation (Heymann 2000, Collins and Mayer 2010).[4] Studies on low-income women raising children post-welfare reform suggest that generous work supports and good jobs are essential as part of social changes needed to allow low-income women to meet the demands of both paid work and motherhood (Seefeldt 2008, Weigt 2010). A major hurdle in addressing the needs of all women is that overall the United States provides fewer social provisions for families with children compared to other nations, leaving solutions to meeting the demands of work and family to private individuals rather than adequate public support for working families (Budig, Misra, and Boeckmann 2012). But as Levine demonstrates and we learned from the stories throughout this book, policies must be accompanied by greater understanding of low-income women's lives. Including the broadly shared moral and cultural forces that differentially shape their work and family decisions.

MEETING THE NEEDS OF FAMILIES

We should do more to help working families. But, we are likely to find this task even more difficult if our solutions do not account for the social, cultural and moral context within which poor and working-class mothers make choices. Maureen Perry-Jenkins's (2012) study of working-class mothers finds that in contrast to fitting one's preferences to the options determined by class position women who "have to" work for wages when their ideal options would include staying home with children face spillover effects caused by the mismatch between their preferences and the constraints of low-wage jobs. As her study suggests, explanations dividing mothers into those who choose to work or those who have to work are too simplistic to capture the complexity of women's work and family lives whether married middle-class professional mothers, working-class mothers, or poor and low-income women reliant on low-wage jobs and/or public assistance.

Anne Marie Slaughter (2012) commenting on women's work lives, states that gender is still embedded in our brains as it organizes the workplace in ways disadvantaging women, particularly those who wish to combine paid work with motherhood. I agree, but even more intractably, gender is embedded in our hearts shaping the most fundamental choices people make about caring for children and providing for families. Understanding why meeting the demands of work and family generates more stress than the balance families desire requires understanding the gendered cultural structures that generate work and family conflict for low-income and working-class women and their relationship to middle-class women, who also confront conflict between the demands of work and family. Attention to the work and family choices of low-income and working-class women and more advantaged women—commonalities and difference—can advance our understanding of the enduring moral salience of gender in shaping the lives of women.

The reality of today's work and family relations—where a majority of mothers combine paid work and caregiving responsibilities—brings increasingly widespread acceptance of women working outside the home. Advocates for working families argue that it is time to recognize that for most working parents, conflict between work and family boils down to the lack of real social support for families working for wages and doing the important work of caring for children not whether mothers should stay home (Coontz 2013). I agree. But, calling attention to the need to do more to help all families meet their obligations to provide and care does not put an end to the moral, ideological, and cultural struggle over gendered expectations for women and mothers, or the end of the struggle within the hearts and minds of poor and low-income women themselves. Even low-income mothers choose to "opt out." However, the social conditions in which they make their choices, the devotional schemas that shape the meaning of their options and their identities as worker and mothers differ from those mothers whose lives inform contemporary understandings of work family conflict.

Rather than portray low-income women on and off welfare as either villains or victims, the stories of mothers in this book illustrate how decisions about paid work and caring for children are filtered through broadly shared definitions of work and family life tied to moral identities as workers and mothers—facets of low-income women's work and family lives obscured in the contemporary work-life debate. Addressing the needs of all women requires attention to the moral and ideological dimension of work and family commitments as well as the economic conditions that differentiate the experience of poor and low income in work and family decisions.

NOTES

1. The influence of gendered cultural structures can be seen in Groysber and Abrahams (2014) article in *The Harvard Business Review* on managing work-life demands including family life for executive men and women. Men were more likely to emphasize provider roles, whereas women were concerned with providing role models for children, especially daughters. Women interviewees also turned to cultural models of motherhood in saying the hardest part of reconciling work life demands was feelings of guilt for missing out on aspects of children's lives. Also see the comments from professional mothers who stayed home to raise children in response to Stephanie Coontz's 2013 column in the *New York Times* "Why Gender Equality Stalled" about changes in women and men's work and family lives. Several commentators described the choice to leave careers as one of self-sacrificing, self-fulfilling devotion to children.

2. See Judith Levine's (2013), *Ain't No Trust: How Bosses, Boyfriends, and Bureaucrats Fail Low-Income Mothers and Why It Matters*. Also Child Trends (2013) report on class differences in center-based day care.

3. See (Edin and Lein 1997, Clampet-Lundquist et al. 2004, London, Scott, Edim, and Hunter 2004) for studies on work and family issues for low-income women on and off welfare.

4. See (Brauner and Loprest 1999, Cancian and Meyer 2000, Corcoran et al. 2000, Loprest 2001, Seefeldt 2008), for studies on women leaving welfare for low-wage jobs.

Acknowledgments

This book would not be possible without the assistance of many individuals. I am deeply indebted to the participants in the Women's Programs for sharing their experiences with me. I wish to thank my colleague Michael Harrod for his helpful comments, advice, and generous gift of time throughout the course of writing this book. I am grateful to my colleagues Ruthi Erdman and Sandra Martinez for their comments and suggestions on several chapters. I also wish to thank Holly Alexander for her expertise in editing the introductory chapters.

This book is based on my dissertation research at Washington State University and I am grateful for the advice and support of my committee, especially my chair Mary Blair-Loy, Julie Kmec, and Gregory Hooks.

For their generous gift of time and expertise in survey research, I wish to thank Danna Moore and Ken Miller of the Social & Economic Science Research Center (SESRC). I also extend thanks to Chris Blodgett of the Washington State University Children and Families Institute, and the director and staff members of the Women's Programs in Spokane Washington.

A National Science Foundation Dissertation Improvement Grant SES-0327030 2003–2004, supported research for the study. Quotations and revised paragraphs from my previously published article "Morality and Work Family Conflict in the Lives of Poor and Low-Income Women," *The Sociological Quarterly* (50): 2009 are integrated into chapters 3, 4, 5 and used with permission.

Methodological Appendix

I undertook this study to explore what I refer to as the paradox in the work-family debate regarding the work and family commitments of low-income and poor mothers after the restructuring of the welfare system under PRWORA. The issue of work-family conflict resonates with the U.S. public, but much of the focus is on the work and family lives of married middle-class and professional mothers in dual-earner households. Previous studies and commentary tell us a great deal about both the practical demands and stresses of families being "torn" between work and family demands and navigating new expectations about men's and women's roles. We know less about mothers who *have to* work and the moral and emotional forces shaping their decisions about providing and caring for children. I use the case of workfare welfare policy and a sample of low-income women to analyze low-income women's self understanding and actions and the relationship among broadly shared cultural models of paid work, family responsibilities, and welfare assistance for poor women and children.

In this study, rather than having to choose whether to rely on survey data, with which I could do quantitative analysis, *or* to gather interview data where I could hear from women themselves, I combined both qualitative and quantitative methods: in-depth interviews combined with survey responses. So in addition to analyzing rich qualitative narratives, I was able to expand analyses to quantitative data and compare the patterns in the interview data with survey responses. Survey data is widely used in social science research and is valuable for investigating patterns and analyzing relationships across a larger chunk of the population of interest. Yet, given the questions I was interesting in exploring, a strictly quantitative study could not capture the emotions, complexity, and ambivalence that characterize women's work and family commitments. This became clear early on. For example, surveys were returned with handwritten notes in the margins, or accompanied by letters and notes telling me more about the details of respondents' lives. Several women called me to talk about difficult circumstances in their past and current situations. Women also shared success stories about children, education, newfound independence, and relationships. Open responses from surveys included thank-you notes for asking these questions about poor women's work and family lives.

SAMPLE POPULATION

All participants resided in a large, predominantly white (89.5 percent), working-class Northwest city. The city's service agencies serve both the clientele within the city and also residents of the rural communities in several surrounding states. The sample for this study includes rural and urban residents and variation across age, education, reliance on public assistance, and marital status. Many studies on poor and working-class women and public assistance programs focuses on minority women. Some of the best work in poverty research points out the racialized gendered nature of poverty and how this has shaped public assistance programs for poor women and children (Abramovitz 1998, Mink 1998, Gordon 1994). However, public discourse and media depictions associating poverty with racial minorities have contributed to the perception of families that rely on welfare as a largely homogeneous group, consisting of young, black, never married single mothers who refuse to work (Schram 2000). The predominantly white population of the Northwest city where this study took place avoids this tendency of associating work and family patterns of impoverished women exclusively with urban ghetto communities.

Subjects for both survey data and interviews were recruited from women enrolled or who had been previously enrolled in one of three programs consisting of workshops, intensive pre-employment training and comprehensive services to low-income women undergoing major transitions in their lives and preparing to enter or reenter the workforce in the years 1996 to 2004. The three programs include young, low-income single mothers, "displaced homemakers" (long-term homemakers either divorced, widowed, separated, or who had a disabled spouse, who were making the transition from home to the workforce), and low-income women who expressed a desire to enter nontraditional jobs.

The three programs—labeled collectively Women's Programs—were set up to provide comprehensive services to individuals re-entering the job market or returning to school. The Women's Programs recruited participants through the community college district website and extensive outreach throughout the community: newspaper advertising, presentations at community organizations, Head Start programs, fliers at food banks, homeless shelters, referrals from social welfare agencies, and referrals from former program participants. These programs serve women with incomes up to 175 percent of the federal poverty level, women who receive Social Security disability income, the underemployed, and women who earn minimum wage.

I selected this sample to capture some of the diversity and variation among low-income women and to avoid a sample that is overly representative of women with severe obstacles to paid work and family disorganization, thus biasing my sample in ways that reinforce stereotypes of impoverished women. In stating this, my intent is not to dismiss the considerable disadvantage of poor women on or off welfare compared to others, but I also wanted to avoid portraying poor women as overwhelmingly victimized by circumstances beyond their control. A substantial minority of women in my sample did face formidable obstacles to their ability to work and care for their children: substance abuse, mental and physical disabilities, and domestic violence in addition to severe financial constraints. Overall the sample included a diverse array of low-income women who vary by age, marital status, number of children, financial stability, history of public assistance, employment, education, and rural and urban residency.

Bear in mind that this sample also contains some biases worth noting. Because it is limited to women who have enrolled in a training program, the sample is biased toward women with some ability, motivation, or impetus (whether personal or institutional) to attend a job skills and training program. Although not everyone in the sample had to complete the program, and some may have enrolled and never attended, it is likely to exclude the most disadvantaged groups of impoverished women. This would include women without phones, with severe mental disorders, substance abuse, domestic violence, or other formidable obstacles to enrollment in a basic skills program. Within the sample population, women with greater residential mobility who were initially included in the sample were less likely to be contacted and thus able to respond. Mail returns and disconnected and wrong phone numbers occurred throughout the data collection process. Therefore, the study is over representative of low-income women with more stable residential mobility.

Interview Process

Interview data are semi-structured interviews of thirty-nine women conducted from June 2003 through May 2004. (See table A.1.) I used three primary recruitment strategies. (1) I made initial contact with respondents by phone. In this phone call, I explained the nature of the study and asked respondents if they wished to participate in an interview. Twenty-five participants were contacted this way. (2) Seven respondents were selected through completion of a self-administered survey that asked them to return a card if they wished to participate in an interview. (3) Seven others were currently enrolled in a class and invited to take part in the study. All respondents were offered $25.00 to complete interviews.

At the beginning of each interview, I told participants that there were no right or wrong answers to the questions that were to follow. I was interested in their experiences, perceptions, and views on work participation and caring for children and programs that support or constrain their ability to do so. The interviews were open-ended and semi-structured around several major topics: experience and views regarding child care and workforce participation, family background, expectations about men and women's work and family commitments, program participation, and views on welfare reform. I wanted to ensure that I covered basic background information and topics related to work and family life but also keep interviews largely unstructured in that women were free to discuss any area of work and family life they felt was important and that I should hear. I modified the interview schedule through pretesting of seven households to allow for greater flexibility on the part of the respondent to describe their experience, yet still maintain the structure necessary to compare across groups and complement the survey questionnaire data.

I continued the interview process until theoretical saturation was reached and interviews offered no new information that required investigation (Glaser and Strauss 1967). Interviews ranged from one hour to three hours in length, were tape-recorded with participant's permission, transcribed verbatim, and coded into appropriate categories. All participants' names are pseudonyms, and any identifying information has been removed to protect confidentiality.

Most of the interviews took place in respondents' homes with the exception of eight interviews where that was not possible for various reasons. Two were conducted over the phone, due to illness, and six were completed in the lounge area at the training center. Two of these six respondents were living in transitional shelters and preferred not to schedule the interview there due to the lack of privacy. Two others also cited the lack of privacy in their living arrangements that they felt would hamper the interview process.

After each interview I noted the neighborhood, a description of the home, the physical and personal characteristics of the respondent and any interaction with children and other family members or individuals that were present or arrived during the interview process. I met many small children. I also met many family pets: dogs and cats and, in one household, a young pet pig left when an adult daughter moved away. The presence of small children generally entailed setting up activities that would keep them occupied, most often a video to watch, some type of food or drink offering, and/or coloring books or playing with a child during the interview. At one home, I followed a two year old out the front door into the parking lot of the apartment and brought

Respondent	ON TANF	Ever AFDC	Marital status	Race/Ethnicity	Age	Education	Employed	No. children
1.	N	Y	Married	Am. Indian	32	Some college	N	5
2.	Y	Y	Divorced	W	49	Some college	N	4
3.	N	N	Widowed	W	26	Some college	N	2
4.	N	N	Cohab	B	43	GED	Y	3
5.	Y	Y	Separated	W	41	Some college	N	4
6.	N	Y	Divorced	W	38	HS deg	Y	2
7.	N	N	Separated	W	43	Some college	Y	2
8.	N	Y	Divorced	W	33	HS deg	N	1
9.	Y	Y	Divorced	W	42	HS deg	Y	1
10.	N	N	Separated	W	40	AA	N	3
11.	N	N	Divorced	W	30	HS deg	Y	2
12.	N	Y	Divorced	W	49	vocational	N	1
13.	N	N	Married	W	52	vocational	Y	1
14.	Y	Y	Cohab	W	32	No degree	N	3
15.	N	Y	Cohab	W	23	HS deg	N	2
16.	Y	Y	Unmarried	W	23	HS deg	N	1
17.	N	Y	Cohab	W	23	HS deg	N	1
18.	N	Y	Unmarried	W	23	HS deg	N	2
19.	N	Y	Separated	W	31	GED	N	2
20.	Y	Y	Unmarried	W	26	HS deg	N	1
21.	Y	Y	Unmarried	W	33	No degree	Y	1

22.	N	Y	Unmarried	W	23	Some college	Y	1
23.	Y	Y	Unmarried	W	28	No degree	N	2
24.	N/GAU*	Y	Divorced	Am. Indian	29	No degree	N	3
25.	Y	Y	Unmarried	W	24	No degree	N	1
26.	Y	Y	Unmarried	W	22	Some college	N	1
27.	N/GAU	Y	Divorced	W	42	Some college	Y	1
28.	N	Y	Unmarried	W	24	Some college	N	2
29.	Y	Y	Unmarried	W	24	GED	Y	2
30.	N	Y	Unmarried	W	40	Some college	Y	2
31.	N	N	Cohab	Biracial B/W	54	Some college	Y	3
32.	N	N	Married	W	30	No degree	N	1
33.	N	N	Married	W	35	HS deg	Y	2
34.	N	Y	Divorced	W	48	Some college	Y	3
35.	N	N	Married	W	57	HS deg	Y	1
36.	N	N	Widowed	W	62	Some college	N	3
37.	Y	N	Divorced	W	35	HS deg	N	2
38.	Y	Y	Unmarried	B	23	No degree	N	1
39.	N	N	Divorced	W	49	Some college	Y	1

* GAU = General Assistance

him back to his grandmother when he ran outside after older children left the door ajar. At other times the interviews were scheduled during naps or while children attended school. Older children who appeared were generally introduced and then directed to other activities in another part of the home.

The in-depth interviews allowed me to gain far greater insights into the topic and more complex understandings than I would have been able to gain through survey data alone. The interviews covered basic background information and topics related to work and family life but were largely unstructured in that women were free to discuss any area of work and family life that they felt was important and that they felt I should hear.

Interview data provide a lens into the broad cultural frameworks that shape and guide the work and family decisions of this sample of low-income women (Lamont 2000). Although interviews may elicit socially desirable responses, at the same time they illuminate the gendered moral and emotional forces that shape the work and family decisions of low-income women— the issue I was interested in exploring. Thus, mothers' interpretations of appropriate models of work and motherhood are useful in documenting the shared understandings that influence action (Blair-Loy 2001). The findings in this study are not assumed to be generalizable to other populations. However, the patterns uncovered here can inform knowledge about the particular contours of work and family decisions from the experience of a group of women who more often occupy the margins of work and family debate than the center as they do in the analyses presented here.

SURVEY DESIGN AND SAMPLE

I designed the self-administered mail survey to supplement the qualitative component and allow analysis of whether themes and associations that appear in the qualitative sample are mirrored in the quantitative sample, net of relevant control variables. Including the survey in this project was a means of comparing the insights or theories developed in the qualitative component across a larger group. The larger sample and fixed variables in the questionnaire also allowed for descriptive statistical analyses, inappropriate in analysis of a small qualitative sample.

Survey Instrument

The survey data include information on demographic data, life history, current and past work experience and attitudes and practices surrounding gender, family life, work, and welfare. The first section of the survey asked questions about respondents' experience in the Women's Programs. These questions were developed in collaboration with the manager of the Women's Programs with the goal of gathering data on former program participants for use by the Women's Center in evaluating their programs. This initial section included open-ended questions about perceived achievements and road-blocks encountered during respondent's program participation and additional skills and educational training attained after completing the program.

The second section of the survey asked about employment status, wages and job characteristics. These questions were developed from prior survey research, including additional questions about employment, child care, future educational and occupational goals, psychological well-being, views on paid work, family, and welfare dependence. The questions were also informed by the qualitative interviews. In addition, I led a focus group with former graduates of the programs to discuss the survey questionnaire in terms of how receptive they were to the content of questions and the overall relevance of the project to low-income women's lives. The mail survey was conducted from September 2003 through May 2004.

Administering the Survey

I used the Tailored Design Method of Survey Research (TDM) (Dillman 2000) in designing and administering the survey questionnaire. Although the TDM yields consistently high response rates in general populations, studies of poor and low-income women pose considerable difficulties due to more transient living arrangements (Groves and Couper 2002). In the sampling process, I oversampled the more recent program participants in the cohorts from 1999-2004 because these groups had more recent addresses and phone numbers and were more likely to be found than the older cohorts. (See table A.2 for descriptive statistics.)

The initial survey mailing resulted in one-third of the surveys returned as undeliverable. I used several additional strategies to address this issue and to increase response rates. These included attempted phone contacts for non-respondents, adding more recent cohorts to the sample, and administering the survey in person to the most recent cohorts in the program.

The phone contacts were of little value in increasing the response rate of the initial sample due to problems with wrong and disconnected numbers. Although low response rates remained a problem with the more recent cohorts, more recent information reduced the number of mail returns and dis-connected and wrong phone numbers. The total sample numbers 909, with 257 completed surveys, yielding a raw response rate of 29 percent and a response rate of 41 percent after adjusting for mail returns and non-eligible respondents. The response rate compares favorably with response rates of mail surveys on low-income women leaving welfare (Acs and Loprest 2002).

Table A.2. Descriptive Statistics of Survey Sample

Descriptive statistics	Percent	Mean
Received welfare after 1997	47.64	
Never received TANF welfare	44.88	
Employed	54.94	
Divorced/Separated	45.02	
Married	23.51	
Cohabiting	6.37	
Widow	11.55	
Never married	14.68	
Age		41
High school diploma	84.05	
Age children (range two months–twenty-six years)		10.4
Income category 1=10,000 or less 2=10,001 to 15,000 3=15,001 to 25,000 4=25,001 to 35,000 5=35,001 to 45,000 6=45,001 or more		2.57
Race/ethnicity		
White	81.32	
Black	2.0	
Hispanic	2.8	
Native American	7.6	
Asian	3.2	
Other	4.8	
Number of cases	257	

QUANTITATIVE ANALYSIS

Responses from the survey questionnaire were analyzed using Stata statistical analysis software and coded into appropriate variables for quantitative analyses. This data, as a supplement to the interview data, forms the basis of the quantitative findings.

Dependent Variables

Dependent variables were constructed using factor analysis to group different variables (survey questions addressing similar concepts) into a single measure of views on paid work and family attachments and welfare policies. The first dependent variable (column two, table 6.4) indicates orientation toward the *work commitment* schema's definitions of the compatibility of mothers' paid work and child care. For this outcome, I combined responses to three statements in the survey that measure views on women's workforce participation. "Working for pay is one of the most important things a mother can do for her family," "When a mother works outside the home, she sets a good example for her children," and "A working mother can establish just as warm and secure a relationship with her children as a mother who does not work," (alpha = .72). Higher values indicate favorable views on combining work outside the home with child care.

The second outcome (column three, table 6.4) variable denotes orientation toward *family commitment's* definition of children and mothers obligations. This is derived from combining five statements, where agreement indicates more traditional views on men's and women's work and family roles. "Taking care of the home and raising children is the most important job for a woman," "When children are born, mothers should not work outside the home," "It is better for everyone if the man in the household has a job outside the home and the woman takes care of the family," "Preschool children suffer when their mothers work outside the home," and "Mothers should not work full-time when their youngest child is under age 5," (alpha = .79).

The final and third dependent variable (column four in table 6.4) measures support for *workfare welfare policy*. I combine three statements, "Women with young children who receive welfare should be required to work for pay," "Welfare makes people work less than they would if there was not a welfare system," and "Women with young children who receive welfare should be able to stay home and care for their children," (alpha = .63). The last statement in the scale is reverse coded. Higher values on this measure indicate support for workfare welfare policies requiring paid work in exchange for welfare benefits.

Independent Variables

Several independent variable measures are included to identify individual and demographic characteristics predicting views on work outside the home, traditional family, and welfare. Marital status is among several individual-level characteristics relevant to views on paid work and child care in addition to education, age, employment, income, and presence of a preschool child in the home.

Marital status is measured with four dummy variables coded (1, 0). The categories are married, never married, and cohabiting. The omitted category is divorced/separated. Whether a mother is employed or not is also an important factor in consideration of work and family attachments. *Employment* is measured by a dummy variable (employed = 1, unemployed = 0). *Age* is measured in years. A dummy variable controls for the *presence of a young child* in the home (1 = child five years old and younger in the home, 0 = children older than five years of age).

Women without a high school diploma are far more likely to be living in poverty and not work compared to others. In this sample, 85 percent of mothers had a high school diploma or GED. Further, women with some post-secondary training or educational attainment are more likely to be working and less likely to rely on welfare compared to others. *Educational attainment* is measured with a dummy variable (1 = high school diploma or higher, 0 = less than high school education). I also include a measure of *work satisfaction* derived from survey question "The work I do outside the home is one of the most satisfying parts of my life." Higher values indicate agreement. Finally, to measure the impact of receiving public assistance I include a dummy variable (coded 1, 0) for whether the respondent received cash welfare benefits under TANF (1 = receiving benefits after TANF was implemented).

References

Abramovitz, Mimi. 1996. *Regulating the Lives of Women: Social Welfare Policy from Colonial Times to the Present.* Boston: South End Press.

Acs, Gregory and Pamela Loprest. 2002. "Studies of Welfare Leavers: Data, Methods, and Contributions to the Policy Process." Pp. 387–414 in *Studies of Welfare Populations: Data Collection and Research Issues: Panel on Data and Methods for Measuring the Effects of Changes in Social Welfare Programs,* edited by Robert A. Moffitt, Constance F. Citro, and Michele Ver Ploeg. Washington, DC: National Academy Press.

Allen, Amy. 2012. "The Mommy Wars Redux." *New York Times,* May 27. Accessed March 15, 2014. http://Opinionator.Blogs.Nytimes.Com/2012/05/27/The-Mommy-Wars-Redux-A-False-Conflict/?_Php=True&_Type=Blogs&_R=0.

Belkin, Lisa. 2003. "The Opt-Out Revolution." *New York Times,* October 26.

Bernard, Jesse. 1981. "The Good Provider Role: Its Rise And Fall." *American Psychologist* 36 (1):1–12.

Bernard, Tara Siegel. 2013. "Choosing Child Care When You Go Back to Work." *New York Times,* November 22. Accessed December 5, 2013. http://Www.Nytimes.Com/2013/11/23/Your-Money/Choosing-Child-Care-When-You-Go-Back-To-Work.Html?_R=0.

Bianchi, Suzanne, John P. Robinson, and Melissa A. Milkie. 2006. *Changing Rhythms of American Family Life.* New York: Russell Sage Foundation.

Blair-Loy, Mary. 2001. "Cultural Constructions of Family Schemas: The Case of Women Executives." *Gender & Society* 15: 687–709.

———. 2003. *Competing Devotions: Career and Family among Women Executives.* Cambridge, MA: Harvard University Press.

Blankenhorn, David. 1995. *Fatherless America: Confronting Our Most Urgent Social Problem.* New York: Basic Books.

Boris, Eileen. 1998. "When Work Is Slavery," *Social Justice* 25 (Spring): 28–46.

Boushey, Heather and Bethney Gundersen. 2001. *When Work Just Isn't Enough: Measuring Hardships Faced by Families after Moving from Welfare to Work.* Washington, DC: Economic Policy Institute.

Brauner, Sarah and Pamela Loprest. 1999. *Where are They Now? What States' Studies of People Who Left Welfare Tell Us.* Washington, DC: The Urban Institute.

Budig, Michelle and Paula England. 2001. "The Wage Penalty for Motherhood." *American Sociological Review* 66:204–225

Budig, Michelle J., Joya Misra, and Irene Boeckmann. 2012. "The Motherhood Penalty In Cross-National Perspective: The Importance Of Work–Family Policies And Cultural Attitudes." *Social Politics* 19 (2) (Summer):163–193. doi:10.1093/Sp/Jxs006.

Cancian, Maria and Daniel R. Meyer. 2000. "Work after Welfare: Women's Work Effort, Occupation, and Economic Well-Being." *Social Work Research* 24 (2):69–86.

Cancian, Maria, Robert Haveman, Daniel R. Meyer, and Barbara Wolfe. 2002. *Before and After TANF: The Economic Well-Being of Women Leaving Welfare.* Madison, WI: Institute For Research On Poverty.

Child Trends. 2013. "Child Care Indicators And Trends." April 2013 *Child Trends Data Bank.* http://www.childtrends.org/wp-content/uploads/2012/07/21_Child_Care.pdf.

Clampet-Lundquist, Susan, Kathryn Edin, Andrew London, Ellen Scott, and Vicki Hunter. 2004. "'Making a Way out of No Way': How Mothers Meet Basic Family Needs While Moving from Welfare to Work." In *Work Family Challenges for Low-Income Parents and Their Children,* edited by Anne. C. Crouter and Allen Booth, 203–42, Mahwah, NJ: Lawrence Erlbaum Associates.

Cohen, Philip N. and Suzanne Bianchi. 1999. "Marriage, Children, and Women's Employment: What Do We Know?" *Monthly Labor Review* 122 (12):22–31.

Cohn, D'Vera, Gretchen Livingston, and Wendy Wang. 2014. "After Decades of Decline, a Rise in Stay-at-Home Mothers." Washington, DC: Pew Research Center.

Collins, Jane L. and Victoria Mayer. 2010. *Both Hands Tied: Welfare Reform and the Race to the Bottom in the Low-Wage Labor Market.* Chicago: University of Chicago Press.

Collins, Patricia Hill. 1996. *Black Feminist Thought: Knowledge, Consciousness, and the Politics of Empowerment.* New York: Routledge.

Coltrane, Scott. 1996. *Family Man: Fatherhood, Housework, and Gender Equity.* New York: Oxford University Press.

Coontz, Stephanie. 1997. *The Way We Really Are: Coming to Terms with America's Changing Families.* New York: Basic Books.

———. 2006. "Myth of the Opt-Out Mom." *Christian Science Monitor,* March 30. Accessed February 6, 2012. http://www.csmonitor.com/2006/0330/p09s01-coop.html.

———. 2013. "Why Gender Equality Stalled." *New York Times,* February 26. Accessed March 1, 2013. http://www.nytimes.com/2013/02/17/opinion/sunday/why-gender-equality-stalled.html?pagewanted=all&_r=0.

Corcoran, Mary, Sandra K. Danziger, Ariel Kalil, and Kristin S. Seefeldt. 2000. "How Welfare Reform Is Affecting Women's Work." *Annual Review Of Sociology* 26:241–69.

Crittenden, Anne. 2001. *The Price of Motherhood.* New York: Metropolitan Books.

Damaske, Sarah. 2011. *For the Family? How Class and Gender Shape Women's Work.* New York, New York: Oxford University Press.

Deutsch, Francine M. 1999. *Halving It All: How Equally Shared Parenting Works.* Cambridge: Harvard University Press.

Dillman, Don A. 2000. *Mail and Internet Surveys: The Tailored Design Method. 2nd Edition.* New York: John Wiley and Sons.

Dodson, Lisa and Ellen Bravo. 2005. "When There Is No Time or Money: Work, Family, and Community Lives of Low-Income Families." In *Unfinished Work: Building Equality and Democracy in an Era of Working Families,* edited by Jody Heymann and Christopher Beem, 122–55. New York: The New Press.

Douglas, Susan J. and Meredith W. Michaels. 2004. *The Mommy Myth: The Idealization of Motherhood and How It Has Undermined All Women.* New York: Free Press.

Edin, Kathryn and Laura Lein. 1997. *Making Ends Meet: How Single Mothers Survive Welfare and Low-Wage Work.* New York: Russell Sage.

Edin, Kathryn and Maria Kefalas. 2005. *Promises I Can Keep: Why Poor Women Put Motherhood before Marriage.* Berkeley: University Of California Press.

Edin, Kathryn and Timothy J. Nelson. 2013. *Doing the Best I Can: Fatherhood in the Inner City.* Berkeley: University of California Press.

England, Paula. 2005. "Emerging Theories Of Care Work." *American Journal Of Sociology* 31:381-399.

Epstein, Cynthia Fuchs. 1988. *Deceptive Distinctions: Sex, Gender and the Social Order.* New Haven: Yale University Press; New York: Russell Sage Foundation.

Floyd, Ife and Liz Schott. 2013. "TANF Cash Benefits Continue to Lose Value," October 21. *Center on Budget and Policy Priorities.* Accessed November 1, 2013. http://www.cbpp.org/files/10-21-13tanf.pdf

Folbre, Nancy. 1994. *Who Pays for the Kids? Gender and the Structures of Constraint.* New York: Routledge.

———. 2001. *The Invisible Heart: Economics and Family Values.* New York: The New York Press.

Fraser, Nancy. 1989. *Unruly Practices: Power, Discourse, and Gender in Contemporary Social Theory.* Minneapolis: University of Minnesota Press.

Friedan, Betty. 1963. *The Feminine Mystique.* New York: Norton.

Fry, Richard and Paul Taylor. 2012. "The Rise of Residential Segregation by Income," *Pew Research Center Social and Demographic Trends*, August 1. Accessed March 1,2014.

Garey, Anita Ilta. 1999. *Weaving Work and Motherhood.* Philadelphia, PA: Temple Universtiy Press.

Gerson, Kathleen. 2002. "Moral Dilemmas, Moral Strategies, and the Transformation of Gender: Lessons from Two Generations of Work and Family Change." *Gender & Society* 16 (1):8–28.

Glaser, Barney and Anselm Strauss. 1967. *The Discovery of Grounded Theory: Strategies for Qualitative Research.* Chicago: Aldine Press.

Glenn, Evelyn Nakano. 1994. "Social Constructions of Mothering: A Thematic Overview." In *Mothering: Ideology, Experience and Agency,* edited by Evelyn Nakano Glenn, Grace Chang, and Linda Rennie Forcey, 1–29. New York: Routledge.

Gordon, Linda. 1990. *Women, the State, and Welfare.* Madison: The University of Wisconsin Press.

———. 1994. *Pitied But Not Entitled: Single Mothers and the History of Welfare 1890–1935.* Cambridge: Harvard University Press.

———. 2002. "Who Deserves Help? Who Must Provide?" In *Lost Ground: Welfare Reform, Poverty and Beyond,* edited by Randy Albelda and Ann Withhorn, 9–26 Cambridge: South End Press.

Groves, Robert M. and Mick P. Couper. 2002. "Designing Surveys Acknowledging Nonresponse." In *Studies of Welfare Populations: Data Collection and Research Issues: Panel on Data and Methods for Measuring the Effects of Changes in Social Welfare Programs,* edited by Robert A Moffitt, Constance F. Citro, and Michele Ver Ploeg, 13–54. Washington, DC: National Academy Press.

Groysberg, Boris and Robin Abrahams. 2014. "Manage Your Work, Manage Your Life." *Harvard Business Review 92*(3)58–66 EBSCO (94490465).

Guilty Moms. 2009. *Dr. Phil Uncensored.* CBS Television Distribution.

Handler, Joel F. 1995. *The Poverty of Welfare Reform.* New Haven: Yale University Press.

Handler, Joel F. and Yeheskel Hasenfeld. 1991. *The Moral Construction of Poverty: Welfare Reform in America.* Newbury Park: Sage Publications.

———. 1997. *We the Poor People: Work, Poverty and Welfare.* New Haven: Yale University Press.

Harris, Edward and Joshua Shakin. 2013. "The Distribution of Major Tax Expenditures in the Individual Income Tax System." *Congressional Budget Office.* Washington, DC: Congressional Budget Office. May 2013. https://cbo.gov/sites/default/files/cbofiles/attachments/TaxExpenditures_One-Column.pdf.

Hart, Mechthild U. 2002. *The Poverty of Life-Affirming Work: Motherwork, Education, and Social Change.* Connecticut: Greenwood Press.

Haskins, Ron. 2006. "Welfare Reform, Success or Failure? It Worked." *The Brookings Institution*, March 15. Accessed May 7, 2012. http://www.brookings.edu/research/articles/2006/03/15welfare-haskins.

Hays, Sharon. 1996. *The Cultural Contradictions of Motherhood.* New Haven: Yale University Press.

———. 2003. *Flat Broke with Children: Women in the Age of Welfare Reform.* Oxford University Press.

Hennessy, Judith. 2005. "Welfare, Work, and Family Well-Being: A Comparative Analysis of Welfare and Employment Status for Single Female-Headed Families Post-TANF." *Sociological Perspectives* 48(1):77–104.

———. 2009. "Morality and Work-Family Conflict in the Lives of Poor and Low-Income Women." *Sociological Quarterly* 50:557–580.

Heymann, Jodie. 2000. *The Widening Gap: Why America's Working Familes are in Jeopardy and What Can Be Done About It.* New York: Basic Books.

Hirschman, Linda. 2006. *Get to Work: A Manifesto for Women of the World.* New York: Penguin Books.

Hochschild, Arlie Russell. 1997. *The Time Bind: When Home Becomes Work and Work Becomes Home.* New York: Henry Holt.

Hochschild, Arlie Russell, with Anne Machung. 1989. *The Second Shift: Working Parents and the Revolution at Home.* New York: Viking.

Ireland, Mardy S. 1993. *Reconceiving Women: Separating Motherhood from Female Identity.* New York: Guilford Publications

Jacobs, Jerry A. and Kathleen Gerson. 2004. *The Time Divide: Work, Family, and Gender Inequality.* Cambridge, MA: Harvard University Press.

Johnson, Jennifer. 2002. *Getting by on the Minimum: The Lives of Working Class Women.* New York: Routledge.

Jones, Bernice. 2012. "Introduction: Women Work and Motherhood in American History." In *Women Who Opt-Out: The Debate Over Working Mothers and Work-Family Balance*, edited By Bernice D Jones, 3–30. New York: New York University Press.

Jones, Jacquelyn. 1986. *Labor of Love, Labor of Sorrow: Black Women, Work, and the Family, from Slavery to the Present.* New York: Random House.

Kantor, Jodi and Jessica Silver-Greenberg. 2013. "Wall Street Mothers, Stay-Home Fathers." *New York Times*, December 8, 2013, 2, A.

Karger, Howard Jacob and David Stoesz. 2010. *American Social Welfare Policy: A Pluralist Approach*, 6th edition. San Francisco: Allyn & Bacon.

Katz, Michael. 1996 [1986]. *In the Shadow of the Poorhouse: A Social History of Welfare in America. Tenth Anniversary Edition.* New York: Basic Books.

Korteweg, Anna C. 2003. "Welfare Reform and the Subject of the Working Mother: Get a Job, a Better Job, Then a Career." *Theory And Society* 32:445–80.

Lamont, Michele. 2000. *The Dignity of Working Men: Morality and the Boundaries of Race, Class and Immigration.* New York: Russell Sage Foundation and Cambridge, MA: Harvard University Press.

Lein, Laura, Deanna T. Schexnayder, with Karen Nanges Douglas, and Daniel G. Schroeder. 2007. *Life after Welfare Reform and the Persistence of Poverty.* Austin: University of Texas Press.

Levine, Judith. 2013. *Ain't No Trust: How Bosses, Boyfriends, and Bureaucrats Fail Low-Income Mothers and Why It Matters.* Berkeley: University of California Press.

Limoncelli, Stephanie. 2002. "Some of Us are Excellent at Babies: Paid Work, Mothering and the Construction of Need in a Welfare to Work Program." In *Work, Welfare and Politics: Confronting Poverty in the Wake of Welfare Reform*, edited by Frances Fox Piven, Joan Acker, Margaret Hallock, and Sandra Morgen, 81–93. Eugene: University of Oregon Press.

London, Andrew S., Ellen K. Scott, Kathryn Edin, and Vicki Hunter. 2004. "Welfare Reform, Work-Family Tradeoffs, and Child Well-Being." *Family Relations* (53):148–58.

Loprest, Pamela. 2001. "How Are Families That Left Welfare Doing? A Comparison of Early and Recent Welfare Leavers." *Assessing the New Federalism.* Washington, DC: Urban Institute.

Lorber, Judith. 1994. *Paradoxes of Gender.* New Haven: Yale University Press.

McCormack, Karen. 2004. "Resisting the Welfare Mother: The Power of Welfare Discourse and Tactics of Resistance." *Critical Sociology* 30(2):355–383.

McMahon, Martha. 1995. *Engendering Motherhood: Identity and Self-Transformation in Women's Lives.* New York: The Guildford Press.

Mead, Lawrence M. 1997. "The Rise of Paternalism," in *The New Paternalism: Supervisory Approaches to Poverty*, edited by Lawrence M. Mead, 1-38. Washington, DC: The Brookings Institution.

Mink, Gwendolyn. 1995. *The Wages of Motherhood: Inequality in the Welfare State, 1917–1942.* Ithaca: Cornell University Press.

———. 1998 *Welfare's End.* Ithaca: Cornell University Press.

Morgen, Sandra, Joan Acker, and Jill Weigt. 2009. *Stretched Thin: Poor Families, Welfare Work, and Welfare Reform.* Ithaca: Cornell University Press.

Morrell, Carolyn. 1994. *Unwomanly Conduct: The Challenges of Intentional Childlessness.* New York: Routledge.

Munger, Frank. 2002. "Democratizing Poverty," in *Laboring Below the Line: The New Ethnography of Poverty, Low-Wage Work, and Survival in the Global Economy*, edited by Frank Munger, 290–312. New York: Russell Sage Foundation.

Murray, Charles A. 1984. *Losing Ground: American Social Policy, 1950–1980.* New York: Basic Books.

———. 2012. *Coming Apart: The State of White America, 1960–2010.* New York: Crown Forum

Naples, Nancy A. 1997. "The 'New Consensus' on the Gendered 'Social Contract': The 1987–1988 U.S. Congressional Hearings On Welfare Reform." *Signs* 22(4):907–945. doi: 10.2307/3175224.

Nelson, Margaret K. 2005. *The Social Economy of Single Motherhood: Raising Children in Rural America.* New York: Routledge.

Newman, Katherine. 1999. *No Shame in My Game*: *The Working Poor in the Inner City.* New York: Alford A Knopf.

O'Connor, Alice. 2000. "Poverty Research and Policy for the Post-Welfare Era." *Annual Review of Sociology* 26:547–62.

Office of the Press Secretary. February 26, 2002. "President Announces Welfare Reform Agenda St. Luke's Catholic Church Washington, DC." Accessed July 2, 2012. http://www.whitehouse.gov/news/releases/2002/02/print/2002022611.html.

Parker, Kim. 2012. "Women, Work And Motherhood A Sampler Of Recent Pew Research Survey Findings." April 13. *Pew Research Social & Demographic Trends*.

Pavetti, La Donna and Gregory Acs. 2001. "Moving Up, Moving Out, or Going Nowhere? A Study of the Employment Patterns of Young Women and the Implications for Welfare Mothers." *Journal of Policy Analysis and Management* 20(4):721–36.

Pearson, A. Fiona. 2007. "The New Welfare Trap: Case Managers, College Education, and TANF Policy." *Gender & Society* 21(5):723–748. Doi: 10.2307/27641007.

Perry-Jenkins, Maureen. 2012. "The Challenges to and Consequences of Opting Out." In *Women Who Opt Out: The Debate Over Working Mothers and Work-Family Balance*, edited by Bernice D. Jones, 103-117. New York: New York University Press.

Peskowitz, Miriam. 2005. *The Truth Behind the Mommy Wars: Who Decides What Makes a Good Mother?* Emeryville, CA: Seal Press.

Piven, Frances Fox and Richard A. Cloward. 1993. *Regulating the Poor: The Functions of Public Welfare.* New York: Vintage Books.

Quadragno, Jill. 1994. *The Color of Welfare: How Racism Undermined the War on Poverty.* New York: Oxford University Press.

Quart, Alissa. 2013. "Crushed by the Cost of Child Care." *New York Times* (August 17). Accessed August 30, 2013. http://opinionator.blogs.nytimes.com/2013/08/17/crushed-by-the-cost-of-child-care/.

Reese, Ellen. 2005. *Backlash against Welfare Mothers: Past and Present.* Berkeley: University of California Press.

Risman, Barbara. 1998. *Gender Vertigo: American Families in Transition.* New Haven, CT: Yale University Press.

Rose, Nancy E. 2000. "Scapegoating Poor Women: An Analysis of Welfare Reform." *Journal of Economic Issues* 34(1):143–157.

Rubin, Lillian. 1994. *Families on the Fault Line: America's Working Class Speaks about the Economy, Race, and Ethnicity.* New York: HarperCollins Publishers.

Sandberg, Sheryl. 2013. *Women, Work, and the Will to Lead.* New York: Alfred A. Knopf.

Schlafly, Phyllis. 2004. "Feminism Is Mugged by Reality." *The Phyllis Schlafly Report* (38)5 (December). Accessed February 6, 2012. http://www.eagleforum.org/psr/2004/dec04/psrdec04.html.

Schor, Juliet B. 1998. *The Overspent American: Upscaling, Downshifting, and the New Consumer.* New York: Basic Books.

Schram, Sanford F. 2000. *After Welfare: The Culture of Postindustrial Social Policy.* New York: New York University Press.

Seefeldt, Kristin S. 2008. *Working After Welfare: How Women Balance Jobs and Family in the Wake of Welfare Reform.* Kalamazoo, MI: W.E. Upjohn Institute for Employment Research.

Senior, Jennifer. 2014. *All Joy and No Fun: The Paradox of Modern Parenthood.* New York: HarperCollins Publishers.

Sewell, William H. Jr. 1992. "A Theory of Structure: Duality, Agency, and Transformation." *American Journal of Sociology* 98:1–29.

Shaw, Kathleen M., Sara Goldrick-Rab, Christopher Mazzeo, and Jerry A. Jacobs. 2006. *Putting Poor People to Work: How the Work-First Idea Eroded College Access for the Poor.* New York: Russell Sage Foundation.

Sidel, Ruth. 2006. *Unsung Heroines: Single Mothers and the American Dream.* Berkeley: University of California Press.

Skocpol, Theda. 1992. *Protecting Soldiers and Mothers: The Political Origins of Social Policy in the United States.* Cambridge, MA: Harvard University Press.

Slaughter, Anne Marie. 2012. "Why Women Still Can't Have It All." *The Atlantic* (July/August).

Solinger, Rickie. 1999. "Dependency and Choice: The Two Faces of Eve." *Social Justice* 25(1):1–27.

———. 2001. *Beggars and Choosers: How the Politics of Choice Shapes Adoption, Abortion and Welfare in the United States.* New York: Hill and Wang.

Somers, Margaret and Fred Block. 2005. "From Poverty to Perversity: Ideas, Markets, and Institutions over 200 years of Welfare Debate." *American Sociological Review* 70:260–287.

Stone, Pamela. 2007. *Opting Out?: Why Women Really Quit Careers and Head Home.* Berkeley: University of California Press.

U.S. Bureau Of Labor Statistics. 2013. BLS Reports, *A Profile Of The Working Poor 2011* (April). Report 1041 Accessed August 23, 2013. http://www.bls.gov/cps/cpswp2011.pdf.

U.S. Census Bureau. 2013. Current Population Reports, *Income, Poverty, and Health Insurance Coverage in the United States: 2012,* by Carmen DeNavas-Walt, Bernadette D. Proctor, and Jessica C. Smith, 60–245. U.S. Government Printing Office, Washington, DC. http://www.census.gov/prod/2013pubs/p60-245.pdf.

U.S. Congress. 1996. *Personal Responsibility and Work Opportunity Reconciliation Act of 1996.* Public Law 104-93, H.R.3734.

U.S. Department of Health and Human Services Administration for Children and Families. 2006. "Federal Register. 45 CFR Parts 261, et al. Reauthorization of Temporary Assistance for Needy Families Program; Interim Final Rule." Accessed August 17, 2006. http://www.acf.hhs.gov/programs/ofa/law-reg/tfinrule.html.

U.S. Department of Health and Human Services. Office of Planning Research and Evaluation, Administration for Children and Families. Table L10 Family Cap Policies, 1992-2012 (July) Accessed October 16, 2014. http://www.acf.hhs.gov/sites/default/files/opre/databook_2012_final_nov2013_003.pdf.

———. 2013. Office of Family Assistance. TANF Financial Data Table A.1.: Federal TANF and State MOE Expenditures Summary by ACF-196 Spending Category, FY 2012. August. Accessed May 1, 2014. http://www.acf.hhs.gov/programs/ofa/resource/tanf-financial-data-fy-2012.

U.S. Department of Labor Bureau of Labor Statistics. 2013. Economic News Release. *Employment Characteristics of Families,* April 2013. Accessed May 20, 2014. http://www.bls.gov/news.release/archives/famee_04262013.htm.

Usdansky, Margaret, Rachel Gordon, Xue Wang, and Anna Gluzman. 2012. "Depression Risk among Mothers of Small Children: The Role of Employment Preferences, Labor Force

Status, and Job Quality." *Journal of Family and Economic Issues 33*:83-94. Accessed November 22, 2013 doi110.1007/s10834-011-9260-5.

Wallis, Claudia. 2004. "The Case for Staying Home." *TIME*. March 22, 2004, 51–58.

Warner, Judith. 2005. *Perfect Madness: Motherhood in the Age of Anxiety*. New York: Penguin Group.

———. 2013. "Ready to Rejoin the Rat Race?" *New York Times*, August 11.

Watkins-Hayes. 2009. *The New Welfare Bureaucrats: Entanglement of Race, Class, and Policy Reform*. Chicago: University of Chicago Press.

Weaver, R. Kent. 2000. *Ending Welfare as We Know It*. New York: Brookings Institution Press.

Weber, Max. 1958. *The Protestant Ethic and the Spirit of Capitalism*. New Jersey: Prentice Hall, Inc.

———. 1958a. "Science as a Vocation." In *From Max Weber: Essays in Sociology,* edited by H. S. Gertz and C. Wright Mills, 129-156. New York: Oxford University Press.

Weigt, Jill. 2006. "Compromises To Carework: The Social Organization of Mothers' Experiences in the Low-Wage Labor Market after Welfare Reform." *Social Problems 53*(3):332-351. doi: 10.1525/Sp.2006.53.3.332.

———. 2010. "'I Feel Like It's a Heavier Burden . . .': The Gendered Contours Of Heterosexual Partnering After Welfare Reform." *Gender & Society 24*(5):565–590. Accessed May 10, 2014. doi: 10.1177/0891243210382865.

Williams, Joan. 2010. *Reshaping the Work-Family Debate: Why Men and Class Matter*. Cambridge: Harvard University Press.

Wilson, William J. 1996. *When Work Disappears*. New York: Alford A. Knopf.

Winston, Pamela. 2002. *Welfare Policymaking in the States: The Devil in Devolution*. Washington, DC: Georgetown University Press.

Wuthnow, Robert. 1996. *Poor Richards Principle: Recovering the American Dream through the Moral Principle of Work, Business, and Money*. Princeton, NJ: Princeton University Press.

Index

Abramovitz, Mimi, 72
ADC, 22–24, 26
AFDC, 1, 22, 24, 26, 30, 32, 98, 100, 114, 128, 148
Aid to Dependent Children (ADC), See ADC
Aid to Families with Dependent Children (AFDC). See AFDC
American views on work and family. *See* U.S. public's views

bad jobs, 50, 51, 52, 114, 134, 145
Biology. *See* sex differences
Blair-Loy, Mary, 5–6, 8, 9, 147
breadwinner role: for women, 35, 103, 148; male breadwinner, 21, 26, 75, 90, 148
Bush, George W. Pres., 43

career mothers, 86, 89; value of children to, 86–87. *See also* children; motherhood; professional mothers; "mommy wars"
care work, 109
caseworkers. *See* welfare caseworkers
children: as priority, 90, 91; better off if mom's work, 97; harmed from mothers working, 81, 105; high cost of, 119, 143; mothers' responsibility, 92, 119; need mother's care, 75, 77–78, 78, 79; value to poor mothers, 119; young

children, 77–78
Clinton, President, 32
Collins, Jane and Victoria Mayer, 145
conservative family values ideology, 30, 54, 57, 88; as backlash against feminism and gay rights, 30. *See also* family values
contemporary trends in work and family life, 3, 17n1, 37, 141
Coontz, Stephanie, 2, 30, 37
cultural models, 9–10, 10. *See also* gendered cultural schemas
cultural schemas, 8, 41. *See also* Devotion Schemas

Damaske, Sarah, 50, 146
day care. *See* paid child care
deserving poor, 20, 22, 23, 27, 34. *See also* motherhood; stigma
Devotion Schemas, 5–6, 8; family devotion schema, 9; impact on elite women, 6, 8, 147; influence on poor mothers, 10, 41–42; poor mothers' schemas, 9, 147; work devotion schema, 9. *See also* family commitment schema; work commitment schema
disadvantage of poor mothers, 6, 14, 22, 24; compared to middle class and professional mothers, 5, 144
Douglas, Susan and Meredith Michaels, 84, 102

mothers

welfare office, 13, 16, 108, 109, 151; demands of, 42, 72, 85, 90, 108, 111, 122; humiliation at, 100–102; lack of understanding of mothers' obligations, 88, 110, 119, 120–121, 150; message to poor mothers, 33, 40, 64; moral authority challenged, 59, 111, 120, 152. *See also* welfare system; welfare, welfare caseworkers

welfare policy history: and gender, 20, 23, 28, 31; and worthy mothers, 21, 22; as reflection of work and family relations, 148; Maternalist Policies, 20–21; Moral uplift, 22, 34; Mothers' Aid, 22; Progressive Era, 20; and welfare caseload increase, 25. *See also* ADC; AFDC; welfare

welfare policy makers: and restrictive welfare provisions, 24; out of touch with poor mothers lives, 110, 116. *See also* welfare

welfare queens, 29. *See also* welfare mothers

welfare reform, 32, 110; impact on work and family arrangements, 33, 88, 123; problems for poor women, 70, 83, 85. *See also* TANF; WorkFirst

welfare system: and gender, 20, 65, 148; and gendered cultural structures, 65, 118, 152; as gendered paradox for poor mothers, 7, 111, 118, 120, 151; dislike of, 105, 106, 120; does not help poor mothers, 107–108, 113; impact on work and family relationships, 19, 80, 104, 121, 144; moral failings of, 16, 110, 117; penalties for caring for children, 121; punishes mothers, 108, 120. *See also* welfare; TANF; PRWORA; work requirements

Williams , Joan, 2

Women's Programs, 160

work and family, 64; as opposite, 3, 7, 12, 69, 70, 70–71; contradictory expectations, 1, 5, 14, 19; meaning of choices, 2, 4, 5; moral concerns, 2, 5; paradox for poor mothers, 9, 39, 97, 142, 143–144. *See also* work-family conflict; work-family debate; work-

family balance

work and family choices, 82, 146, 153; as moral dilemma, 85; conditions differentiating poor mothers' choices, 85, 93, 153; elimination of choice for poor mothers, 83; evaluation of choices, 82, 84, 85, 117; moral salience of, 65, 83, 84, 85, 87, 145, 146; moralizing, 83, 84; middle-class vs. poor mothers, 83, 84, 85

Work Commitment Schema, 10; ambivalence toward, 68–69; challenges to, 68, 70, 149; defined, 43; differs from elite mothers' schema, 44; moral vision for poor mothers, 149; relationship to welfare policy, 43, 44; rewards and obligations, 65, 68

work ethic, 23, 25, 27, 29, 31, 99, 115; masculine, 16, 43, 110, 146; of low-wage workers, 50, 104; poor mothers accountability to, 54, 68, 106, 108, 116, 117, 141, 145; valorization of, 43, 99, 151

work-family balance, 1, 6, 85, 141, 144, 154

work-family conflict, 2, 6, 72; as moral dilemmas for poor women, 5, 52, 93, 147; comparison of middle-class married mothers and welfare mothers', 35, 98, 119, 144; moral and cultural foundations of, 8, 9, 40, 41, 42, 46–47; welfare policies' impact on, 6–7, 40, 73, 88–89. *See also* morality; welfare; work and family

work-family debate: differences between low-income and poor women and married middle-class and professional women, 2, 4, 78; moral and cultural forces shaping poor women's choices, 40, 57. *See also* work-family conflict

work-family policy, 153; and welfare reform, 1

WorkFirst, 56, 112, 128, 129, 130, 133; resentment of, 113, 120. *See also* TANF

Work Incentive Program (WIN), 26

work outside the home: as sign of character and responsibility, 49, 57; meaning of, 50, 51; provides roles models for